Loss Prevention Guide

NORTH

BILLS OF LADING
A GUIDE TO GOOD PRACTICE
Third Edition

Stephen Mills

THE NORTH OF ENGLAND P&I ASSOCIATION

First edition published in 1998 ISBN 0 9531785 2 8

Second edition published in 2005 ISBN 978-0-09558257

Third edition published in 2014 by The North of England P&I Association Limited
The Quayside, Newcastle upon Tyne, NE1 3DU, United Kingdom

Telephone +44 191 232 5221
Fax +44 191 261 0540
Email loss.prevention@nepia.com

All rights reserved. No part of this publication may be reproduced, stored in a retrieval system or transmitted in any form or by any means (electronic, mechanical, photocopying, recording or otherwise) without the written permission of the publisher.

Copyright © The North of England P&I Association Limited 2014

The moral right of the Author has been asserted.

ISBN 978-0-9574936-0-5

Author: Stephen Mills

Printed and bound in the UK by Anchorage Press

The publisher and author wish to thank the United Nations Department of Public Information for permission to publish the Hamburg Rules, The Controller of Her Majesty's Stationery Office for permission to publish the Hague-Visby Rules (permission reference 98001663) and The Baltic and International Maritime Council for permission to publish the Congenbill Editions 1994 and 2007.

This publication is intended for general guidance only to assist in the avoidance of disputes and problems arising from improper use of bills of lading. Whilst care is taken to ensure the accuracy of any information no warranty of accuracy is given and users of the information contained herein are expected to satisfy themselves that it is relevant and suitable for the purposes to which it is applied or intended to be applied. No responsibility is accepted by the Author, The North of England P&I Association or by any person, firm, corporation or organisation who or which has been in any way concerned with the furnishing of data, the development, compilation or publication thereof, for the accuracy of any information or advice given herein or for any omission herefrom, or for any consequences whatsoever resulting directly or indirectly from, reliance upon or adoption of guidance contained herein.

CONTENTS

Chapter	Page
INTRODUCTION	**3**
Loss prevention and bills of lading	3
Notes on the third edition	4
How to use this guide	4
General notes	6
QUICK REFERENCE	**7**
How to use this section	7
The bill of lading – a quick guide to its role and its problems	7
PRACTICAL GUIDANCE	**11**
Signing bills of lading *(paragraphs 1 – 21)*	11
Delivering the cargo at discharge port *(paragraphs 22 – 34)*	19
A typical bill of lading – the BIMCO Congenbill *(paragraphs 35 – 55)*	22
THEORY	**34**
History and context *(paragraphs 56 – 104)*	34
Signing the bill of lading *(paragraphs 105 – 199)*	45
Sources of information for the bill of lading *(paragraphs 200 – 214)*	67
Movement of the bill of lading under the sale contract *(paragraphs 215 – 225)*	70
The voyage – deviation, delivery, loss and damage to cargo *(paragraphs 226 – 245)*	73
Delivery of the cargo *(paragraphs 246 – 265)*	77
Other matters *(paragraphs 266 – 279)*	81
Other documents and variations *(paragraphs 280 – 294)*	85
Security issues *(paragraphs 295 – 296)*	88
Sanctions *(paragraphs 297 – 298)*	88

ELECTRONIC BILLS OF LADING — 89

Background *(paragraphs 299 – 308)* — 89
P&I cover *(paragraphs 309 – 319)* — 91
The master's role *(paragraphs 320 – 323)* — 93
Charterparty requirements *(paragraph 324)* — 94

LEGAL NOTES — 95

APPENDICES — 106

I	Glossary	106
II	Standard letter of authority to issue bills of lading	109
III	P&I club circulars on standard letters of indemnity	110
IV	Standard letters of indemnity	113
V	Hague Rules	117
VI	Hague-Visby Rules	122
VII	Hamburg Rules	127
VIII	List of countries applying the conventions	139
IX	UK Carriage of Goods by Sea Act 1992	142
X	P&I club circulars on electronic (paperless) trading systems	147
XI	International Group of P&I Clubs frequently asked questions of August 2013 on paperless trading	149

BIBLIOGRAPHY — 151

INDEX — 152

INTRODUCTION

LOSS PREVENTION AND BILLS OF LADING

In 1996 the North of England P&I Association issued a simple questionnaire to readers of its loss prevention newsletter *Signals*. It asked for their experiences with regard to the issue of bills of lading and subsequent delivery of cargo against those bills of lading. The majority of answers were received from shipowners' offices or from masters, with agents, operators, financiers and others also responding.

A number of specific problems set a recurring theme

- pressure on the master to issue clean bills of lading
- disagreement between ship's and shore figures
- agents signing bills of lading without reference to the mate's receipts or in excess of their authority from the master
- requests to deliver the cargo without production of the original bill of lading.

A general point also emerged which can be summarised by one member's comment

'I have noticed a distinct casualness by shippers, receivers and their agents at load/discharge ports about the importance to the master of bills of lading. Conclusion: they are ignorant of its legal purposes.'

Strong words, but possibly true. Although the bill of lading is a key document in a transaction where the cargo and freight together may be worth several millions of dollars, masters who are diligent or cautious in their handling of that document may often be seen by others as obstructive or awkward. If masters are to stand their ground and justify their stance, then they may need to know not only what they have to do, but why they are doing it.

Masters need to be fully aware of the importance and function of bills of lading

The aim of this guide is to assist ship's officers, operators and managers in the understanding of bills of lading and the problems and practical issues surrounding their everyday use. The hope is that they will then be able to deal with these situations and the many others that arise in connection with what is a vital and unique document.

NOTES ON THE THIRD EDITION

Although it is 16 years since the first edition of this guide was published, many of the issues concerning bills of lading remain unchanged: disputes between shipowners and shippers as to condition or as to quantity; delivery without production of the bill of lading; incorporation of terms from often unidentified charterparties; splitting, backdating, amending bills of lading; additional information which the shippers ask to be shown on the bill of lading, but which the shipowner is under no duty to include. The list goes on.

Everyone concerned in the bill of lading transaction and the sale and credit contracts which underlie it, as well as the insurers of the goods and the carriers, are equally committed to a smooth and successful transaction. It remains the purpose of this guide to assist in achieving that common goal.

But there have been changes and developments since the first and second editions were published: the *Rafaela S* has (to an extent) clarified the law relating to 'straight' bills of lading; COGSA 1992 has been applied to a number of title to sue issues and received some clarification in the process; the International Group of P&I Clubs' standard letters of indemnity have been tested and updated by P&I club circulars; the Hamburg Rules have faded, but the Rotterdam Rules are showing at least a glimmer of light – and if and when enacted will be the subject of a fully updated version of this guide.

At last, the electronic bill of lading is establishing its place in international trade with rapid recent growth in use and acceptance. A new section on electronic bills has been added to this guide, very much from the perspective of the P&I clubs.

The format and purpose of the guide remains the same. It is not a legal text book. It is a practical guide offering practical assistance to those in the front line, but hopefully with a sound legal foundation which is, albeit briefly, explained in the Legal Notes.

HOW TO USE THIS GUIDE

The guide has five main colour-coded sections

- quick reference (red)
- practical guidance (orange)
- theory (green)
- legal notes (blue).
- electronic bills of lading (purple).

Quick reference

The quick reference section is for those occasions when guidance is needed quickly and there is no opportunity to read about or understand the underlying principles of the bill of lading. On these occasions, the quick reference section indicates the part of the book which is most likely to help. It is a source of reference and reassurance and should not be seen as a substitute for seeking proper guidance from owners, their P&I clubs or their lawyers.

Practical guidance

The practical section gives specific guidance on signing, and refusing to sign, bills of lading and delivery of cargo. It then analyses from a practical viewpoint each part of the Congenbill, a widely used bill of lading. A specimen bill is included in this section.

Common problem areas are examined and some guidance given as to how these problems should be handled from the point of view of the master, shipowner or operator.

Each paragraph has a unique number for ease of cross-referencing.

Theory

The theory section examines the evolution of the bill of lading from its simple beginning to its modern role as a fundamental document in the international sale and carriage of goods. The traditional three-part analysis of the bill of lading as a receipt, a contract of carriage and a document of title is not followed – instead there is analysis of the path the bill of lading will follow from its issue to fulfilment and the problems that can be met along the way.

The analysis includes the problems in describing the nature, quantity and condition of the goods put on board the vessel; the array of express and implied terms, statutes, codes and conventions within which the bill of lading operates; and the relationship of the bill of lading with the underlying sale contract.

It is not essential to read the theory section in order to understand the practical section. Again, each paragraph has a unique number for ease of cross referencing.

Masters rarely sign bills of lading even though they have legal responsibility for them

Legal notes

Both the practical guidance and theory sections are supplemented by legal notes indicated by a ⚖ symbol in the text. To avoid distraction, these notes are gathered together in a separate section. The purpose of these notes, essentially legal in nature, is to identify for those who may be asked to assist the master (e.g. shipowners, clubs or their lawyers) the legal basis of the advice being offered by this guide.

Electronic bills of lading

This section records the progress that has been made in the use of electronic bills of lading, their legal functionality and the response of the P&I clubs to the increasing use and appeal of such systems.

Where the advice given in this guide may vary in respect of electronic bills of lading, this is indicated by reference to a paragraph number in the electronic bills of lading section of this guide.

GENERAL NOTES

Readers should also note the following.

Law

Advice in this guide is based on English law.

'Clausing' and 'endorsing'

In this guide the verb 'to clause' means to write on a bill of lading a comment which casts doubt on the apparent good order and condition of the cargo. The verb 'to endorse' means to stamp and or sign the back of a bill of lading in order to effect legal transfer of rights under the bill of lading to another person. This distinction is made throughout the guide, but it is recognised that within the industry the word 'endorse' is often used to describe both functions.

'Shipowner' and 'carrier'

The words 'shipowner' and 'carrier' should be used synonymously as it is assumed that the shipowner is the master's employer and, when masters issue a bill of lading, they will bind the shipowner as carrier. However, in certain circumstances, other parties such as charterers or freight forwarders may be the legal if not physical 'carriers'.

Role of the master

The assumption made throughout this guide – and indeed the assumption made in most printed forms of charterparty and bill of lading – is that the master will check and sign the bill of lading at the port of loading and will receive the bill of lading in return for delivery of the goods at the discharge port. This is because legal responsibility for the bill of lading usually lies with the master and the shipowner.

However, for practical and commercial reasons, there may be an array of charterers, agents, brokers and freight forwarders between the master and the bill of lading and a master may rarely or never see a bill of lading unless a problem occurs.

QUICK REFERENCE

HOW TO USE THIS SECTION

All words and expressions shown in **bold print** are in the index at the end of this guide. The index refers to unique paragraph numbers in the practical guidance and/or theory and/or electronic bills of lading sections where these subjects and terms are described and discussed in more detail.

THE BILL OF LADING – A QUICK GUIDE TO ITS ROLE AND ITS PROBLEMS

In most international sales transactions where the goods are to be carried by sea, the seller of the goods promises to do two things

- put the goods on board a ship
- provide the commercial documents required by the contract, the central one usually being the bill of lading.

All the master can do is describe the apparent order and condition of the cargo – in this case the outer covers of the rolled steel cargo are in 'apparent good order and condition'

The bill of lading says a lot of things to those who come into possession of it.

- It helps to identify the owner of the goods – in this respect it is often referred to as being a **document of title**.
- It identifies the party who can receive the goods – again as a **document of title**.
- It is a means of **transferring title** from one person to another.
- It provides information on
  - the **description** of goods
  - the **condition** of goods
  - the **quantity** of goods
  - the **loading port** and **date** of shipment
  - the **discharge port**
  - the name of the ship
  - whether **freight** has been paid
  - the **terms of carriage** under which the cargo is being carried
  - delivery instructions (e.g. the **notify party** or **consignee**).

In this respect the bill of lading is both a **receipt** for the goods shipped and evidence of the **contract of carriage**.

As the various functions of bills of lading are essential to international sale transactions, it is important that information given in each bill is meaningful and consistent in expression. Attempts to ensure this have given rise to agreed **codes and conventions** and recognised practices.

Agreed **codes and conventions** include

- **UCP 600** (Uniform Customs and Practice for Documentary Credits)
- **Hague Rules**
- **Hague-Visby Rules**
- **Hamburg Rules**
- **Incoterms.**

Recognised practices include widely accepted terminology for **clausing** (e.g. in respect of **steel cargoes**) and the use of widely understood abbreviations. These include **FOB**, **CFR** and **CIF** and (less frequently) EXW, FCA, FAS, CPT, CIP, DAF, DAP and DDP, all of which are **Incoterms**.

It is important that the information in a bill of lading is correct. However, masters when issuing the bill of lading may (justifiably) wish to limit their responsibility for information which they are not in a position to check for accuracy. This has given rise to the use of commonly used **words of description** in bills of lading such as

- 'weight, measure, quantity, condition, contents and value unknown'
- 'shipper's load and count'
- 'apparent order and condition'
- 'said to be'.

Sometimes attempts are made, or pressure put on the master, to hide information that will make the bill of lading less attractive to the buyer of the cargo. This gives rise to requests for the issue of **clean bills of lading** when, because of the condition of the cargo, the bills should be **claused**. These requests (which should be refused) are often made with promises of **letters of indemnity** which say they will protect the issuer of the bill of lading.

A number of important questions need to be addressed.

- Must the master sign any bill of lading **as presented**?
- Who prepares the bill of lading?
- Who else has the right of **signing the bill of lading** on the master's behalf?
- What is the **authority of charterers** or **agents**?
- What is the master to do when asked to deliver the cargo to a **change of destination** from that named in the bill of lading?
- Can the master deliver the cargo **without production of the bill of lading**?
- Can the master deliver to one person where more than one person demands **delivery** under the bill of lading?
- What are the difficulties with **straight bills of lading** and **sea waybills**?

All these questions are discussed in the practical guidance and theory sections. In addition, the following more specific topics are covered

- the **purpose** of the bill of lading in a practical and legal sense
- what **information** the bill of lading must contain
- the sources of the most accurate information, in particular
    - the **mate's receipt**
    - the **shipping note**
    - the **shipper**
    - **surveyors** and **inspectors**
    - the **draught survey**
    - (for liquid cargoes) **ullages**
    - certificates of origin, quantity and quality.

In addition there is discussion of situations frequently encountered. These include

- **blending or co-mingling** liquid cargoes
- **mixing** dry cargoes
- **multiple sets of bills of lading**
- **backdating (ante-dating, pre-dating)** or **post-dating** bills of lading
- **amending** bills of lading
- conflict with **mate's receipts**
- the relevance of the **sale contract**
- where **pressure** or **duress** is put on the master to sign
- requests for **shipped** or **received for shipment** bills of lading
- describing the **quality** of the cargo
- offers of **letters of indemnity**
- the relationship with **letters of credit**

- the bill of lading and the **charterparty**
- how a person acquires a bill of lading: **endorsement** and **consignment**
- responsibility for **packaging and marking** of cargo
- terms as to **freight**
- cargo damaged after loading but **before issue of bills of lading**
- **delay** to the vessel
- **delay** in issuing the bills of lading
- **charterer's bills of lading**
- **place of issue** other than at the loading port
- **lost** bills of lading
- bills of lading **'for custom's purposes only'**
- bills of lading showing **final destination** which is an **inland** destination
- whether an original bill can be carried in the **ship's bag**
- **security issues**
- **sanctions.**

There is also a brief discussion of types of bills of lading and related documents including

- **ship's delivery orders**
- **sea waybills**
- **groupage, house** or **service** bills of lading
- **straight** or **non-negotiable** bills of lading
- **shipped** and **received for shipment** bills of lading
- **split** and **switch** bills of lading.

There is also a new section on

- **electronic bills of lading.**

PRACTICAL GUIDANCE

SIGNING BILLS OF LADING

1. One of the most important functions of a bill of lading is that it provides information as to the description of the goods, the condition of the goods, the quantity of the goods, the loading port and date of shipment, the discharge port, the name of the ship, whether freight has been paid and the terms of carriage. As these functions are essential to trade it is important that information given in a bill of lading is accurate. Failure to ensure accuracy can give rise to liability of the shipowner.

2. The essential rule is that in no circumstances, other than those described at paragraph 18(a), should masters sign a document which they knows to be untrue, or which they believe may be untrue, or where they have not given careful thought to the facts contained in the documents ⚖.

3. The following matters are important. If the master cannot contact or obtain guidance from the shipowner, the following general principles should be applied.

(a) The master must ensure that the information on the bill of lading agrees with that on the mate's receipt(s).

Where there is liberty to carry cargo on deck it is essential that the bill of lading states that the cargo actually is being carried on deck. In such circumstances it would also be usual for the shipowner to insert protective clauses placing the risk of deck cargo on the shipper

(b) The master must check the facts about the cargo. It would be unusual for the master or the ship's agent to prepare the bill of lading. The bill of lading is usually prepared by the shipper or the shipper's agent. It is accordingly essential for the master to check the information about the cargo in the bill of lading. Masters will not know all of the facts about the cargo that appear on the bill of lading which they are being asked to sign. This problem is dealt with specifically in the section entitled 'Information in the bill of lading' (paragraph 4).

(c) The master must check the facts about the voyage. If the place or date of loading is incorrect, or if the discharge port is outside the charterparty range, the master should refuse to sign.

(d) Refusal to sign. It is recognised that refusal is not always safe or practical. Where in this practical guidance section of the book masters are advised to refuse to sign, they should refer to paragraph 18 for guidance.

(e) The advent of electronic trading systems, using electronic bills of lading, will have an impact upon these problems and their solutions. In particular, the control of the content of the bill of lading may, under an electronic trading system, shift to the shipowner's office. However, the master remains the 'eyes and ears' of the shipowner and therefore communication of any of the above issues by the master to the shipowner's office would be prudent.

Information in the bill of lading

4. This section deals with ways of describing the cargo and the voyage. It is intended to give masters guidance where they are unable to obtain guidance from the shipowner. It may also assist the master in identifying what is a usual and what is an unusual situation.

(a) Some of the information in the bill of lading is within the master's knowledge, for example, the port of shipment, the date of completion of loading of the parcel described in the bill of lading, and the date of issue of the bill of lading. If these facts are not correct the master should refuse to sign the bill of lading.

(b) Some information in the bill of lading may not be within the precise knowledge of the master; for example the quantity or weight or the actual condition of the goods loaded. The following rules may assist.

Quantity

(i) The master should if possible add the words 'shipper's figures' or 'shore figures' to any statement as to quantity or weight on the bill of lading.

(ii) If the ship has its own figures and these differ from those in the bill of lading, but the difference between the two figures can reasonably be explained by the practical imprecision of ullaging, draught surveys or tallying, then the ship's figures should be written alongside the shipper's figures; and/or the words 'weight and quantity unknown' added.

(iii) If the master does not know the weight or quantity loaded (because there are no reasonable means of measuring or checking or if the difference between the shipper's figures and the ship's figures is more than could reasonably be explained by the practical imprecision of ullaging, draught surveys or tallying) then the master should refuse to sign the bill of lading, and reference should be made to the detailed guidance at paragraph 141.

(iv) The practice of issuing a bill of lading containing a quantity which the master does not believe is correct accompanied by a letter of protest declaring reservations about that figure, is not recommended. See paragraph 141.

Condition

(v) Usually masters only know the apparent condition of the cargo. Accordingly if they can see no apparent problem with the goods when loaded they should mark the bill of lading 'received in apparent good order and condition'.

(vi) If masters can see that the goods are damaged in some way then they should say so. A more difficult question is where masters think that the goods may be defective or substandard, for example because they appear dirty, or mixed with foreign particles or debris, or are discoloured or odorous. They may need guidance. See paragraph 204. If such comments are appropriate they should do their best to explain in ordinary language in writing on the face of the bill of lading what they believe is wrong with the condition of the cargo – see paragraphs 165 and 166 for the importance of care in doing this. If they require to add an additional sheet of paper then they should state (in writing on the bill of lading) how many sheets

Containers are usually sealed and the master would not have an opportunity of inspecting the contents. It is therefore crucial that the master makes a suitable remark on the mate's receipt and bill of lading to indicate any obvious damage to the container itself. In a serious case such as this it may be appropriate to arrange for the container to be opened prior to shipment and the contents inspected of paper are attached to each bill of lading. They should seek guidance from the P&I club or its local correspondent or agent or from a surveyor as to the precise wording to be used.

(vii) It is always useful to describe the nature of the packaging of goods, for example 'in paper bags' or 'polythene sacks'. If these are torn or damaged the bill of lading should say so, such as 'about 457 bags torn'. If only a rough estimate can be made of the quantity damaged, however, this should be stated, for example 'about 10% torn' or 'about 5000 bags damaged'. Whether it is on the basis of a tally or an estimate, masters must have evidence to support their remarks.

(viii) Special clausings are often used for, for example, timber or steel cargoes and if possible the shipowner or the P&I club correspondent should be consulted. For further discussions see paragraph 185.

(ix) If in situation (vi) or (vii), masters are not permitted by the shipper or charterer to add comments which accurately describe apparent defects in the goods or packing, they should refuse to sign the bill of lading.

Quantity and condition

(x) The words 'weight, measure, quantity, condition, contents and value unknown' are useful and desirable words to add to a bill of lading if they are not already part of the printed form. And see paragraph 296, Security issues.

Quality

(xi) The master need not describe the quality of the cargo (see paragraph 169).

(c) For the avoidance of doubt, masters should place their signature and/or the ship's stamp at the foot of the bill of lading only ⚖.

Other matters at the time of signing

5. Freight / hire / demurrage / liens

Masters may be worried that a bill of lading presented to them does not give the shipowner sufficient protection in terms of freight or hire or demurrage or liens for any of those or they may be worried about other terms of carriage. These are all matters for the shipowner or its P&I club to consider. The master should always check with the shipowner as to whether it requires protective terms to be added but leave the decision to the shipowner. If it is impossible to get guidance from the shipowner then see paragraph 3.

6. Charterparty bills of lading

Wherever there is a reference to a charterparty in the printed form of a bill of lading (for example in the Congenbill, the master should check with the shipowner as to the date of the charterparty to be inserted in the bill of lading. In the absence of guidance see paragraphs 274 – 277.

7. Deck cargo

Except in purpose-built container ships or in special trades where cargo is customarily carried on deck, carriage of cargo on deck should always be checked with the shipowner.

Where cargo is carried on deck it is essential to state on the face of the bill of lading that cargo is being carried on deck. It is for the master to check with the shipowner and for the shipowner to ensure that such carriage is permissible.

8. 'For customs purposes only'

Sometimes, the master is asked to issue bills of lading '*for customs purposes only*'. The issue of additional bills of lading, for any reason, is problematic and should be referred to the shipowner for careful consideration. If the bill of lading to be released is a duplicate of the original bills of lading, then if the shipowner agrees that such a bill can be released, it should be clearly marked with a warning such as: '*For customs purposes only. Not a document of title. Delivery of cargo will not be given against production or surrender of this bill of lading*'.

9. 'Inland destination'

Sometimes, again for customs purposes, the master is asked to issue bills of lading which show the ultimate destination of the cargo and which may be an inland destination beyond the sea discharge port. This is something which should be referred to the shipowner or its P&I correspondent for assistance. If the shipowner considers that it is essential in the trade and for customs purposes that such a destination be shown on the bill, then wording such as the following should be considered: '*The carrier has undertaken carriage to the discharge port named above. The carrier is informed by the shipper that the intended inland destination of the cargo is [name inland destination]. The carrier makes no representation as to the destination of the cargo after the discharge port and the reference to the inland port is included, at the shipper's request, for customs purposes only*'. The alternative and more formal approach is not to permit such a marking on the face of the bill but to leave those involved in the sale and purchase of the cargo to reach a more satisfactory arrangement with customs.

Many types of cargo may be damaged as a result of handling prior to shipment - any such damage should be carefully noted and recorded on the mate's receipt and bill of lading

10. References to sale contract etc.

Sometimes the master is asked by the shipper to show on the face of the bill of lading a sale contract reference number, or a letter of credit reference number, or an invoice number. This is for documentary purposes related to the sale contract. The risk is that the bill of lading containing this information may be treated as an '*ad valorem*' bill of lading (see glossary in appendix I). The master is not under any obligation to include this information on a bill of lading ⚖⚖.

11. Bill of lading carried on board in 'ship's bag'

Bills of lading are often issued in sets of three or four originals (see paragraphs 30 and 50). On occasions, the ship is asked to carry one of these bills of lading on board the ship during the voyage, sometimes with the additional instruction that delivery of the cargo at the discharge port should be given against that document. This is an inherently unsafe practice which is explained in more detail at paragraph 197. The practical advice to masters is that they should resist any request or instruction to carry one original of the bill of lading on board. They should also bring the request to the attention of the shipowner and seek guidance. Practical advice to the shipowner, if it feels compelled to agree to the request, may be that:

(a) All of the original bills of lading should be marked: '*One original bill of lading retained on board against which bill delivery of cargo may properly be made on instructions received from shippers/charterers*'. In this way, the clausing will give notice to any party purchasing any of the bills of lading that delivery may be made in exchange for one original bill of lading retained on board; or

(b) The shipowner should make it clear to the charterer/shipper that the carriage of the bill of lading on board is simply the transportation of the document itself, and the master can take no responsibility for confirming or ratifying the identity of the person to whom that document is handed at the discharge port.

12. 'FIOST' 'Free out' 'Liner terms'

The inclusion of these terms can directly affect the responsibility of the shipowner or charterer for the cargo and for loading and discharging operations. See paragraph 239. If any such abbreviation is used, then these are matters which the master should report and discuss with the shipowner as soon as possible.

13. 'CIF/CFR'

These words, on the face of the bill of lading, may be taken to denote that freight has been paid. If asked to sign a bill of lading bearing these abbreviations, masters should treat them in the same way as they would the marking '*freight pre-paid*'. Also see paragraphs 5, 119, 120, 124 and the glossary in appendix I.

14. How many bills of lading is a 'set'?

The master should check with the shipper and with the charterparty. The master should also check the terms of the bills of lading themselves as they may show the number to be issued. There is no general rule as to how many bills of lading make a 'set'; although three (a top, a second and a third marked 1/3, 2/3, 3/3 respectively) is common ⚖⚖.

Parcels of cargo
15. Sometimes the shipper or charterer will require bills of lading for individual parcels of cargo. Where the cargoes are clearly different in nature, this is not a problem. Where cargoes are homogeneous and a separate bill of lading is requested for each parcel, caution should be exercised where the cargo is not in good condition when loaded (and so clausing of bills of lading will be required) ⚖️. There is also a risk of shortage claims on some of the parcels and over-delivery on others if care is not taken during discharge to allocate and deliver accurate quantities.

16. *Blending/co-mingling of oil cargoes*
(a) Oil cargoes are unusual in that charterers and traders may wish to blend or comingle cargoes shipped from different ports on different dates, and often with different specifications.

(b) Blending and co-mingling may have different meanings. Blending is commonly intended to refer to the active mixing of cargoes of different qualities or specifications to create a new specification. Co-mingling is commonly intended to refer to the mixing of similar cargoes in the same tanks. Blending may give rise to issues such as proper care of the cargo(es), product liability, or even safety; but those issues are beyond the scope of this guide. Blending and co-mingling both give rise to issues of description dealt with below, and the expression 'mixing' is hereinafter used to describe both practices.

(c) If cargoes shipped from separate ports and/or on separate dates and/or of separate origins are mixed then complications arise as to the accurate description of the port of shipment, date of shipment and type of cargo in the bills of lading. Further problems may arise at the discharge port if the cargo mixed in the tanks no longer resembles the cargo described in one or more of the original bills of lading.

(d) Wherever there is mixing of cargo shipped on different dates from different ports and of different types it is essential that the shipowner's instructions are obtained before bills of lading are issued. If the shipowner's instructions cannot be obtained masters should refuse to sign and should explain their reasons for doing so by reference to (c) above.

17. *Letters of indemnity*
It is not for masters to agree to sign a bill of lading containing terms of which they are uncertain in return for a letter of indemnity. That is for the shipowner to decide. If the shipowner cannot be contacted then the master should refuse to sign. It is better for the master to follow the steps at paragraph 18 than to accept a letter of indemnity without the shipowner's authority ⚖️.

Refusal to sign
18. In circumstances where masters feel that they should refuse to sign a bill of lading they should seek guidance from the shipowner or from the P&I club or its correspondent. If no guidance can be obtained, the following general principles should be applied.

(a) If the refusal of the master to sign a document is met with physical threats or coercion against the ship or her master or crew, then the master should sign the document. When the vessel has sailed and upon reaching a position of safety, the master (or the shipowner, if it is now in contact with the master) may give notice of protest to all parties and authorities concerned to the effect that the document has been signed under duress and the shipowner and the master consider themselves not bound by the master's signature. (Of course thought must be given as to whether the ship or master or any sister ship is likely to return to this dangerous regime).

(b) Sometimes legal pressure will be exerted on the master to sign. The most common example will be where the ship is operating under a charterparty. The charterparty may list the master's obligations with regard to signing bills of lading. For example the master may have to sign bills of lading 'as presented'. This and similar expressions do not mean that the master must sign any bill of lading whatever its terms. For example, the master can refuse to sign a bill of lading 'as presented' if it

   (i) contains facts about the cargo which are incorrect and which cannot be satisfactorily dealt with by following the steps in the section entitled 'Information in the bill of lading' (paragraph 4)

   (ii) contains facts about the voyage which are incorrect or names discharge ports outside the charterparty range

   (iii) says that deck cargo is being carried under deck

   (iv) contains terms which the charterparty expressly prohibits in the bill of lading.

(c) However, if masters are required by the charterparty to sign bills of lading 'as presented' they should not refuse to sign a bill of lading simply because it is marked, for example, 'liner out' or because it contains some foreign jurisdiction clause. These are not facts but terms of the shipper's or charterer's trade. They are matters for the shipowner to argue about with charterer if necessary. If masters are requested to sign 'freight pre-paid' bills of lading their position is slightly less clear and reference should be made to paragraphs 115 – 124 and paragraph 279.

(d) Sometimes commercial pressure will be exerted on masters to sign in circumstances where they should, as advised above, refuse to sign. It is for the shipowner to make commercial decisions in response to such pressure. The shipowner may wish to negotiate, or take the commercial risk, or accept a letter of indemnity. Masters, however, do not have these options. They should maintain their refusal to sign. Delay to the vessel or other consequences of threats made by the shipper or charterer may then perhaps be avoided by the following steps.

   (i) Masters should sign the document in the form that they are prepared to give. For example in the case of a bill of lading where the quantity or description of the cargo is in dispute, masters should sign a bill of lading showing the quantity or description which they consider to be accurate. The bill of lading should be left with the ship's agent (and a protecting agent appointed for this purpose if possible). Notice can then be given that a bill of lading for the cargo has been signed and issued and is available for collection.

   (ii) Alternatively, masters should give notice that they have given authority to the ship's protecting agent to sign bills of lading on their behalf subject to instructions and approval from the shipowner when available.

19. The master should not sign blank bills of lading.

20. Where any person coming on board insists that the master takes delivery of a document from them, the master should mark it 'for receipt only'.

P&I club cover

21. All the commentary in paragraphs 1 – 20 and above is important to the shipowner because signing a document, and in particular a bill of lading, which contains incorrect information can expose the ship to liabilities which it would not otherwise face. In addition to facing those liabilities, the shipowner may lose the protection of its P&I insurance if inaccurate bills of lading are signed and expose the shipowner to increased liability.

DELIVERING THE CARGO AT DISCHARGE PORT

22. The master must deliver the cargo to the holder of a 'bearer' bill of lading (see paragraph 224(e)). If a bill of lading shows a named consignee or named endorsee (see paragraphs 223 and 225) the person demanding delivery of the cargo must provide some evidence that it is the person identified in the bill of lading. As the bill of lading would usually be presented through the shipowner's or time charterer's agents who are local to and familiar with the discharge port, the master probably need only be worried about identification of the person demanding delivery if the master has actual reason for believing there has been fraud or that the bill of lading may have been stolen or that the person is not entitled to claim the goods, or if the master has been notified of a competing claim for the goods ⚖. It is also important to check that if the bill of lading requires endorsement in order to be properly transferred, that it has been properly endorsed ⚖.

With bagged sugar cargo the master would usually be restricted to describing the apparent order and conditions of the bags – in this case the consignment would appear to be in apparent good order and condition

23. The problems which usually arise are where

   (a) no bill of lading is available at the discharge port
   (b) delivery of cargo is requested at a port which is not the named discharge port.

24. In the absence of clear guidance from the shipowner or the local P&I correspondent, the master should take note of the following points.

(a) The unavailability of a bill of lading at the discharge port is a problem for the buyers and sellers of the cargo to resolve ⚖.
(b) The master should not agree to discharge the cargo against a letter of indemnity (unless the shipowner has expressly agreed to this).
(c) Delay to the vessel while waiting for the bill of lading will usually be paid for under the charterparty in the form of hire or demurrage (or as part of the laytime which has been paid for in the freight payment). Even if the vessel is threatened with the cost of the delay, that threat should not justify delivery of the cargo without production of the bill of lading or at the wrong port.
(d) Delivery without production of the bill of lading, or at the wrong port, will be a breach of the terms of the shipowner's P&I insurance and there will be no insurance if in consequence a claim is subsequently brought by the 'true' cargo owner.
(e) In some places the cargo can be discharged (at the named discharge port) into the custody of the port or a private warehouse where it will remain under the legal control of the master until the bill of lading has been produced. The master should investigate this, if possible through the P&I correspondent.
(f) In some countries a 'straight', that is non-negotiable, bill of lading is treated differently and its production is not required in order to demand delivery of the cargo. Local legal advice must be sought if delivery of cargo is demanded on this basis (and see paragraph 287).

Other matters at the time of discharge
25. Lost bills of lading
Sometimes a person will claim to be entitled to possession of the cargo and will provide a plausible explanation that the bills of lading have been lost or destroyed. Sometimes the offer of a letter of indemnity (see below) accompanies the explanation. This is both a legal and a commercial problem for the shipowner and its advisors to resolve and masters should not agree to discharge the cargo (unless the shipowner expressly instructs them to do so) ⚖.

26. Letters of indemnity
The giving of letters of indemnity in return for delivery of cargo at the wrong discharge port or without production of the original bill of lading is not wrong, nor is it unusual. It is, however, a matter for the shipowner to decide upon. It is a commercial decision for it to make and one which it will make taking into consideration the fact that it may have no P&I cover as a consequence of doing so.

27. If the letter of indemnity identifies a specific person to whom the cargo is to be delivered it is important to ensure that delivery is given to that person and that steps are taken to check their true identity, with the assistance of the ship's agent or P&I correspondent, or by asking the charterer (who will usually be the person making such request) to confirm that the person making the demand is the person named in the letter of indemnity.

28. Standard letters of indemnity are included in the appendices. These standard forms include counter-signature by a bank. Banks are rarely prepared to sign an indemnity for unquantified amounts. Frequently, therefore, the letter is accepted without a bank's countersignature. Alternatively a limit (e.g. 200 % of the value of the cargo) is placed on the bank's liability under the letter. Again these are commercial decisions for the shipowner to take.

29. *Photocopy or faxed bills of lading*
Sometimes the master is asked to deliver against a copy or faxed bill of lading, the original being unavailable. Unless special arrangements have been made in writing by the shipowner to accept such a bill of lading, delivery should be refused. The usual rule is that delivery shall be given against presentation of at least one original bill of lading.

30. *Multiple originals*
Bills of lading are often issued in sets of three or four originals. The bill of lading will usually provide on its face that production of any one of those originals, will be acceptable. At the same time, the other originals are considered to be void and cancelled even if they have not been collected in by the master or ship's agent.

31. *Retention of the original bill of lading*
The master should retain the original bill of lading against which cargo has been delivered. However, originals are sometimes required by local officials or customs and in those circumstances masters should ensure that they (or their agents) are allowed to see the original bill of lading and that they are allowed to retain a photocopy of the front and reverse side of the original. This should, if possible, be certified by receivers or their agents as follows: *'This is certified to be a true copy of the original bill of lading which is now accomplished'*.

32. *More than one person demanding delivery of the cargo*
This situation may arise where

(a) no bills of lading are available at the discharge port
(b) more than one set of bills of lading has been placed in circulation, all or some of which are unauthorised
(c) the original shipper has parted with the bills of lading and is asserting that the holder has not complied with its obligations under the sale contract, for example it has somehow acquired the bills of lading without making payment.

33. Each of these situations places the master (and the shipowner) in a very difficult position and can give rise to complex legal issues and may involve complex commercial and legal solutions. The best advice that can be given to masters, if they cannot obtain guidance from the shipowner, is as set out in paragraph 24.

34. *Change of destination during voyage*

Sometimes the master may be asked to change destination during the voyage and to proceed to a discharge port other than that named in the bill of lading. That is a matter for the shipowner to give instructions upon. In the absence of clear guidance from the shipowner or the local P&I correspondent, the master should take note of the following.

(a) Even if the governing charterparty gives a range of discharge ports, once a bill of lading has been issued naming a discharge port, that discharge port should be treated as the required destination.

(b) So far as the bill of lading holder is concerned, the diversion of the vessel to a different discharge port will be a deviation, the consequences of which can be serious for the carrier.

(c) Promises by a person seeking to change the destination (be it charterer, shipper, or receiver) that it holds all of the original bills of lading or that the persons holding the bills of lading have agreed to the change, may at best be meaningless and at worst untrue. If such persons are genuinely in a position to make proper arrangements for the change of destination then they should be in a position to provide a letter of indemnity (see (d) below) including an undertaking for the return of all of the original bills of lading.

(d) As stated at paragraphs 26 and 28, the provision of letters of indemnity in return for delivery of cargo at a different destination is not unusual. However, the standard wording for a change of destination letter of indemnity (see appendix IV) expressly provides for the return of all of the original bills of lading and any letter of indemnity which omits this fundamental provision should be regarded as inadequate and rejected.

A TYPICAL BILL OF LADING – THE BIMCO CONGENBILL

35. A standard printed form of bill of lading is reproduced on pages 24 – 25 at half-size. Each item in the bill of lading has been marked with a circled number which refers to the numbers of the paragraphs in the text below. The standard BIMCO Congenbill 1994 is shown because of its widespread use. Brief comment on the Congenbill 2007 has been added where appropriate, and that form is also reproduced for ease of reference on pages 26 – 27. Although many of the terms and conditions shown on the reverse of the bill of lading are relatively short and simple compared with those of a more detailed liner or combined transport bill, the essential information contained in the Congenbill is typical of many bills of lading.

36. *'Shipper'*

The shipper will frequently be the party who prepares the bill of lading and who supplies much of the information to go in it. This information must be checked carefully. Where the Hague or Hague-Visby or Hamburg Rules apply compulsorily (see paragraphs 82 – 93 and appendices V, VI & VII) the shipper is entitled to have a bill of lading containing specified information issued to it upon shipment of the cargo (see paragraphs 133 – 140). The shipper is under an obligation to provide accurate information and if any of that information is inaccurate and leads to liability of the carrier then in some circumstances the shipper can be liable to indemnify the carrier (see paragraph 203).

37. 'Consignee'

The information contained in this section is not primarily the concern of the master. It is a matter between the seller of the goods (often the shipper) and the intended buyer or buyers. Depending upon the nature of the underlying sales transaction typical entries in the consignee box may be the words 'bearer' or 'holder' or the box may simply be left blank; or it may name a consignee; or it may show the words 'to order' with or without the name of the consignee. Each of these affects the transferability of the bill of lading and, with it, control over the delivery of the goods. See paragraph 224. They are not matters which should trouble the master at the time of issue of the bill of lading.

38. 'Notify address'

This is the address (and usually the name) of the person to whom the shipper requires the shipowner to give notice when the goods arrive at their destination. Typically, the notify address will be the consignee or an agent which has been appointed to collect the goods on their arrival, or a bank ⚖.

39. 'Vessel'

The name of the vessel should be shown. This is necessary for the bill of lading to perform its vital function of showing that the goods have commenced their physical transportation from the seller to the buyer ⚖.

40. 'Port of loading'

Part of the description of the goods, which may be important to the buyer, is their origin. The place of loading may be an important indication of the origin of the goods. It is also relevant to the compulsory application of the Hague, Hague-Visby or Hamburg Rules (see paragraph 82 – 93). Whereas the master should ensure that the port of loading is shown in the bill of lading, it is not for the master to investigate the origin of the goods. A broad description of the name of the load port is adequate.

41. 'Port of discharge'

It is usual for the bill of lading to name a single port of discharge. On occasion, and particularly with liquid cargoes, bills of lading may give the option to the shipper or the charterer to nominate a discharge port after sailing. Where a discharge port is named (or, in the latter case, nominated) and the bill of lading issued, then the shipowner is obliged to go there, unless danger prevents this. Even if the vessel is on charter, and the charterparty provides for a range of ports, once the bill of lading has been signed, the safe course of action is to assume that the shipowner's obligation is to carry the cargo to that named discharge port. To do otherwise may amount to a deviation (see paragraph 229) ⚖. The port of discharge may also influence the compulsory application of the Hamburg Rules (see paragraph 92(a)).

CODE NAME: "CONGENBILL". EDITION 1994

Shipper 36

BILL OF LADING
TO BE USED WITH CHARTER-PARTIES

B/L No.

Reference No.

Consignee 37

Notify address 38

Vessel 39   Port of loading 40

Port of discharge 41

Shipper's description of goods 42   Gross weight 43

(of which   on deck at Shipper's risk; the Carrier not being responsible for loss or damage howsoever arising) 44

Freight payable as per CHARTER-PARTY dated 45

FREIGHT ADVANCE.
Received on account of freight: 46

Time used for loading .... days .... hours. 47

SHIPPED at the Port of Loading in apparent good order and condition on board the Vessel for carriage to the Port of Discharge or so near thereto as she may safely get the goods specified above. 48
Weight, measure, quality, quantity, condition, contents and value unknown. 49
IN WITNESS whereof the Master or Agent of the said Vessel has signed the number of Bills of Lading indicated below all of this tenor and date, any one of which being accomplished the others shall be void. 50
FOR CONDITIONS OF CARRIAGE SEE OVERLEAF

Freight payable at 52   Place and date of issue 54

Number of original Bs/L 53   Signature 55

Printed and sold by
Fr. G. Knudtzons Bogtrykkeri A/S, 55 Toldbodgade, DK-1253 Copenhagen K,
Telefax +45 33 93 11 84
by authority of The Baltic and International Maritime Council
(BIMCO), Copenhagen.

BILL OF LADING

Page 1

TO BE USED WITH CHARTER-PARTIES
CODE NAME: "CONGENBILL"
EDITION 1994
ADOPTED BY
THE BALTIC AND INTERNATIONAL MARITIME COUNCIL (BIMCO)

Conditions of Carriage

(1) All terms and conditions, liberties and exceptions of the Charter Party, dated as overleaf, including the Law and Arbitration Clause, are herewith incorporated.

(2) **General Paramount Clause.**
  (a) The Hague Rules contained in the International Convention for the Unification of certain rules relating to Bills of Lading, dated Brussels the 25th August 1924 as enacted in the country of shipment, shall apply to this Bill of Lading. When no such enactment is in force in the country of shipment, the corresponding legislation of the country of destination shall apply, but in respect of shipments to which no such enactments are compulsorily applicable, the terms of the said Convention shall apply.
  (b) *Trades where Hague-Visby Rules apply.*
  In trades where the International Brussels Convention 1924 as amended by the Protocol signed at Brussels on February 23rd 1968 – the Hague-Visby Rules – apply compulsorily, the provisions of the respective legislation shall apply to this Bill of Lading.
  (c) The Carrier shall in no case be responsible for loss of or damage to the cargo, howsoever arising prior to loading into and after discharge from the Vessel or while the cargo is in the charge of another Carrier, nor in respect of deck cargo or live animals.

(3) **General Average.**
General Average shall be adjusted, stated and settled according to York-Antwerp Rules 1994, or any subsequent modification thereof, in London unless another place is agreed in the Charter Party.
Cargo's contribution to General Average shall be paid to the Carrier even when such average is the result of a fault, neglect or error of the Master, Pilot or Crew. The Charterers, Shippers and Consignees expressly renounce the Belgian Commercial Code, Part II, Art. 148.

(4) **New Jason Clause.**
In the event of accident, danger, damage or disaster before or after the commencement of the voyage, resulting from any cause whatsoever, whether due to negligence or not, for which, or for the consequence of which, the Carrier is not responsible, by statute, contract or otherwise, the cargo, shippers, consignees or the owners of the cargo shall contribute with the Carrier in General Average to the payment of any sacrifices, losses or expenses of a General Average nature that may be made or incurred and shall pay salvage and special charges incurred in respect of the cargo. If a salving vessel is owned or operated by the Carrier, salvage shall be paid for as fully as if the said salving vessel or vessels belonged to strangers. Such deposit as the Carrier, or his agents, may deem sufficient to cover the estimated contribution of the goods and any salvage and special charges thereon shall, if required, be made by the cargo, shippers, consignees or owners of the goods to the Carrier before delivery.

(5) **Both-to-Blame Collision Clause.**
If the Vessel comes into collision with another vessel as a result of the negligence of the other vessel and any act, neglect or default of the Master, Mariner, Pilot or the servants of the Carrier in the navigation or in the management of the Vessel, the owners of the cargo carried hereunder will indemnify the Carrier against all loss or liability to the other or non-carrying vessel or her owners in so far as such loss or liability represents loss of, or damage to, or any claim whatsoever of the owners of said cargo, paid or payable by the other or non-carrying vessel or her owners to the owners of said cargo and set-off, recouped or recovered by the other or non-carrying vessel or her owners as part of their claim against the carrying Vessel or the Carrier.
The foregoing provisions shall also apply where the owners, operators or those in charge of any vessel or vessels or objects other than, or in addition to, the colliding vessels or objects are at fault in respect of a collision or contact.

For particulars of cargo, freight, destination, etc., see overleaf.

BIMCO

CONGENBILL 2007
BILL OF LADING
To be used with charter parties
Page 1

Shipper [36]	Bill of Lading No.	Reference No.

Consignee [37]	Vessel [39]

Notify address [38]	Port of loading [40]
	Port of discharge [41]

Shipper's description of goods [42]

(of which on deck at shipper's risk; the Carrier not being responsible for loss or damage howsoever arising) [44]

Gross weight [43]

Freight payable as per CHARTER PARTY dated: [45]	SHIPPED at the Port of Loading in apparent good order and condition on the Vessel for carriage to the Port of Discharge or so near thereto as the Vessel may safely get the goods specified above. [48]
FREIGHT ADVANCE Received on account of freight: [46]	Weight, measure, quality, quantity, condition, contents and value unknown. [49]
	IN WITNESS whereof the Master or Agent of the said vessel has signed the number of Bills of Lading indicated below all of this tenor and date, any one of which being accomplished the others shall be void. [50]
	FOR CONDITIONS OF CARRIAGE SEE OVERLEAF.

Date shipped on board	Place and date of issue [54]	Number of original Bills of Lading [53]

Signature:

(i) .... Master [55]
    Master's name and signature

Or

(ii) .... as Agent for the Master
    Agent's name and signature

Or

(iii) .... as Agent for the Owner*
    Agent's name and signature

.... Owner
*if option (iii) filled in, state Owner's name above

Revised 1994, 2007 (v2.0)

Printed by BIMCO's *idea*

Copyright, published by BIMCO, Copenhagen

This document is a computer generated CONGENBILL 2007 form printed by authority of BIMCO. Any insertion or deletion to the form must be clearly visible. In the event of any modification made to the pre-printed text of this document which is not clearly visible, the text of the original BIMCO approved document shall apply. BIMCO assumes no responsibility for any loss, damage or expense as a result of discrepancies between the original BIMCO approved document and this computer generated document.

CONGENBILL 2007
BILL OF LADING
To be used with charter parties
Page 2

Conditions of Carriage

(1) All terms and conditions, liberties and exceptions of the Charter Party, dated as overleaf, including the Law and Arbitration Clause/Dispute Resolution Clause, are herewith incorporated.

(2) General Paramount Clause
The International Convention for the Unification of Certain Rules of Law relating to Bills of Lading signed at Brussels on 25 August 1924 ("the Hague Rules") as amended by the Protocol signed at Brussels on 23 February 1968 ("the Hague-Visby Rules") and as enacted in the country of shipment shall apply to this Contract. When the Hague-Visby Rules are not enacted in the country of shipment, the corresponding legislation of the country of destination shall apply, irrespective of whether such legislation may only regulate outbound shipments.

When there is no enactment of the Hague-Visby Rules in either the country of shipment or in the country of destination, the Hague-Visby Rules shall apply to this Contract save where the Hague Rules as enacted in the country of shipment or if no such enactment is in place, the Hague Rules as enacted in the country of destination apply compulsorily to this Contract.

The Protocol signed at Brussels on 21 December 1979 ("the SDR Protocol 1979") shall apply where the Hague-Visby Rules apply, whether mandatorily or by this Contract.

The Carrier shall in no case be responsible for loss of or damage to cargo arising prior to loading, after discharging, or while the cargo is in the charge of another carrier, or with respect to deck cargo and live animals.

(3) General Average
General Average shall be adjusted, stated and settled according to York-Antwerp Rules 1994 in London unless another place is agreed in the Charter Party.

Cargo's contribution to General Average shall be paid to the Carrier even when such average is the result of a fault, neglect or error of the Master, Pilot or Crew.

(4) New Jason Clause
In the event of accident, danger, damage or disaster before or after the commencement of the voyage, resulting from any cause whatsoever, whether due to negligence or not, for which, or for the consequence of which, the Carrier is not responsible, by statute, contract or otherwise, the cargo, shippers, consignees or the owners of the cargo shall contribute with the Carrier in General Average to the payment of any sacrifices, losses or expenses of a General Average nature that may be made or incurred and shall pay salvage and special charges incurred in respect of the cargo. If a salving vessel is owned or operated by the Carrier, salvage shall be paid for as fully as if the said salving vessel or vessels belonged to strangers. Such deposit as the Carrier, or his agents, may deem sufficient to cover the estimated contribution of the goods and any salvage and special charges thereon shall, if required, be made by the cargo, shippers, consignees or owners of the goods to the Carrier before delivery.

(5) Both-to-Blame Collision Clause
If the Vessel comes into collision with another vessel as a result of the negligence of the other vessel and any act, neglect or default of the Master, Mariner, Pilot or the servants of the Carrier in the navigation or in the management of the Vessel, the owners of the cargo carried hereunder will indemnify the Carrier against all loss or liability to the other or non-carrying vessel or her owners in so far as such loss or liability represents loss of, or damage to, or any claim whatsoever of the owners of said cargo, paid or payable by the other or non-carrying vessel or her owners to the owners of said cargo and set-off, recouped or recovered by the other or non-carrying vessel or her owners as part of their claim against the carrying Vessel or the Carrier.
The foregoing provisions shall also apply where the owners, operators or those in charge of any vessel or vessels or objects other than, or in addition to, the colliding vessels or objects are at fault in respect of a collision or contact.

For particulars of cargo, freight, destination, etc., see overleaf

42. 'Shipper's description of goods'

Where the Hague or Hague-Visby or Hamburg Rules apply, the shipper is entitled to require the carrier to issue a bill of lading containing specified information about the goods (see paragraph 133 – 140). The buyer of the cargo will rely upon the bill of lading to identify that the goods are on board and in transit. The buyer will in particular rely upon the accuracy of the description given in the bill of lading. The description of the goods is something which the carrier may wish to qualify because of its limited knowledge about their condition and quantity. The use of qualifying words such as those shown at paragraphs 48 and 49 is vital in protecting the master from giving descriptions of the cargo which are binding upon the carrier and which it may have no means of checking accurately. This is one of the most fundamental and frequent areas of disputes and it is dealt with in practical terms in paragraphs 1 – 21 and in more theoretical terms in paragraphs 105 – 186.

43. 'Gross weight'

See paragraph 42. It is important that master state the source of their information as to weight and, if possible, state any conflicting information as to weight which they may have derived from other sources. Qualifying words may be 'shipper's' figures' or 'said to weigh' or, preferably, the words which appear at paragraph 49. This is one of the most fundamental and frequent areas of dispute and it is dealt with in practical terms in paragraphs 1 – 21 and in more theoretical terms in paragraphs 105 – 186.

It is difficult to establish exactly how many roof tiles are broken on these pallets - a reasonable estimate should be made and suitable remark inserted on the bill of lading to describe the apparent order and condition and also to draw attention to the inadequacy of the packaging

44. '(of which [quantity] on deck at Shipper's risk; the Carrier not being responsible for loss or damage howsoever arising)'

Carriage of cargo on deck when the shipper has not agreed to it or where there is no universal custom of deck carriage, is a serious breach of the contract of carriage. If the terms of the bill of lading expressly state that cargo can be carried on deck then it is important to ensure that the bill of lading also states that the cargo actually is carried on deck (see paragraph 187). The standard Congenbill form does *not* contain such an express term giving liberty to the carrier to carry goods on deck and the simple wording shown here is not sufficient to give such a liberty.

45. 'Freight payable as per CHARTERPARTY dated [date]'

There may be a number of charterparties and therefore the master should if possible check with the shipowner to see what date is to be inserted in the bill of lading. The shipowner is in the best position to advise on this. The importance of inserting the date in the charterparty is that many of the protective clauses in the charterparty which are designed to protect the shipowner may in many legal systems be considered to be incorporated into the bill of lading only if the date of the charterparty is shown on the bill of lading (see paragraph 51.1). The significance of this sentence is therefore not limited purely to freight but also extends to a whole range of other protective conditions. For further guidance see paragraphs 274 – 277.

46. 'FREIGHT ADVANCE. Received on account of freight:'

The reference to freight advance is rarely completed. If other terms as to freight have been written on the bill of lading presented to the master for signature, he should seek guidance from the shipowner. For practical guidance see paragraph 18 and for the underlying theory see paragraphs 115 – 124 and paragraph 279.

The apparent order and condition of a solid bulk cargo may require some qualifying words, for example if it is found to be lumpy

47. *'Time used for loading [no.] days [no.] hours.'*

This is rarely completed. If the ship is on charter, masters should not refuse to sign any bill of lading simply because they disagree with the figure inserted here by the shipper, unless they have clear instructions from the shipowner to do so. They should insert their own and the shipper's figures in the bill of lading and issue a letter of protest to the charterer and shipper setting out their own calculation of time used. (This item does not appear in Congenbill 2007).

48. *'SHIPPED at the Port of Loading in apparent good order and condition on board the Vessel for carriage to the Port of Discharge or so near thereto as she may safely get the goods specified above'.*

For 'SHIPPED' see paragraph 39. For 'Port of Loading' see paragraph 40. For 'apparent good order and condition' see paragraph 159. For 'Port of Discharge' see paragraph 41. For 'or so near thereto so she can safely get' see paragraph 233.

49. *'Weight, measure, quality, quantity, condition, contents and value unknown.'*

See paragraphs 42 and 44 and 158 and 168.

50. (first part) *'IN WITNESS whereof the Master or Agent of the said Vessel has signed the number of bills of Lading indicated below all of this tenor and date...'*

As a general rule, the bill of lading may be signed by the shipowner, masters or their agents, charterers or their agents, or the shipowner's loading agent. It is both common sense, and in accordance with UCP 600 (see paragraphs 76 – 79) for the person signing the bill of lading to state the capacity in which they are signing: for example 'charterer as agent for the master' or, in the case of an agent, 'as agent for the master', or 'charterer's agent as agent for the master'. Whether a party has authority to sign, and whether having so signed the bill of lading they create a contract between the shipowner and the shipper (an owner's bill) or between the charterer and the shipper (a charterer's bill) is dealt with in paragraphs 125 – 128 and paragraph 271 – 273. Traditionally the number of bills issued has been three in a set. The number actually issued is shown on the face of the bill of lading in the appropriate box. Also see paragraph 53. However this is not a universal practice and one or any number of bills of lading can be issued and the number shown on the face of each bill of lading. (In Congenbill 2007, the signature box is designed to provide greater clarity as to the identity of the signatory)

50. (second part) *'...any one of which being accomplished the others shall be void.'*

Even though a number of originals may have been issued, presentation of any one original to the master (in the circumstances described in paragraphs 22 and 247) is sufficient and at that moment the function of the bill of lading has been achieved (or 'accomplished') and the other bills of lading become worthless (except as evidence in the event of a dispute, for which reason they should be retained carefully). 'Accomplished' is a reference to the bill of lading having completed its work, and that upon delivery of the cargo and the surrender of the bill of lading, it has become void.

51. 'Conditions of Carriage'

51.1. *All terms and conditions, liberties and exceptions of the charterparty, dated as overleaf, including the Law and Arbitration Clause, are herewith incorporated.*

The conditions of carriage referred to are set out on the back of the bill of lading. The back of the bill of lading is as important as the face and wherever a copy of the bill of lading is requested the front and back should be supplied and carefully examined. The conditions of carriage which are set out on the reverse will be added to by the terms of any charterparty referred to in the 'Freight payable' section overleaf (see paragraph 45). The extent to which the charterparty terms can be incorporated in the bill of lading in this way depends upon the extent of the incorporating words and the words used in the charterparty itself and is a matter of detailed English case law. See paragraphs 274 – 277. (Congenbill 2007 slightly modifies this to include a reference to any Alternative Dispute Resolution clause which may be in the incorporated charterparty).

51.2. *General Paramount Clause*

(a) The Hague Rules contained in the International Convention for the Unification of certain rules relating to bills of Lading, dated Brussels the 25th August 1924 as enacted in the country of shipment, shall apply to this bill of Lading. When no such enactment is in force in the country of shipment, the corresponding legislation of the country of destination shall apply, but in respect of shipments to which no such enactments are compulsorily applicable, the terms of the said Convention shall apply.

(b) Trades where Hague-Visby Rules apply. In trades where the International Brussels Convention 1924 as amended by the Protocol signed at Brussels on February 23rd 1968 – the Hague-Visby Rules – apply compulsorily, the provisions of the respective legislation shall apply to this bill of Lading.

(c) The Carrier shall in no case be responsible for loss of or damage to the cargo, howsoever arising prior to loading into and after discharge from the Vessel or while the cargo is in the charge of another Carrier, nor in respect of deck cargo or live animals.

Mention should be made of contents spilling from bags

The first two paragraphs, (a) and (b), are the mechanism by which the Hague or the Hague-Visby rules will apply contractually. This contractual application is over and above any compulsory application imposed by virtue of the goods having been shipped from, or the bill of lading having been issued in, a country which has given effect to the Hague or Hague-Visby rules. (See paragraphs 80 – 90). The third paragraph, (c), attempts to limit the scope of responsibility. It is permissible under the Hague or Hague-Visby rules for shipowners to limit their responsibility so that they are not responsible before loading or after discharge, and to avoid responsibility in respect of deck cargo or live animals. However, so far as deck cargo is concerned, the simple attempt at exclusion of liability at (c) will not be effective unless the cargo was carried on deck by agreement or by universal custom, and the bills of lading clearly show the cargo has been stowed on deck. If those requirements are not satisfied the shipowner will be liable for any damage caused by the cargo being on deck and may also lose the protection of P&I club cover. (See paragraphs 103 and 187). (Congenbill 2007 adopts BIMCO's latest Clause Paramount, which favours the Hague Visby Rules and SDR protocol (package limitation) over the Hague Rules).

51.3. *General Average*

General Average shall be adjusted, stated and settled according to York-Antwerp Rules 1994, or any subsequent modification thereof, in London unless another place in agreed in the charterparty.

Cargo's contribution to General Average shall be paid to the Carrier even when such average is the result of a fault, neglect or error of the Master, Pilot or Crew. The Charterers, Shippers and Consignees expressly renounce the Belgian Commercial Code, Part II, Art. 148.

This is a standard provision designed to ensure certainty as to the general average regime to apply in the event of general average sacrifice or expenditure, and to identify the place of adjustment. (Congenbill 2007 has removed the reference to 'any subsequent modification' in order to avoid the unintended incorporation of the 2004 Rules, which are less favourable to shipowners. The reference to the Belgian Commercial Code has also been removed).

51.4. *New Jason Clause*

In the event of accident, danger, damage or disaster before or after the commencement of the voyage, resulting from any cause whatsoever, whether due to negligence or not, for which, or for the consequence of which, the Carrier is not responsible, by statute, contract or otherwise, the cargo, shippers, consignees or the owners of the cargo shall contribute with the Carrier in General Average to the payment of any sacrifices, losses or expenses of a General Average nature that may be made or incurred and shall pay salvage and special charges incurred in respect of the cargo. If a salving vessel is owned or operated by the Carrier, salvage shall be paid for as fully as if the said salving vessel or vessels belonged to strangers. Such deposit as the Carrier, or his agents, may deem sufficient to cover the estimated contribution of the goods and any salvage and special charges thereon shall, if required, be made by the cargo, shippers, consignees or owners of the goods to the Carrier before delivery.

This is a standard clause that deals with obligations of all the parties involved in the voyage to contribute to general average. It is a purely legal provision and need not concern the master.

51.5. *Both-to-Blame Collision Clause*

If the Vessel comes into collision with another vessel as a result of the negligence of the other vessel and any act, neglect or default of the Master, Mariner, Pilot or the servants of the Carrier in the navigation or in the management of the Vessel, the owners of the cargo carried hereunder will indemnify the Carrier against all loss or liability to the other or noncarrying vessel or her owners in so far as such loss or liability represents loss of, or damage to, or any claim whatsoever of the owners of said cargo, paid or payable by the other or non-carrying vessel or her owners to the owners of said cargo and set-off, recouped or recovered by the other or non-carrying vessel or her owners as part of their claim against the carrying Vessel or the Carrier.

The foregoing provisions shall also apply where the owners, operators, or those in charge of any vessel or vessels or objects other than, or in addition to, the colliding vessels or objects are at fault in respect of a collision or contact.

This is a standard clause dealing with cross and counter claims in collision cases. It is a purely legal provision and need not concern the master.

51.6 Occasionally, additional terms and conditions will be added even to standard bills of lading such as the Congenbill. A typical term may be a lien clause or a choice of jurisdiction or place of arbitration clause. If the vessel is operating under a charterparty, it will sometimes require additional clauses to be inserted in the bill of lading.

52. *'Freight Payable at [place]'*

This may show a specific place for payment but, if completed, is more likely to show freight payable at 'destination'. (This item does not appear in Congenbill 2007).

53. *'Number of original Bs/L'*

Traditionally the number of bills issued has been three in a set. However this is not a universal practice and one or any number of bills can be issued and shown on the face of the bill of lading itself. Usually the bill of lading will be given a number shown in the top right hand corner of the front of the bill. Bills of lading for carriage to the United States will show an SCAC number (comprising a four digit number and then a second reference of up to twelve letters or numbers), which is unique to the carrier and to the bill of lading.

54. *'Place and date of issue'*

The date of issue is extremely important, as often the value of the cargo or the price to be paid or the effectiveness of the underlying sales transaction will be governed by the date of issue of the bill of lading. See paragraph 188. It is essential that a 'shipped' bill of lading shows the date on which completion of loading occurred in respect of the parcel of cargo identified in the bill of lading. It is not essential that the bill of lading is issued at the port of loading – although, of course, the port of loading must be named. If the place of issue is not the port of loading, the place of issue still has significance because it can affect the compulsory application of the Hague, Hague-Visby or Hamburg rules.

55. *'Signature'.*

See paragraph 50.

THEORY

HISTORY AND CONTEXT

56. Legal text books traditionally define and analyse the bill of lading by its three distinct functions

(a) as a receipt which shows what has been loaded on the ship
(b) as a document of title which shows who can demand the goods at the discharge port
(c) as a contract of carriage.

57. Although this guide adopts the more practical approach of following the life of the bill from its issue to delivery of the cargo, it is useful to keep these three functions in mind. They can most easily be understood by examining the simple origins of the bill of lading.

Evolution

58. When the owner of goods puts them on board a ship as cargo, it will expect to receive from the master a document, signed by the master, confirming that the goods have been received on board. This document or receipt was the first type of bill of lading.

59. In the early days of commerce, the owner of the goods, a merchant or trader of some sort, would often travel with the goods and sell them at their destination. The merchant would tender the bill of lading to the master at the discharge port and in return, the master would release the goods to the merchant or, at personal direction, to the buyer. The function of the bill of lading remained simple.

60. As commerce became more sophisticated the merchants and traders became involved in more shipments and were unlikely to sail with any of them. In those circumstance it became important for them to be able to give the master orders as to delivery of the goods. The delivery order would be written upon the bill of lading and would tell the master with whom he should deal at the discharge port.

61. The law developed alongside these commercial developments and soon recognised the bill of lading as a document which gave certain rights to the person holding it. The transfer of the bill of lading accordingly became the practical method of transfer of ownership of the goods. It became a document of title ⚖️.

62. As the bill of lading was now symbolic of the goods themselves, it was more important than ever for the bill of lading to state clearly the facts about those goods, namely that they had been shipped on board, their general description, their quantity, and their apparent order and condition. The buyer had a sale contract and the buyer wanted to check the detail of the goods before the buyer paid the price. The buyer relied principally on the bill of lading for this. The duty to make the bill of lading accurate was that of the master and so the bill of lading as a receipt became more important and more burdensome to him.

63. The law reinforced the buyer's expectations by recognising that the bill of lading gave the buyer not only the right to demand delivery of the goods, but also the right to sue the shipowner for any failure on its part. The buyer was entitled to expect the goods to be carried safely to their destination. If they were not, the shipowner would be liable. The embodiment in the bill of lading of these liabilities, and reasonable defences to them, was the third function of the bill of lading, as a contact of carriage.

64. With its three inter-woven functions, as a receipt, as a document of title, and as a contract of carriage, the bill of lading plays a unique and important part in any international sales transaction. But there is another important document – the contract of sale. Although the master may never see such a contract, it is important to understand the basic nature of that contract and this is considered in more detail below. But first, the law.

The law

65. This guide assumes the application of English law to the sale transaction and to the bill of lading. Often English law will be chosen by the parties to apply. On other occasions it will govern by implication. Even where English law is not directly or indirectly chosen it provides a useful guide, as to a great extent English law reflects the practical needs of commerce, which in many respects are the same throughout the world.

66. The law applying to a bill of lading will rarely be found simply by looking at the bill of lading itself. Furthermore, if English law applies, it cannot be found in one book or code.

67. In a typical commercial transaction in which a bill of lading is involved the rights and obligations of the parties may come from a number of sources.

(a) Many of the rights and obligations are written on the face and reverse of the bill of lading. So, for example, the name of the load port, the discharge port to which the vessel must proceed, and the basis on which general average is to be adjusted and paid, may be written on the bill of lading and if they are, are known as express terms of the contract.

(b) Sometimes the law finds it sensible to add its own terms to a contract so that it makes good business sense. So, for example, even the simplest bill of lading carries with it an implied term that the carrying vessel will be seaworthy.

(c) Sometimes terms are imposed on the parties to the contract by international convention. When a number of countries agree on a specific set of rights and obligations which should apply to the carriage of goods by sea or to the ownership and operation of ships they will usually set them down in the form of an agreed code or convention. The best known of these conventions, dealing with the rights and obligations applying to the carriage of goods by sea, are the Hague Rules, the Hague-Visby Rules and, more recently, the Hamburg Rules. These conventions may apply as a matter of local law at the place of loading or discharge or issue of the bill of lading. Sometimes they will apply through express choice, see (d) below. (A new convention, the Rotterdam Rules, has been adopted by the United Nations but awaits full ratification and enactment. For a little more detail see paragraph 94).

(d) Sometimes additional rights and liabilities will be included or incorporated by reference being made in the bill of lading to a convention or to another document. So, for example, a bill of lading may expressly refer to the Hague Rules or Hague-Visby Rules or Hamburg Rules or, for example, may refer to a charterparty or the terms of a booking note (particularly in a liner service). If it does then the party holding the bill of lading will be assumed to have knowledge of the terms of that convention or charterparty or booking note, even if the party has not taken the trouble in fact to obtain a copy of it or to look at it.

(e) English statute law and common law. English modern law is based on case law (i.e. an accumulation of the decisions which have been made in cases over the years, sometimes also known as common law), together with statute law. Statutes relevant to the subjects covered in this guide may include the various Sale of Goods Acts (dealing with the relationship between the seller of the cargo and the buyer of the cargo), Merchant Shipping Acts (dealing with the ownership and operation of ships including limitation of liability), the Carriage of Goods by Sea Acts 1924 and 1971 (which are the English enactments of the Hague and Hague-Visby Rules respectively, referred to above) and the Carriage of Goods by Sea Act 1992 (which deals with the transfer of the right to bring actions under a bill of lading, from the shipper of the goods to subsequent holders of the bill of lading).

(f) In addition, attempts have been made from time to time by commercial groups and organisations to standardise sensible and common practices within international

Cardboard cartons can be easily damaged – any damage noted should be recorded on the mate's receipt and bill of lading

trade. UCP600 and the Incoterms are examples of these and are referred to later in this guide. These are nothing more than codes which have attempted to give internationally recognised meanings to particular words and expressions used in sale and finance contracts. The parties may choose to apply then. They are not mandatory and should be distinguished from conventions which have been made law in each country which has created or adopted the convention. UCP 600 and the Incoterms do not have any binding force of law unless expressly chosen, but they do reflect current practices and are good guidance as to what should be done in the absence of any other guidance to the contrary.

68. All the sources, rights and obligations will work together to create the legal environment in which a bill of lading functions. Sometimes the rights and obligations will be considered by the law to be of significant and fundamental importance. On other occasions, they will be considered to be of minor importance. The most important rights and obligations will be considered in the remainder of this guide.

The international sale of goods – background

69. The agreement between a seller and buyer of goods is contained in the sale contract and this will contain whatever arrangement or provision the seller and buyer may choose for their specific purpose and needs. Where the transaction involves the transportation of goods by sea, the bill of lading is one of a number of documents which is customarily used to make that sale contact work. To avoid misunderstandings as to which party is bearing which risk in the sale or carriage of the goods, many attempts have been made to achieve uniformity of terms. Some may be adopted voluntarily, others may apply compulsorily. The most important are Incoterms 2010, UCP600, and the Hague and Hague-Visby Rules.

Incoterms 2010

70. The seller and the buyer decide in their sale contract who will do what. For example, in a simple transaction, the buyer may agree to collect the goods from the seller's factory or warehouse and to undertake all the responsibility and cost for transportation involved in getting the goods safely to their destination. Alternatively, the seller may agree that it will do everything necessary to get the goods to the buyer's chosen destination. The parties can negotiate the words of their contract on each occasion that they work together. However, an attempt world-wide to standardise transactions like these, and most variations in between, can be found in the Incoterms 2010.

71. The Incoterms (an abbreviation for 'International Commercial Terms' and which were devised by the International Chamber of Commerce in 1936) can be adopted voluntarily by the seller and buyer, or, sometimes, by international custom of the trade or by implication. They are usually represented by abbreviations in the sale contract. The abbreviation utilised indicates what obligations are undertaken by the seller as part of the all-inclusive price of the goods. So, for example, in a CIF contract the seller arranges insurance and carriage and the price paid by the buyer will include the cost of the goods, the insurance cost, and the freight.

72. Some of the Incoterms place an obligation on the seller not only to deliver the goods but also to deliver shipping documents to the buyer. The bill of lading is the most common and vital of these shipping documents. The Incoterms where a bill of lading (or similar shipping document) is vital are

- CFR (C & F) cost and freight
- CIF (cost, insurance and freight)
- CPT (carriage paid to...)
- CIP (carriage and insurance paid)
- FOB (free on board).

73. All of the abbreviations are used for convenience between the seller and buyer. They will not usually appear in the bill of lading. They are matters between the seller and buyer of the goods and need not concern the shipowner or master. However, because in each of these cases the bill of lading is one of the key documents in the sale transaction, these are the categories of sale contract where problems are most likely to arise for the ship, and so a little more commentary on the two most frequently used terms, CIF and FOB may be helpful.

74. Under the CIF contract the seller puts the goods on board the ship, pays the freight, and insures the cargo. The seller therefore has rights against the insurance company and rights against the ship. To transfer these rights to the buyer the seller will deliver to the buyer (in return for payment of the CIF price), the insurance policy or certificate, and the shipping documents, one of which is the bill of lading. The legal right and obligations under the bill of lading may be transferred to the buyer by consignment or endorsement. These expressions are explained in paragraph 224.

75. Under the other main Incoterm, the FOB contract, the buyer finds space on a ship for its cargo. The buyer will do this either by finding a suitable liner service or by chartering a vessel in. The buyer will also arrange its own insurance on the cargo. The seller only has to put the goods on board the ship named by the buyer. The seller will obtain a mate's receipt which the seller will deliver to the buyer. The buyer will use this mate's receipt to obtain, through the ship's agent, the bill of lading. There may be a variation of the FOB, contract where the seller has to obtain and provide to the buyer the bill of lading, rather than the mates' receipt. The sale contract decides this ⚖.

UCP600

76. Any international sale transaction requires payment to be made by the buyer to the seller. This can be done by cash, or by various collection arrangements under which the seller's bank holds the key documents and releases them only when it has received payment from the buyer, or, most frequently, through some kind of documentary credit arrangement. A documentary credit arrangement involves the buyer of the goods making an arrangement with its bank to issue a promise (a letter of credit) to the seller that the bank will pay against receipt of the shipping documents. One such shipping document is the bill of lading. To ensure the ease of arranging such documentary credits, the International Chamber of Commerce devised in 1933 a code for the Uniform Customs and Practice for

Documentary Credits ('UCP Rules'). These rules, with the current edition being known as UCP600, apply by reason of being adopted by the banks or chambers of commerce or simply by incorporation of the UCP600 terms in the documentary credit itself.

77. UCP600 Articles 20 to 22 list the information that an 'ocean' or 'port to port' bill of lading (or charterparty bill of lading, or seawaybill) must contain so that it can pass through the banking system in a smooth and efficient way.

78. As between the buyer and the seller, therefore, there are a number of requirements which the bill of lading must satisfy because the Incoterms have been adopted in the sale contract or because UCP600 requires it. These are all matters for the seller and the buyer and they are not for the master to worry about.

79. The master will rarely (or probably never) see, and should not expect to see, the sale contract between the buyer and the seller or the terms of any documentary credit.

Conventions dealing with the care of cargo

80. The quest for certainty, however, goes beyond the terms of the sale contract and the financial arrangements which have been made for payment. The parties to the sale contract will also need to know that the goods will be transported carefully and on a seaworthy ship, and that if they are not that they will have some right of action against the carrier. As these rights may be transferred through the hands of the various persons holding the bills of lading during the transaction, each will need to have some idea of the risks and rights which accompany the sea voyage.

81. In an attempt to create uniformity of rights and obligations of shipowners and cargo owners, a large number of countries involved in the carriage of goods by sea (either as shipowners or as merchants or as both) have agreed from time to time to set out these rights and obligations in the form of agreed conventions. There are many conventions in the maritime world but the principal ones relevant to the issues in this guide are now discussed below.

Hague and Hague-Visby Rules

82. The terms of the Hague Rules were drafted at the Hague in 1921 and adopted by a number of countries in a meeting in Brussels in 1924. Additional countries then also agreed to adopt the rules as applying compulsorily to carriage by sea in which their country was involved. Various amendments were made over the years and a revised convention was made following a meeting at Visby in 1963 which led to the adoption by the member countries in 1968 of the revised rules known as the Hague-Visby Rules.

83. The English version of the original Hague Rules is set out in appendix V. The English version of the Hague-Visby Rules is set out in appendix VI. The countries which have agreed to apply the Hague and Hague-Visby Rules are listed in appendix VIII.

84. The intention of the conventions is to provide a balanced regime of rights and obligations so that the cargo owner can expect a certain standard of care from the shipowner in maintaining its ship and in caring for the cargo; and the shipowner can be protected from claims where, despite its maintenance and care, the cargo is damaged.

85. The method of application of the conventions is basically as follows. Countries which have chosen to apply the Hague or Hague-Visby Rules enact legislation in their own country (for example in the UK the Carriage of Goods by Sea Acts of 1924 and 1971) which says that the terms of the convention are to apply as if they were part of the national law. The convention itself sets out the voyages to which the Hague or Hague-Visby Rules will apply compulsorily. In very broad terms these are voyages from contracting states or where the bill of lading has been issued in a contracting state. The term 'contracting states' is simply a way of describing countries which have agreed to apply the conventions.

86. Quite often the seller and buyer of goods, or a carrier of goods, will decide that even where one or other of the conventions does not apply compulsorily (for example because the shipment is not from a contracting state), they would still like the well-understood regime of the conventions to apply to the voyage in question. In those circumstances, the parties can in the bill of lading choose to apply the terms of the convention by incorporating them by way of contractual clauses written in to the contract. An example of a contractual clause which provides that the Hague or Hague-Visby Rules are to apply contractually, in any case where there is no compulsory application, can be found on the back of the standard printed Congenbill (see paragraph 51.2).

The timber inside these packages cannot be seen by the master it is therefore important that a clear remark is made on the mate's receipt and bill of lading that the outer packaging is wet, stained and damaged

87. The rights and liabilities of the shipowner under the conventions are in essence simple, although in their application over the years, the case law has become quite complex. The obligations placed on the shipowner are

(a) to exercise due diligence to make its ship in all respects seaworthy (see paragraph 237)

(b) to care for the cargo while it is in its custody (see paragraph 238).

88. In return for the shipowner accepting these obligations, it is afforded some defences. The convention recognises that cargo can be lost or damaged even in circumstances where the shipowner has exercised due diligence to make its ship seaworthy, or where events beyond the shipowner's control occur, such as some inherent problem with the cargo, or some latent problem with the vessel which it could not by the exercise of due diligence identify, or due to perils of the sea beyond those which the shipowner could have expected on the voyage undertaken. There are many specific and general defences, all of which are listed in Article 4 rules 1 and 2 in both the Hague and Hague-Visby Rules.

89. The conventions also recognise that even where the shipowner is liable, it is in the interests of the trading community as a whole that the shipowner should, unless it is completely reckless, be able to limit its ultimate liability to an amount related to the quantity and value of the cargo being carried. To leave the shipowner with open ended liability could make shipowning and operating unviable. The conventions therefore specify a maximum level of liability according to the weight of the cargo or the number of packages. This is often referred to as 'package limitation'.

90. All of these principles are embraced in the Hague and Hague-Visby conventions. Their precise application is not straightforward and it is not the role of this guide to examine the complexities which have arisen out of the drafting and application of the conventions. However, one very important point about the Hague and Hague-Visby Rules is that they impose on the shipowner an obligation as to the content of the bills of lading which are to be issued when goods have been shipped on board its vessel, and they state what reliance can be placed upon that information by the holder of the bill of lading. This particular aspect of the Hague and Hague-Visby Rules is perhaps the most important for the purposes of this guide and it is dealt with specifically in paragraphs 133 – 139.

The Hamburg Rules

91. Despite the widespread adoption and understanding of the Hague and Hague-Visby Rules, there has been a move, principally among countries which trade as merchants rather than shipowners, to impose a rather more onerous regime compulsorily upon shipowners. This has led to the adoption by a number of countries of a competing regime known as the Hamburg Rules. These were devised in a United Nations convention in 1978 and had gained sufficient support to come in to force in 1992. The terms of the Hamburg Rules are set out in appendix VII and the countries which have ratified or adopted them are set out in appendix VIII.

92. The Hamburg Rules attempt compulsorily to exclude the application of the Hague or Hague-Visby Rules. The main regime of rights and obligations as set out in the Hamburg Rules can essentially be described as follows.

(a) The intended scope of application of the Hamburg Rules is wide. The basis of their application still depends upon contracting states having agreed to apply the convention as a matter of their national law, but the scope of application includes voyages not only from but also to ports in contracting states.

(b) The Hamburg Rules provide a cargo claimant with a greater number of options as to where the claimant can commence its action, even to the extent of overriding arbitration provisions.

(c) The period of responsibility is far greater then under the Hague/Hague Visby regime and puts the carrier under a liability throughout the time that it has the cargo, as distinct from the 'tackle to tackle' responsibility which is the basic provision in the Hague and Hague-Visby Rules.

(d) Most importantly, the basis of liability is that the carrier is presumed to be at fault if the goods are damaged or lost, or if there is delay in delivery. The carrier, to avoid liability, must then prove that it, its servants and its agents took all measures which could reasonably be taken to avoid the occurrence in question. The only exception to the presumed fault principle is where loss, damage or delay has been occasioned by fire and in these circumstances the burden will lie upon the claimant to show that the fire or the loss, damage or delay resulted from the carriers' fault.

(e) Limits of liability are about 25% higher than under the Hague-Visby Rules.

(f) Liability for delay is expressly imposed, and the cargo is deemed to be lost if it is not delivered within 60 days of the appropriate time for delivery.

93. It is worth stating that the Hamburg Rules have not yet had a wide impact and there is little sign of their displacing the Hague and Hague-Visby Rules. However, for the purposes of this guide it is worthwhile to note the information which under the Hamburg Rules, the shipper is entitled to demand in a bill of lading – see paragraph 140.

The Rotterdam Rules

94. Although the Hamburg Rules have not achieved a wide impact and have done little to displace the Hague or Hague Visby Rules, nevertheless the United Nations Commission on International Trade Law continues to hold the belief that the adoption of uniform but updated rules to govern modern international contracts of carriage would play a fundamental role in promoting trade and economic development, domestically and internationally. In sessions in 2001 and 2002 the Commission thus decided to start work on a new convention, which resulted in the Rotterdam Rules.

95. The Rotterdam Rules will come into force one year after the twentieth ratification by a signatory country. Any country which has adopted the convention will then be expected to treat the convention as having force in that state, and recognising that it is in force in other contracting states. At the same time the contracting country will be expected to withdraw from the other previous conventions that it has adopted, that is the Hague, Hague Visby or the Hamburg Rules, whichever is applicable.

96. As with the Hague, Hague Visby and Hamburg Rules, the intention of the Rotterdam Rules is to provide a balanced regime of rights and obligations so that the cargo owner can expect a certain standard of care from the shipowner in maintaining its ship and in caring for the cargo; and the shipowner can be protected from claims where, despite its maintenance and care, the cargo is damaged. However, the Rotterdam Rules attempt a far more detailed approach and seek to take into account modern transport practices, including containerisation, door-to-door transport contracts and the use of electronic transport documents. As with the Hamburg Rules, the balance shifts away from the shipowner in that defences are reduced, and package limitation of liability is increased to a higher limit when contrasted with any of the preceding conventions.

97. It is intended to publish a detailed and revised version of this guide when the twentieth acceptance signature by a contracting country as referred to at paragraph 95 occurs.

COGSA 1992

98. Finally, mention should be made of the UK Carriage of Goods by Sea Act 1992. Despite its name, this is not a close relative of the Carriage of Goods by Sea Acts 1924 and 1971 referred to earlier, which gave effect to the Hague and Hague-Visby Rules respectively. The Carriage of Goods by Sea Act 1992 (COGSA 92) is not an act designed to give effect to an international convention and it does not relate to the allocation of rights and obligations between merchants and carriers in carrying cargo. Its role is to give legal effect to the intended transfer of rights and responsibilities under the bill of lading as it passes from holder to holder and thereby identify who is the party who can legally bring an action against (or 'sue') the shipowner under a bill of lading. It is therefore of relevance in determining who can demand delivery of the goods ⚖⚖.

99. It is not necessary to look into the intricacies of COGSA 92 for the purpose of this guide. Suffice to say that COGSA 1992 does not try to link the passing of title to sue with the ownership of the cargo, but simply says that the lawful holder of the bill of lading can sue. If it transpires that the holder is not the owner of the cargo, but the true owner is the one who has suffered loss if the cargo is lost or damaged, then the holder must sue and hold the proceeds for the benefit of the true owner. By the same reasoning, the holder of the bill of lading is the person to whom the master should deliver the cargo, save where there are suspicious circumstances such as those described in paragraph 22 ⚖⚖.

100. As a final complication, COGSA 1992 does take the opportunity of correcting an old anomaly in English case law. COGSA 1992 now supplements the provisions of the Carriage of Goods by Sea Acts 1924 and 1971 in one respect; namely that when a bill of lading states that goods have been received on board, the shipowner is now prevented (estopped) from denying that statement, even though in fact the goods were not shipped on board. The case law before COGSA 92 stated that a master had no authority to sign a bill of lading for cargo which had not been put on board. The act now adopts the policy that if a person buys a bill of lading which, by its very nature, says that goods have been shipped, then they

are entitled to rely on that statement and to sue the shipowner if the goods 'shipped' do not arrive ⚖️.

The shipowner's insurance

101. If the shipowner accepts cargo on board its ship, and does not meet the shipowner's basic obligations of carrying that cargo to its destination safely and there delivering the cargo to the rightful receiver, then the shipowner can expect to face claims from the cargo owner for loss, damage or wrongful delivery. To obtain some protection in respect of these liabilities, the shipowner will arrange P&I (protection and indemnity) insurance so that if it pays these liabilities, the P&I association (commonly known as a 'P&I club') will reimburse it.

102. However, the P&I clubs will expect a certain standard of conduct from the shipowner not only in the way that it maintains its ship, and in the nature of the business it undertakes, but also in the manner in which it conducts itself with regard to the issue of bills of lading and its compliance with obligations under that bill of lading.

103. So far as the master is concerned, this standard of conduct is laid down by the P&I club in the P&I rules contained in the P&I rule book which will usually be issued annually and ideally be on board the vessel. Typical rules would say as follows.

(a) That, as to the issue of bills of lading, a shipowner may not be entitled to protection from its P&I club in circumstances where bills of lading are issued by it which

- do not show the correct date
- do not contain an accurate description of the cargo or its quantity or condition

(b) That, as to the voyage, the shipowner may not be entitled to protection from its P&I club if

- there is a deviation from the contractual voyage
- cargo is carried on deck in circumstances where an express right to carry the cargo on deck has not been agreed between the shipowner and the cargo owner

Cardboard cartons can be easily damaged if wet – any such damage must be clearly recorded at the time of loading and noted on the mate's receipts and bills of lading

- carriage is on terms less protective to the shipowner than the Hague or Hague-Visby Rules (unless the Hamburg Rules have applied unavoidably by operations of law).
(c) That, as to the completion of the voyage, the shipowner may not be entitled to protection from its P&I club if
    - the cargo is delivered at the wrong discharge port
    - the cargo is delivered to a person who has not been able to produce one of the original bills of lading
    - under a waybill or non-negotiable bill, delivery has been given to someone other than the person named in that document as the person to whom delivery should be made.
(d) That, where electronic bills of lading are used, the shipowner may not be entitled to protection from its P&I club if the claim would not have arisen if a traditional paper bill of lading had been used. For more detail see the section on electronic bills of lading and in particular paragraphs 308 – 312.
(e) In addition to the rules, the P&I club will also issue regular circulars which are distributed to all members and which may contain guidance on the subject of bills of lading.

104. Each of the points made by the rules is, of course, of the utmost importance for the master to understand. The rules clearly reflect the legal and commercial expectations of the sellers and buyers of the goods as described in the following chapters in this guide. The P&I club rules do not impose on the commercial transaction anything which is not already there. They do, however, clearly illustrate and reflect in their terms the importance and relevance of the issues to which this guide is dedicated. They should therefore always be in the forefront of masters' minds, from the moment that they make preparation to receive cargo at the loading port until they have delivered the cargo and the bill of lading has fulfilled its purpose.

SIGNING THE BILL OF LADING

105. In this section the legal principles underlying the practical guidance given in the practical guidance section are explained.

106. The general guidance given in this section will often apply equally to a paper bill of lading as to an electronic bill of lading. However, where there are likely to be different considerations for an electronic bill of lading, the relevant cross-reference to the electronic bills of lading section of this guide is provided.

107. The questions examined in more detail in the following pages include the following.

- Must there be a bill of lading?
- Who prepares it?
- Must masters sign any form of bill of lading presented to them?
- Who else can sign?
- Can the master or bill of lading holder correct mistakes?

- What information must the bill of lading contain?
- What terminology should be used to describe the cargo?
- Does this terminology make the bill of lading 'unclean' or 'claused'?
- What if the shipper refuses 'unclean' or 'claused' bills of lading?
- Are letters of indemnity a solution?
- What is the significance of the date of issue?
- What is the significance of the place of issue?

108. Loading cargo will almost inevitably lead to the issue of a bill of lading. That bill of lading will be drawn up by the shippers. It will contain facts which the master, by the his signature, will be treated as represented by him to be correct. That representation will be seen not only by the shipper, who should be well aware of the true nature and quantity of the cargo shipped ⚖, but also by the ultimate buyer of the cargo who, when they acquire the bill of lading, will rely very heavily on the statements of facts contained in the bill and the master's apparent adoption of them by putting the his signature, or that of his authorised agent, to the bill. These representations are made in part in the capacity of the bill of lading as a receipt (the description, quantity and condition of the goods) and in part in its capacity as a contract of carriage (that the goods will be carried to the named discharge port) and in part in its capacity as a document of title (that the goods will be delivered to the holder of the bill of lading).

109. In practical terms it is perhaps useful for the master at this early stage to consider what information he may be able to collect and from what sources (see paragraphs 200 – 214). The master is not expected to have an expert eye or to call for any scientific analysis when observing the condition of cargo coming on board. In particular the master is not expected to make any observation as to the quality of cargo coming on board. So, for example, the master is not interested in enquiring or ascertaining whether the cargo is, for example, number 2 or number 3 corn, or low or high sulphur fuel oil. The master will be expected, however, to apply common sense and act as a reasonably careful and observant master in identifying defects in the condition of the cargo; for example the presence of foreign contaminants, water, mould, insects, discoloration or smell, and broken packaging and accurately recording those defects on the bill of lading ⚖. On some occasions, the master may be expected to do this before loading has commenced ⚖ (see paragraph 181). In order to put the information available to the master in context it is useful first to consider the issues that may arise at the time of signing the bill of lading.

Does the master have to issue a bill of lading?

110. When goods are shipped there will usually be a bill of lading. If none is tendered to the master for signature and no letter of authority has been given by him, he should enquire what arrangements are being made for the issue of bills of lading.

111. The shipper of the goods will, when the goods have been shipped, require the issue of a bill of lading, usually following the issue of a mate's receipt. At common law there is probably no obligation on the master to issue a bill of lading containing any particular information, or indeed to issue any bill of lading at all ⚖.

112. However, there are usually very strong practical reasons why the master will wish to issue a bill of lading. It is useful for the master to have a document which will indicate to whom delivery is to be given at the discharge port, and which records the apparent order and condition of the goods when they were shipped on board. In some countries the ship may not be permitted to sail until a bill of lading has been issued or, at least, authority has been given in writing to the ship's agent to sign bills of lading on the master's behalf. In addition to those practical reasons for signing and issuing a bill of lading, the Hague, Hague-Visby and Hamburg Rules require a master, if called upon to do so by the shipper (or charterer), to issue a bill of lading containing specific types of information. This is looked at in more detail in paragraph 133 – 140 (with regard to the Hague, Hague-Visby and Hamburg Rules) and 116 – 122 (with regard to charterparties).

Who prepares the bill of lading?

113. The bill of lading will usually be prepared (but not signed) by the shipper, or its agent, or forwarding agent. It will rarely be prepared by the shipowner or the shipowner's agent or the master. Whoever prepares the bill, it is important for the master to check the bill of lading carefully (or to ensure that any agent acting on his behalf is instructed also to check carefully) the following information.

(a) The description (that is quantity and condition) of the cargo (as to which see paragraphs 133 – 170). The important step is to ensure that the bills of lading are in accordance with the mate's receipt(s). Any description or clausing in the mates' receipts (see paragraphs 211 – 214) should be included in the bill of lading.

(b) The date and place of shipment (see paragraphs 188 and 189) should be correct.

114. A failure by the master properly to check this information can bind the carrier to the accuracy of the bill of lading, and can lose any right of indemnity which the carrier may otherwise have had against the person who prepared (inaccurately) the bill of lading.

Must masters sign any form presented to them?

115. As a matter of basic principle the master is probably under no obligation to issue a bill of lading. Therefore if a bill of lading is issued the master does have some control over the information which it contains. However, this basic principle will rarely apply because under the Hague, Hague-Visby or Hamburg Rules, the shipper can and invariably does demand a bill of lading. The Rules list the information required. See paragraph 133 – 140.

116. Frequently the master's duty to sign or authorise the signature of the bill of lading is also prescribed by the terms of a charterparty. For example, a charterparty will often provide that the master is to sign bills of lading 'as presented' to him by the charterer or its agents.

117. What this means is that the master is bound to sign a bill of lading in the ordinary form for that trade. It is important to note, however, that a master does not have to obey a request by a charterer to sign bills of lading 'as presented' which contain inaccurate or unverified information as to the description, quantity, condition of the cargo, or as to the date or place of shipment. The charterer cannot require the master to sign bills of lading

which are simply untrue or careless in respect of these matters. Matters such as these, all of which are dealt with under paragraphs 133 – 189, are matters of fact and these facts cannot be varied simply by the charterer requiring the master to sign a bill of lading 'as presented' if the bill of lading 'as presented' is factually incorrect.

118. In addition to matters of fact, there are also probably other situations in which the master does not have to sign a bill of lading 'as presented' despite a charterparty saying that he must do so. These types of situation are listed below simply to sound 'alarm bells' for the master if any of these situations arises, but it is of the utmost importance that the master does everything he can to discuss the matter with the P&I club correspondent or the shipowner rather than simply refusing to sign the bill of lading. The law is complex and the consequences of refusing to sign a bill of lading can be serious.

119. Important 'alarm bell' situations include requests for the issue of the following under an 'as presented' charterparty clause:

- *A bill of lading for a destination outside charterparty limits*. The master has the right and probably the duty to refuse to sign a bill of lading which names a port of discharge outside the charter trading limits.
- *A bill of lading presented to the master for signature which does not incorporate terms which the charterparty expressly requires to be included*. The master will probably be entitled to refuse to sign.
- *A bill of lading misrepresenting the condition, quantity or nature of the cargo* (see discussion above). The master should not sign.
- *A bill of lading bearing the incorrect date*. A master is not bound to sign a bill of lading bearing an incorrect date and should not do so.
- *A bill of lading which states that the cargo has been loaded under deck when in fact the cargo has been loaded on deck*. The master has a duty not to sign.
- *A bill of lading which states that freight has been pre-paid*. If the vessel is under a voyage charterparty it is arguable that the master does not have authority to sign freight pre-paid bills of lading. For more discussion see paragraph 279. If the ship is operating under a time charterparty then see paragraph 120.

120. The following are situations where the master may have doubts about whether he should sign bills of lading 'as presented'. However, all of these situations are more properly dealt with by the shipowner having the right to an indemnity from the charterer and in the event of uncertainty or the absence of guidance from the shipowner the master should sign in these situations:

- Where a bill of lading contains a demise or 'identity of carrier' clause.
- Where a bill of lading is marked 'freight pre-paid'. The master may not usually refuse to sign these, nor require a lien clause in the charterparty to be incorporated in the bills of lading, simply to protect the owner's position on charterparty freight or hire.
- Where a bill of lading contains a foreign jurisdiction clause. The fact that a bill of lading contains a jurisdiction clause which is different from that in the charterparty will not entitle the master to refuse to sign bills of lading.

121. For practical guidance in all these situations the master is referred to paragraphs 1 – 21.

122. There are many variations of charterparty clauses requiring a master to sign 'as presented'. The most common variation is that the master is required to sign bills of lading 'as presented without prejudice to this charterparty'. Another common variation is where the master is required to sign bills of lading 'as presented, in conformity with mate's or tally clerk's receipts'. Those words probably add nothing to the discussion and guidance given above ⚖.

Duress or pressure to sign
123. A contract will be unenforceable if it has been made unwillingly and in response to threats against a person or their goods, or in response to economic duress, which can include a threat to break a contract or to bring some other illegitimate pressure to bear. Whether or not a particular threat amounts to duress, so that the contract can be treated as unenforceable, is a matter of law and fact and may include the question of whether the party under threat had any other choices available to it. Duress is mentioned in this guide because there may be occasions when masters feel compelled to sign a bill of lading in terms which they are not happy with, and where masters may be justified, once the threat has passed, in announcing that they does not consider themselves bound by the bill of lading. This possibility is recognised in the practical advice given at paragraph 18(a) ⚖.

Freight, hire, demurrage, liens, Hamburg Rules, etc.
124. A master may be worried that a bill of lading presented to him does not give the shipowner sufficient protection in terms of freight, or hire, or demurrage, or liens for any of those, or the master may be worried that it provides for carriage to be under the Hamburg Rules rather than the Hague-Visby Rules, or the master may be concerned about other conditions which it imposes. They are all matters for the shipowner or its P&I club to consider and advise upon. The general rule should be that where the master's worries relate to the terms and conditions of carriage and payment of freight, then despite his concerns, and if he can get no instruction from the shipowner, the master should issue the bill of lading in the form presented to him and at the same time he should write to the charterer stating that he has signed the bill of lading without being able to obtain guidance from the shipowner and reserving all rights of indemnity which it may have. This is so, notwithstanding the comment in paragraph 111. It is likely that under a voyage charterparty or a time charterparty the shipowner would be entitled to some kind of indemnity from the charterers if they have required the master to issue bills of lading which are too onerous ⚖. The opposite, refusing to sign such a bill of lading, potentially is without justification and could place the shipowner in breach of contract with potential liability to the charterer for damages.

Who is to sign the bills of lading? (see paragraph 322(a) for electronic bills of lading)
125. The bill of lading will usually be prepared by the shipper and will be presented to the master for signature. ⚖ Alternatively, they may be presented to the master's agent or to the charterer's agent.

126. The master should always proceed from the starting point that he alone has authority to sign bills of lading on behalf of the shipowner. If authority is to be given to a ship's agent or to a charterer, then the master should proceed on the assumption that the authority would be given by him in a clear letter setting out the scope of that authority. A letter of authority is contained in appendix II.

127. As a matter of law the position is much more complex than that. Authority may be given to the charterers or their agents to sign bills of lading by virtue of the terms inserted in the time or voyage charterparties. Also, there are circumstances in which these persons appear to have authority to sign bills of lading (which can bind a shipowner to a holder of the bill of lading) even though no authority has expressly been given to them either under the charterparty or by any letter of authority from the master ⚖️. For more discussion see paragraph 273.

Issue of unauthorised bills of lading

128. There may be occasions when a charterer or an agent issues bills of lading without authority from the master or the shipowner. The reason may be fraudulent, for example, to sell the cargo to as many buyers as there are sets of bills of lading. More frequently, the reason is likely to be to ensure that the bill of lading complies with the requirements of the letter of credit, for example as to date of shipment or description of cargo where the actual time of loading or condition of the cargo makes the true bill of lading unacceptable under the terms of the credit. Often the master will not know that an unauthorised bill of lading is in circulation; he will know only of the issue of the true bill of lading. Sometimes the matter will go undetected. On other occasions the receivers or the customs authorities (who often will demand a copy of the original issued bill of lading and the cargo manifest for their own administrative purposes) will identify the problems. The only practical advice that can be given to a master once he becomes aware that there is or may be an unauthorised bill of lading in circulation is to notify the shipowner. The reference to the bill of lading being 'unauthorised' means that the master or the shipowner has not given authority to anyone to issue bills of lading in these terms. It does not mean, however, that in the hands of an innocent buyer of the authorised bill of lading it is worthless. As stated in paragraph 127 and at paragraph 273, there are circumstances in which a bill of lading which has been issued without actual authority can nevertheless appear to have been issued with authority and bind the shipowner. The shipowner's only right of recourse is against the unauthorised issuer ⚖️.

Can the master correct the bill of lading at the time of the signature?

129. A master should proceed on the basis that at the time of signature he can unilaterally vary the terms of any bill of lading presented to him only in the circumstances where he could refuse to sign an 'as presented' bill of lading. These are described in paragraphs 115 – 122. The master can of course correct a bill of lading at the time of signing, if it is agreed that the bill of lading as presented is not factually correct.

Correcting mistakes and amending bills of lading after issue (see paragraph 322(b) for electronic bills of lading)

130. There may on occasion be an opportunity to correct bills of lading after they have been issued if it is found that they contain inaccurate information. However, the shipowner will only be able to do this if all of the original bills of lading are accessible. In that situation the master can either ask for the return of the original bills so that accurate bills can be issued, or he can mark the original bills with an amendment and signature, again with the shipper's co-operation. If the bills of lading are not accessible for amendment or replacement, the best the master can do is issue a notice to the shipper, correcting the information. Such a notice should require the shipper to give similar notice to any other party to whom it delivers, consigns or endorses the bill. The charterer cannot forbid this ⚖. The master has no authority to sign a second bill of lading for goods for which a bill of lading has already been signed ⚖.

131. There is no power in a charterer or shipper to instruct the master to amend bills of lading after they have been signed and released where the bill of lading cannot be retrieved. Where they can be retrieved, the shipper's or charterer's right to require amendment is a matter of debate and is very much a matter for the shipowner and its lawyer to decide ⚖. Sometimes a charterer may ask a shipowner to issue new bills of lading after discharge. Such a request is inconsistent with the three main functions of a bill of lading: first it is evidence of the contract of carriage (for example the promise is to carry it to a certain destination and there to deliver it); second it is a receipt (reporting to the buyer on the apparent order and condition of the goods); third, it is a key to the right to the possession of the goods – essentially the lawful holder of the bill can call for delivery. Issuing a bill of lading after discharge performs none of these functions. If the cargo is no longer in the custody of the shipowner, it can neither deliver it in accordance with the terms of the contract (because it has no control over the cargo) nor can the shipowner direct to whom the possession should be given (because it does not possess the cargo). Furthermore, the shipowner cannot say anything about the current apparent order and

The wet staining of these 'bulk bags' would suggest that the contents may also be damaged - it is crucial that the master draws attention to the staining in the remarks inserted on the mate's receipt and bill of lading

condition of the goods, or even of their whereabouts. For that reason, the bill of lading so issued would be a fictitious document. Furthermore, there is authority that a bill of lading must be issued on shipment: i.e. without undue delay and in accordance with the usual course of business. Where bills of lading are issued a long time after shipment, or (as in one reported case) after transhipment onto another vessel, the bills of lading were found to be incapable of good tender under the sale contract. While the shipowner is not interested in the sale contract, it does not want to get involved in issuing a sham piece of paper and the consequence of his doing so are both unpredictable, and potentially dangerous ⚖️.

132. Sometimes a person will claim to be entitled to possession of bills of lading, or to have been in possession of the bills of lading, but that they have now been lost or destroyed. This person may ask the master to issue a new bill of lading in substitution for the lost or destroyed bill. The master should not agree to the issue of a new bill of lading ⚖️.

What information must the bill of lading contain?

133. The master may not be under an obligation to issue a bill of lading at all or to issue a bill of lading containing precise descriptions of the goods loaded. However, for practical considerations and because the provisions of the Hague, Hague-Visby or Hamburg Rules will very often apply to the shipment, it is assumed that the master is under an obligation to sign a bill of lading and that it will contain some degree of description of the goods. The master has no authority to certify the quality, as distinct from the condition, of goods shipped ⚖️.

134. Under the Hague and Hague-Visby Rules (Article 3 rule 3) the carrier must, on demand of the shipper, issue a bill of lading showing

> 'The leading marks necessary for identification of the goods as the same are furnished in writing by the shipper before the loading.... [and.....
> ....the number of packages or pieces, or the quantity, or weight .... as furnished in writing by the shipper.... [and......
> The apparent order and condition of the goods....'.

135. Article 3 rule 4 goes on to say

> 'Such a bill of lading shall be prima facie evidence of the receipt by the carrier of the goods as therein described...'

And the Hague-Visby Rules add the following words to that provision:

> 'However, proof to the contrary shall not be admissible when the bill of lading has been transferred to a third party acting in good faith.'

136. What the provision means is that under the Hague and Hague-Visby Rules the information in the bill of lading describing the quantity and condition of the cargo amounts to a promise that what the bill of lading says can be relied upon as evidence of what was shipped on board. The Hague-Visby Rules take the matter further so that where the bill of

lading has been transferred from the original shipper (who should know the condition and quantity of the goods ⚖) to a buyer, the carrier cannot deny the truth of the statements which the master or agent has made in the bills of lading.

137. The provision places a heavy burden to place on the carrier ⚖ but there are a number of points in Article 3 rule 3 which help the master. These are:

(a) As to the condition of the goods, the obligation of the master is limited to their *apparent* order and condition. See paragraph 160.

(b) As to the quantity of the goods:

  (i) Firstly, the information as to marks, quantity and weight is as furnished 'by the shipper' and so there is no reason why the bill of lading should not make this plain.

  (ii) Secondly, there is a proviso at the end of Article 3 rule 3 as follows

  'no carrier master or agent of the carrier shall be bound to state or show in the bill of lading any marks, number, quantity or weight which he has reasonable ground for suspecting not accurately to represent the goods actually received, or which he has had no reasonable means of checking'.

So there will occasions when the master is justified in refusing to issue a bill of lading: or in doing so in clearly quantified terms. Also see paragraph 141.

138. Because of this it is important for the master to consider carefully how to describe the quantity and condition of the goods. The ingenuity of shipowners and masters in using protective or restrictive words in bills of lading which promise no accuracy, has resulted in a number of phrases being accepted in practice which successfully limit at least some of the shipowner's responsibility for what is described in the bill of lading. These are discussed at paragraphs 141 – 168.

139. When done carefully and honestly the use of such protective or restrictive words should not be in contravention of the obligations of the Hague or Hague-Visby Rules. This is because of the proviso that the carrier does not have to state the marks, number, quantity or weight ⚖ if it has reasonable grounds for suspecting that they do not accurately reflect the goods actually received or where it has no reasonable means of checking the facts ⚖. For more detailed discussion see paragraphs 141 – 169.

140. The corresponding provisions under the Hamburg Rules appear in Articles 15 and 16 and can be seen in appendix VII. The information which must be included in the bill of lading is more extensive than in the Hague or Hague-Visby Rules (see Article 15) ⚖ but, like the Hague and Hague-Visby Rules, it is permissible under the Hamburg Rules for the master to use protective or restrictive words which promise no accuracy (Article 16) and therefore the discussion in paragraphs 141 – 168 is relevant. Finally it should be noted that the Hamburg Rules provide (at Article 16 rule 2) that if the master does not note on the bill of lading the apparent condition of the goods he is deemed to have noted on the bill of lading that the goods were in apparent good condition ⚖.

How to describe the cargo quantity and condition?

141. With regard to description of quantity, the carrier must, as stated at paragraph 134, show the number of packages or pieces, or the quantity or weight as furnished in writing by the shipper. The shipper is the person most interested in having the bill of lading show a weight which accords with the shipper's sale contract. If the master disputes the shipper's figure, he should follow the guidance below.

142. The key issue for any master when ship and shore figures do not match when loading cargo is to decide whether he can issue an accurate bill of lading. An accurate bill of lading is one that will not deceive the receiver into thinking that it is getting something that the ship, in fact, is not able to deliver.

143. The vital decision for the master to take, therefore, when faced with a discrepancy between ship and shore figures, is to decide whether that discrepancy is within an acceptable margin. If it is within an acceptable margin, then either of the figures could conceivably be correct. It would not, therefore, be wrong to use the shore figure if compelled to do so.

144. By contrast, to issue a bill of lading with a figure which a master knows to be false, or where he has no belief in its truth, or where he has simply decided to make no effort at all to check its accuracy, would be to issue an inaccurate bill ⚖️.

145. What is an acceptable margin will vary according to the facts and circumstances of each loading. There is no universal margin acceptable for all cases. This may vary according to the type of cargo. For example, for petroleum cargoes, if on comparison of shore and ship figures there is a discrepancy of more than 0.3%, then this needs to be investigated ⚖️. What is an acceptable margin for dry bulk cargoes will vary according to the nature of the cargo and the ship.

146. It is important to remember that the only relevant criteria are those applicable at the load port. While there will often be a difference between ship figures from load port to discharge port (for example, for petroleum, this may be in the region of 0.2%), and while other cargo will lose volume or weight in the course of a voyage (giving rise to discussions about 'customary allowance' or acceptable 'in-transit loss'), there is no justification for using these to give guidance on what may be an acceptable margin at the load port.

147. If, on an objective assessment of the figures, the discrepancy is within an acceptable margin, then the master's position should be relatively straightforward.

(a) The first option is to show:
   (i) the ship's figures; or
   (ii) both figures.
(b) If neither is acceptable to the shipper (as is likely to be the case), then there is nothing wrong in the shore figure being shown on the bill of lading, in particular:
   (i) the owner will preserve its right to an indemnity from the shipper (or charterer) if the shore figure is inaccurate (see paragraph 154; and

(ii) the owner will retain P&I cover on the basis that it has not included an 'incorrect' description of the cargo (see paragraph 154).

(c) In any event, the master should also try to include on the bills of lading any or all of the phrases **'weight...(etc)...unknown'**, **'said to be'**, **'shippers' figures'** or any of the similar phrases discussed at paragraphs 155 – 158.

(d) Finally, to be sure of evidencing the care that has to be taken to issue an accurate bill of lading where there is a known discrepancy, the master should issue a letter recording all of the steps he has taken, and recording that while he considers the discrepancy to fall within an acceptable margin, the owner nevertheless relies upon the shipper's guarantee and indemnity in respect of the figures it has supplied. (This is in accordance with the Hague Rules – see paragraph 154).

148. Where the discrepancy does not fall within an acceptable margin then:

(a) the master should immediately give notice that he is willing to issue a bill of lading showing the ship's figure and that the ship is ready to sail; but if that is not acceptable then

(b) call for a recalculation of the shore figures and a joint re-measurement of the ship's figures. This may lead to a reduction in the discrepancy to within an acceptable margin, whereupon paragraph 147 above can be followed. If the discrepancy continues to fall outside the acceptable margin, then the master should

(c) insist on ship's figures or, if rejected

(d) insist that the bill of lading contains both ship and/or shore figures; or if rejected

(e) refuse to sign until an acceptable figure has been identified and agreed (any such refusal can be justified on the grounds set in the proviso to Article 3 Rule 3 of the Hague Rules – see paragraph 154); and/or

(f) sail and leave the matter to be debated while the ship makes its way to the discharge ports. On a cautionary note, however, it is important that before the ship sails, every opportunity has been given to the shipper, charterer and independent surveyor to check or verify the ship's measurements and to take their own, and that all such steps or offers to assist are recorded in written notices.

(g) If not allowed to sail, the master should record this in a suitable letter of protest.

(h) The master should not sign a bill of lading with a figure which is not true or not credible. If such a bill of lading is signed, a letter of protest will not provide protection.

149. Throughout the process at 147 or 148, it is essential that a clear record is maintained in documentary form (and with the assistance of P&I correspondents and surveyors) of all steps taken by the ship, measurements and calculations, and any other factors relevant to any potential disputes between the owner, charterer, shipper and receiver. In particular, in the event of disputed quantities at load port, an independent surveyor should be appointed to verify all measurements and calculations at an early stage.

Letters of protest

150. There is a widespread practice of using letters of protest to record discrepancies between ship and shore figures. This is a useful way of recording the difference between ship and shore figures when they are within the acceptable margin and reinforces the process recommended at paragraph 147(d).

151. However, the use of letters of protest can be counter-productive for owners in circumstances where the discrepancy falls outside the acceptable margin. Typically (but incorrectly), in such a situation, the master issues the bill of lading with the shore figure and then subsequently issues a letter of protest stating what he believes to be the correct (ship's) figure. The difficulty with this is twofold:

(a) It clearly evidences a belief on the part of the master that the bill of lading figure is wrong. It therefore immediately suggests that it is a bill of lading that the master should not have signed.

(b) It also does little to assist the shipowner's defence against the receiver. The receiver has not seen the letter of protest, it has only seen the bill of lading. The bill of lading states that a higher figure was shipped. The shipowner is not in a position to deny that figure (see the conclusive evidence rule at Article 3 Rule 4 of the Hague-Visby Rules – paragraph 154).

Are letters of indemnity a solution?

152. If the bill of lading contains a figure which the master does not believe to be true, then that bill of lading will deceive the receiver. A letter of indemnity promising to indemnify the owner for issuing such a bill would usually be unenforceable. (The Hamburg Rules opens the door slightly for such a letter at Article 17.3 but remains highly problematic).

153. The protective or restrictive words of description at paragraphs 155 – 158 should always be used where possible, but these will not provide protection where the figure inserted in a bill of lading is obviously wrong.

Hague / Hague-Visby Rules

154. The theory behind the guidance at paragraphs 147 and 148 is as follows:

(a) The Hague and Hague-Visby Rules recognise that there is such a thing as an acceptable margin, or to put it another way, an acceptable level of inaccuracy.

(b) Hague-Visby Rules, Article 3 Rule 3, require a shipowner on demand to issue a bill of lading which contains both the description of the apparent good order and condition of the cargo, and a description as to quantities.

(c) Unlike the obligation placed on the master with regard to good order and condition (where it is the master who must determine its apparent condition), it is the shipper who must furnish the figure that is inserted in the bill. Furthermore, the shipper guarantees the accuracy of that figure, (Article 3 Rule 5).

(d) Thus, the Hague-Visby Rules contemplate the shipper supplying the figures.

(e) Hague-Visby Rules go on at Article 3 Rule 5 to say that the shipper will indemnify the carrier against any loss arising or resulting from *'inaccuracies'* in the figures supplied. Thus the Hague-Visby Rules contemplate that the shipper's figures might prove to be inaccurate but that they may still be inserted in the bill of lading.

(f) The question then is what degree of inaccuracy is contemplated as being acceptable. The answer lies in the proviso to Article 3 Rule 3 of the Hague-Visby Rules, which provides that the master is not bound to put a figure in the bill of lading *'which he has reasonable ground for suspecting not accurately to represent the goods actually received, or which he has no reasonable means of checking'*.

(g) What the Hague-Visby Rules contemplate is that the master will carry out a check. If the master cannot check the figure (which seems unlikely), he should follow the procedure at paragraph 148. If the master can check, he is to use that as a benchmark for assessing the reasonable accuracy (or truthfulness) of the shipper's figures.

(h) Clearly, the master has no reasonable means of checking with any precise accuracy the shore figure, nor the shore mechanisms for measurement. What the master does have is his own tools on board the ship (draught survey, ullaging, etc.) which enable him to form a rough view of the figure that has come on board. The master then has to compare that rough view with the figure proffered by the shipper, and see what is the difference. If that difference is within normal measurement error, then the master can follow paragraph 147. If it does not, the master should follow the procedure at paragraph 148.

(i) Finally, it should be noted that whatever figure is inserted in the bill of lading will be treated as conclusive evidence of what was loaded, so far as any receiver of the cargo is concerned. The receiver has accepted the bill of lading in reliance upon the figures stated in it, and the shipowner cannot later try to argue or produce evidence (e.g. a letter of protest) that the figure was incorrect. (Article 3 Rule 4).

Protective or restrictive words of description – quantity

155. 'Shipper's figures' or 'shipper's load and count' or 'said by shipper to contain'
Each of these expressions is a way of pointing out that no verification has been made by the ship of the quantity of cargo loaded and that the figures have been provided by the shipper ⚖. However, the statement 'weight, measure, quantity, quality and condition unknown' (below) is more informative and is better protection for the carrier.

156. 'Said to be', or 'said to weigh' or 'said to contain'
An English judge has said that the words 'said to be' when used alone probably afford no protection to the shipowner, but it is suggested that in conjunction with other expressions such as those at paragraphs 155 – 168, these and similar expressions remain useful ⚖.

157. Notwithstanding the view expressed on the effectiveness of the words 'said to be', there seems to be a general recognition in English law that expressions such as 'said to contain' or 'said to weigh' (and, by logical inference, the words 'said to be') all should generally have the same effect as the reservation 'contents unknown' or 'weight number quantity unknown'. All of these expressions are useful although wherever possible the wider reservation at paragraph 158 should be used ⚖.

158. 'Weight, measure, quantity/unknown'
Although statements made in a bill of lading are representations or warranties by the carrier, where the above expression is added the representation as to, for example, weight, measure or quantity, is a representation as to nothing at all. It is a statement that the bill of lading is making no evidential statement as to (in this example) the weight, measure or quantity ⚖. This expression is usually used in its extended form, see paragraph 168.

Words of description – condition
159. With regard to condition, the carrier must, as stated at paragraph 134, issue a bill of lading showing the apparent order and condition of the goods.

Protective or restrictive words of description – condition
160. 'Apparent good order and condition'
In this description of the goods shipped on board the word 'apparent' is important. It says what it means. The master has looked at the external appearance of the packaging or of the container of the goods and has not opened, and often will not be able to open or see inside, the packages and will not look beyond the external appearance of the goods ⚖.

161. Therefore, the only promise made by the carrier is that the external appearance of the goods is in the condition described.

162. If the goods are discharged with external (i.e. apparent) damage, of course, the cargo claimant can then rely upon the bill of lading to show that when the goods were put on board they were in external (i.e. apparent) good condition. The carrier must then explain how the goods came to be damaged. But where the goods are discharged in the same external, (i.e. apparent) condition as when loaded, but are found internally damaged (for example on opening boxes) the cargo claimant must explain how the goods came to be damaged if it wishes to blame the shipowner.

163. For example, if a box of apples is described in a bill of lading as being 'in apparent good order and condition', the box may be in good condition but the apples may be damaged. The statement on the bill of lading is only that the box is in good condition. It says nothing about the condition of the apples. This does not mean that a cargo claimant cannot bring a claim for damage to the apples. What it does mean is that the cargo claimant must first find evidence to show that the damage occurred while in the carrier's care. The cargo claimant may be able to do this by showing the report of a survey, an inspection certificate, or simply an event during the course of carriage which, sensibly viewed, shows that the damage complained of probably occurred on board the ship.

164. If the master observes the goods as they come on board and by reasonable observation forms the reasonable view that they are defective or substandard, for example because they appear dirty, mixed with foreign particles or debris, or are discoloured or odorous, then the master must record ('clause') these observations on the face of the bill of lading or, if the observations are lengthy, by more detailed report, showing the existence of this clearly on the face of the bill of lading ⚖.

165. The word 'good' must also be treated with caution. A cargo described in the bill of lading, for example, as 'scrap' or as 'hot rolled steel coils with pitting and gouging' can be confirmed in the bill of lading as 'in good order and condition'; that is the description is accurate, or 'good' or 'proper' ⚖.

166. It is most important for the master to resist attempts by the shipper or charterer to persuade him not to clause bills of lading in circumstances where he believes the cargo is defective or substandard. See the practical guidance at paragraph 4. However, it is equally important for the master to be accurate in describing the extent of such damage. The description of apparent order and condition must be reasonable. The master must note the apparent condition of the cargo not with the ability of an expert surveyor but with the diligence of a reasonably careful and observant master ⚖. The master must decide whether, in all the circumstances, the cargo, insofar as he can see it in the course and circumstances of loading, appears to satisfy the description of its apparent order and condition in the bills of lading as tendered to him for signature. If the master disagrees with the description of the cargo's apparent order and condition as set out in the bills of lading tendered to him for signature, then he should qualify that description by wording which reflects reasonably closely the actual apparent order and condition of the cargo ⚖. Importantly, the master should also identify the extent of any defective condition which he, as a reasonably observant master, considers it to have. For example, if the master believes there is discolouration in the cargo then he should describe the extent of that discolouration. If the master believes it is contaminated by foreign substances he he should give his best estimate of the extent of that contamination by foreign substances ⚖. If the master wishes to qualify those comments by the limitation of his ability to observe the cargo, for example if the master's observations are limited to what he can see of the presence of foreign materials from the surface of the stow, then he should say in his clausing of the bills of lading that his observations refer to the surface of the stow.

167. The goods include their packaging and therefore if the packaging is damaged the bill of lading should say so. However the clausing in respect of defective packages should be as precise as possible so that 'some bags torn' or 'some bags damaged' would be more effective if qualified by an estimate as to the amount torn, for example 'about 10%' torn or 'about 500 bags torn'. Furthermore, a general clausing such as 'packages insufficient' will probably not be sufficient to override a general statement that the goods have been loaded on board in apparent good order and condition ⚖.

168. *'Weight, measure, quantity, condition, contents and value unknown'*
This is a widely accepted wording and appears in the Congenbill printed form which appears in this guide. Its purpose and effect is as discussed in paragraph 158. Wherever a master is asked to sign a bill of lading which does not contain these words in the printed form, then he should endeavour to add this phrase to the bill of lading.

Words of description – quality

169. The master's obligation is limited to describing the cargo in purely generic terms (e.g. 'sugar', 'coal', 'grain'). The Hague and Hague-Visby Rules make no requirement for a description of quality (see paragraph 134). The Hamburg Rules require the bills to show 'the general nature of the goods' (see paragraph 140). Where none of these Rules applies, the master's position is as set out in paragraphs 111 and 112, namely that he does not have to issue bill of lading, and that if he does he is not under any obligation to include any specific information save for the basic generic description.

What is the moment at which the goods are to be described?
170. A shipped bill of lading describes the condition of the goods at the time of shipment. This may be illustrated by the following examples.

(a) If cargo has been loaded, but before the bills of lading have been issued the cargo has been damaged (e.g. by fire), then the bill of lading would have to record that the goods had been received on board in apparent good order and condition. There is no legal requirement, therefore, to show the damage by fire on the bill of lading. If, however, it is decided that the bill of lading should sensibly record that the cargo has since loading been damaged by fire and by water, then that notation would not make the bill 'unclean' because it would not cast doubt on the condition of the goods at the time of shipment ⚖.

(b) The same general principle applies to damage done to the cargo by stevedores during loading. In factual terms this may be a more difficult situation because it may be

Very large claims can arise in respect of alleged damage to and rusting of steel cargo unless the damage and extent of rusting is accurately recorded on the mate's receipt and bill of lading at the time of loading

unclear, if the stevedores are handling the cargo from quay to hold, when the damage actually occurred, and there may be complex contractual arguments about who is responsible for the stevedores and at what moment the goods were 'received on board'.
(c) With the mixing (blending or co-mingling) of oil cargoes, the cargo which passes through the ship's manifold may not be the cargo which is ultimately in the tanks, because that cargo has been mixed with cargo already in the tanks. More detailed advice on this is given at paragraph 266. However, as the cargo at the manifold was received in good order and condition it should be described as such. It may be prudent to add a comment that the cargo has been loaded in a tank containing other, perhaps different quality, cargo and that this has been done 'following instructions from [charterers][shippers]'.

Clean bills of lading

171. The reason that a shipper is a reluctant to have any kind of comment on the bill of lading which states that the goods or the packaging are defective is because this will prevent the bill of lading from being 'clean'. A clean bill of lading is one which does not cast doubt on the condition of the goods at the time of shipment. For example, the Uniform Custom and Practice for Documentary Credits (UCP600, see earlier at paragraphs 76 – 79) describes and defines a clean transport document as one which bears no clause or notation which expressly declares the defective condition of the goods and/or the packaging, it does not require the word 'clean' to appear on the bill of lading ⚖.

172. In order to issue a clean bill of lading a master does not have to say that the goods are in good condition. It is sufficient for the master to say that they are in apparent good order and condition. A clean bill of lading is simply saying that the external appearance of the goods and/or packaging is good. The word 'good' does not necessarily mean that the goods appear to be perfect, simply that they are properly and accurately described. See paragraphs 160 – 167. The bill of lading described in paragraph 165 would therefore be a clean bill of lading. It is important to remember this in the discussion that follows at paragraphs 173 – 181.

173. The bill of lading describes the condition of the cargo when shipped. If, therefore, the cargo is damaged after loading but before the bill of lading is issued, the bill of lading will have to show that the cargo was received on board in good order and condition although a comment may be added that it has since been damaged ⚖. See also paragraph 170(a).

174. It is worth mentioning at this stage that occasionally a master is asked to issue bills of lading containing the expression 'clean on board'. This seems to be a practice which has grown out of the blurring together of two distinct requirements of documentary credits, namely that the bill of lading must be 'clean' and that the cargo must be 'on board'. The practice of describing cargo as 'clean on board' should be discouraged in favour of the more meaningful and appropriate use of 'apparent good order and condition' to describe the cargo, and the separate use of 'on board' to show that it has been shipped. See also 'shipped on board' and 'received for shipment' bills of lading in the glossary.

Claused bills of lading

175. A clean bill of lading can be issued when the master has no reason to doubt the apparent good order and condition of the cargo when shipped. Beware the note of caution at paragraph 165 as to the meaning of 'good' in this context. If the master does have doubt about it, then he should issue a claused bill of lading (sometimes called a foul bill of lading or a dirty bill of lading). Such a bill of lading may not be acceptable to the buyer or may not be capable of passing through the finance or letter of credit arrangements which have been made for the sale contract. This is essentially the shippers' problem as discussed below. The clausing, however, must be accurate, as discussed at paragraphs 164 – 167.

What terminology makes the bill of lading 'unclean' or 'claused'?

176. If it is apparent to the master that the goods are in fact damaged or not accurately described by the shipper in its draft bill of lading, so that he feels compelled to write on the bill of lading words which describe the cargo as in some way damaged or defective or deficient, then the bill of lading is described as a 'claused', 'foul' or 'dirty' bill of lading.

177. As stated at paragraph 172 the words 'apparent good order and condition' (which are printed on the Congenbill (see paragraph 49) or which are frequently typed or written on the bill of lading) do not render the bill of lading unclean, dirty, or foul. They would, however, if they were followed by or replaced by the words such as 'cargo wet' 'cargo rotting' 'some bags torn', 'some bags mouldy' etc. They would then cast doubt upon the condition of the goods. However, where the words do not expressly cast doubt of the condition on the goods but simply say that the master after the exercise of reasonable skill and care feels unable to give an unqualified description, then bills of lading containing words of general reservation will still usually be acceptable. So, for example, words such as 'condition unknown', 'quality, condition unknown' or variations of these, will not usually offend the requirements of the letter of credit or the sale contract ⚖.

178. Saying that the weight, measure or even condition is unknown does not question the apparent good order and condition of the goods ⚖.

What if the shipper is unwilling to be issued with an 'unclean' or 'claused bill of lading?

179. Sometimes charterers or shippers attempt to apply pressure on the master to 'negotiate' the wording of his clausing (to cast less doubt on the cargo) or not to clause at all. As long as the final wording accurately describes the cargo, this is an acceptable practice. If, however, the master is not happy with the wording being put forward by the shipper or charterer because it does not accurately describe the cargo, then he is justified in insisting on the clausing which he requires or words of similar effect.

180. The master is justified in refusing to sign the bill of lading in circumstances where the shipper/charterer will not accept an accurate description of the cargo even where the charterparty requires him to sign bills of lading 'as presented'. See paragraphs 115 – 122. Refusing to sign and avoiding any delay which this may cause to the vessel are discussed in the practical section of this guide, at paragraphs 1 – 21.

181. There are some charterparties ⚖ which require the master to issue clean mate's receipts and bills of lading. On other occasions the charterer's voyage instructions seek to impose a similar obligation ⚖. It must be emphasised that in these circumstances the master must reject any cargo if he believes that the description put forward by the shipper or charterer does not accurately describe the cargo, and that therefore the bill of lading should be claused ⚖. The standard which the master must apply when observing and rejecting the cargo is that described at paragraphs 165 and 167. The position the master should adopt where defective cargo has been loaded is, in the absence of guidance, that set out at paragraphs 179 and 180.

Are letters of indemnity a solution?

182. As a practical way of resolving the difficulties associated with a shipper being burdened with a claused bill of lading, the shipper will often request the master to issue clean bills of lading in respect of defective goods in return for a letter of indemnity from the shipper promising to indemnify owners in respect of any liability incurred to the consignee. Whilst this might seem like the obvious solution in circumstances where the shipper knows that the consignee will accept the goods in that condition, for example with slightly rusted steel cargoes, it is fraught with danger. This is because such a letter will be treated by English law as unenforceable ⚖.

183. Although letters of indemnity remain in use as a perceived practical solution to the difficulties arising from the issue of a claused bill of lading, their acceptance is not recommended. The entire risk of the letter of undertaking is with the shipowner. It stands to lose its ship if the claim is big enough and the shipper does not volunteer payment under the otherwise unenforceable letter of indemnity ⚖.

184. A further consequence of the master signing clean bills of lading for defective cargo is that the insurance cover from the P&I club may be lost. Thus there will be no indemnity from the club in respect of cargo claims made against a shipowner arising from the issue of clean bills of lading in circumstances where the bills should have been claused. See paragraphs 101 – 104.

Other solutions

185. A practice is developing in some trades of including in the bill of lading a definition of 'good order and condition' which makes it clear that the use of those words does not imply that the cargo is free from the type of defect which commonly affects the cargo in question, for example, rust on metal goods or moisture damage to timber. It is legitimate to use such a clause to clarify the statement of fact in the bill of lading to remind its holder that some defects (e.g. visible rust or moisture on steel cargoes) are often likely to be present. However, such a clause will not be allowed to be used to contradict or undermine the statement that the cargo is in good order and condition. It should not be used as a means of issuing an apparently clean bill of lading where the cargo has defects beyond those commonly found ⚖.

186. The final and the most appropriate answer to the issue of bills of lading for cargo shipped in less than good condition is for shippers to make sure consignees issue a letter of

credit with amended terms enabling payment out to be made against bills of lading which record that damaged condition. In many cases where masters stand their ground and insist on identifying damaged cargo in the bill of lading by clausing, shippers will frequently, but after much protestation, follow this, the proper, course of action.

Deck cargo

187. Another contractual aspect which it is important to note on the face of the bill of lading is whether cargo is or is not carried on deck. In trades where the Hague or Hague-Visby rules apply, the carrier's obligations to care for the cargo in accordance with the Hague or Hague-Visby standards of care will apply to deck cargo unless

(a) there is an express agreement in the bill of lading (or a universally recognised custom) to carry the cargo on deck; and
(b) the bill of lading clearly states that the cargo has been placed on deck.

Only if both requirements (a) and (b) are complied with can the carrier lay down its own standards of care for the carriage of the cargo – usually that such deck carriage will be entirely at the merchant's risk ⚖. If either of the above ingredients is missing then the carrier cannot exclude itself from the Hague or Hague-Visby Rules standards of care and it is highly likely that the simple act of placing such cargo on deck in these circumstances (unless it can safely be, or by universal custom is usually, carried on deck) will be a breach of these standards giving rise to liability on the carrier ⚖ and insurance cover from the P&I club may be lost. The situation under the Hamburg Rules is broadly similar. Again the carrier is entitled to contract out of the Hamburg Rules standard of care but to do so the carrier must show an agreement with the shipper that the goods may be carried on deck and include a clear statement in the bill of lading to that effect. The consequences of the carrier failing to satisfy these requirements are set out in the Hamburg Rules, and are broadly similar to those described above with regard to the breach of the Hague or Hague-Visby Rules. It is not within the scope of this guide to identify what cargo can or cannot safely be carried on deck. In the context of the issue of bills of lading the fundamental point is to ensure that the two points highlighted at (a) and (b) above are complied with and, if they are, and the Rules thereby excluded, that a clear set of terms of carriage and/or exclusions of liability take their place ⚖.

What is the significance of the date of issue or the date of loading?

188. Often the value of the cargo or the price to be paid or the effectiveness of the underlying sales transaction will be governed by the date of completion of loading. Usually this will also be the date of issue of the bill of lading ⚖. It is essential that a 'shipped' bill of lading shows the date on which completion of loading occurred in respect of the parcel of cargo identified in the bill of lading ⚖. If the date of issue and date of loading are different, both should be shown on the bill of lading. Any attempt by the charterer or shipper to persuade the master to issue a bill of lading showing a date other than the date on which completion of loading occurred, must be resisted. Such a bill of lading is misleading and incorrect. Any offer by the charterer or shipper of a letter of indemnity to protect the shipowner from the consequences of ante-dating or post-dating a bill of lading should be refused. Any such letter of indemnity will be unenforceable because it is designed to persuade the master or shipowner to issue a false bill of lading, and any demand by the charterers that the master must sign such an ante-dated or post-dated bill of lading 'as presented' can properly be resisted (see paragraph 103).

What is the significance of the place of issue and place of loading?
189. The significance of the place of issue of the bill of lading is that it can trigger the compulsory application of the Hague, Hague-Visby or Hamburg rules. See paragraphs 82 – 93 and appendices V – VIII. It should be noted that the place of issue does not have to be the same as the place of loading. The place of loading must always be shown. The significance of the place of loading is that it is part of the description of the goods, which may be important to the buyer as it shows their origin. It is also relevant to the compulsory application of the Hague, Hague-Visby or Hamburg Rules (see paragraphs 82 – 93). It may also be relevant for reasons of customs, trade restrictions, embargoes, or sanctions.

When must the bill of lading be presented for signature?
190. When the cargo has been loaded the shipper must present the bill of lading (to the master or the master's agent) for signature within a reasonable time ⚖.

Parcels of cargo
191. Sometimes the shipper or charterer will require bills of lading for individual parcels of cargo. Where the cargoes are clearly different in nature, this is not a problem. Where cargoes are homogeneous it should not be a problem to issue a bill of lading for each parcel. However, caution should be exercised where the homogeneous cargo is not in good condition when loaded and clausing of bills of lading will be required ⚖; and there is the risk of shortage claims on some of the parcels and over-delivery on others if care is not taken during discharge to allocate and deliver accurate quantities.

Can the master wait until the ship is fully loaded before signing any bills of lading?
192. The master must sign a bill of lading in respect of each parcel shipped within a reasonable time of presentation. The master is not allowed to delay signing until all the cargo for the vessel has been shipped unless it is a single parcel ⚖. The shipper can ask for a 'received for shipment' document when the goods come into the control of the shipowner if this is earlier than the moment of loading. See 'shipped' and 'received for shipment' bills of lading which are described in the glossary at appendix I.

To whom are the bills of lading to be released?
193. Almost invariably a mate's receipt will have been issued by the ship upon receipt of the goods. As a general rule the person who holds the mate's receipt is the person who is entitled to receive the bills of lading when released by the master or the master's agent in exchange for a return to the master or the master's agent of the mate's receipt. In the unlikely event that the mate's receipt actually shows the name of the cargo owner then the bills of lading can be delivered to that person ⚖. If no mate's receipt has been issued then the shipper of the goods is entitled to the bills of lading when issued.

Other information on the bill of lading

194. Sometimes, the master is asked to issue bills of lading *'for customs purposes only'*. The issue of additional bills of lading, for any reason, is problematic and should be referred to the shipowner for careful consideration. If the bill of lading to be released is a duplicate of the original bills of lading, then if the shipowner agrees that such a bill can be released, it should be clearly marked with a warning such as: *'For customs purposes only. Not a document of title. Delivery of cargo will not be given against production or surrender of this bill of lading'*.

195. *'Inland destination'*

Sometimes, again for customs purposes, the master is asked to issue bills of lading which show the ultimate destination of the cargo and which may be an inland destination beyond the sea discharge port. This is something which should be referred to the shipowner or its P&I correspondent for assistance. If the shipowner considers that it is essential in the trade and for customs purposes that such a destination be shown on the bill, then wording such as the following should be considered: *'The carrier has undertaken carriage to the discharge port named above. The carrier is informed by the shipper that the intended inland destination of the cargo is [name inland destination]. The carrier makes no representation as to the destination of the cargo after the discharge port and the reference to the inland port is included, at the shipper's request, for customs purposes only'*. The alternative and more formal approach is not to permit such a marking on the face of the bill but to leave those involved in the sale and purchase of the cargo to reach a more satisfactory arrangement with customs.

Care must be taken to describe accurately the extent of rusting on each steel coil

196. Sometimes the master is asked by the shipper to show on the face of the bill of lading a sale contract reference number, or a letter of credit reference number, or an invoice number. This is for documentary purposes related to the sale contract. The risk is that the bill of lading containing this information may be treated as an '*ad valorem*' bill of lading. See glossary at appendix I. The master is not under any obligation to include this information on a bill of lading ⚖.

197. Bill of lading carried on board in 'ship's bag'

Bills of lading are often issued in sets of three or four originals (see paragraphs 30 and 50). On occasions, the ship is asked to carry one of these bills of lading on board the ship during the voyage, sometimes with the additional instruction that delivery of the cargo at the discharge port should be given against that document. This is an inherently unsafe practice. Where a set of original bills of lading has been issued, endorsement or consignment of any one original bill of lading may be sufficient to give the holder the right to demand possession of the cargo. Masters have no means of knowing that the person to whom they are delivering the bill of lading which has been carried on board is the named consignee. If that person is not the named consignee, then they could only become the holder by endorsement. If they are neither the named consignee nor the proper holder by way of endorsement, then they have no right to demand possession of the cargo. However, the master is physically in possession of a bill of lading (the one carried in the ship's bag) and this may give rise to competing demands between that person and other (possibly lawful) holders of the other original bills of lading which have passed through the sale and purchase or finance chain. There is, therefore, an inherent risk of delivery of the cargo to the wrong person, which would prejudice the shipowner's P&I cover. Practical advice for the master and the shipowner is given at paragraph 11.

198. 'FIOST' 'Free out' 'Liner terms'

The inclusion of these terms can directly affect the responsibility of the shipowner or charterer for the cargo and for loading and discharging operations. See paragraph 239. If any such abbreviation is used, then these are matters which the master should report and discuss with the shipowner as soon as possible.

199. 'CIF/CFR'

These words, made on the face of the bill of lading, may be taken to denote that freight has been paid. If asked to sign a bill of lading bearing these abbreviations, the master should treat them in the same way as he would the marking '*freight pre-paid*'. Also see paragraphs 5, 119, 120, 124 and the glossary in appendix I.

SOURCES OF INFORMATION FOR THE BILL OF LADING

Shipper

200. If the shipper requires a bill of lading then it must furnish the master with details of the number of packages or pieces or quantity or weight of the goods, and it must give this information in writing. Furthermore, it is responsible for ensuring that the goods themselves bear the necessary leading marks for identification. All of this is set out in the Hague, Hague-Visby and Hamburg Rules (see paragraphs 82 – 93 and 133 – 140), and if none of these applies, the master is probably entitled to demand this information (see paragraph 111 and 112).

201. If the master is not satisfied that the marks, numbers, quantity or weight provided by the shipper accurately represent the goods actually received, or if he has no reasonable means of checking the information, or if he has reasonable grounds for suspecting that the information does not accurately represent what was shipped, then he does not have to insert in the bill the information given by the shipper. See paragraph 137.

202. Incoterms 2010 (see paragraphs 70 – 75) similarly place the duty on the shipper to mark the goods. If no marks appear on the mate's receipt or shipping note, then it would be sensible to show on the bills of lading 'no marks'.

203. The Hague and Hague-Visby Rules say that if the master relies on the information given by the shipper, and it is incorrect and the shipowner suffers a loss because of this, then the shipper must indemnify the shipowner for that loss. Whether that right of indemnity will be of any value will depend upon the law and jurisdiction where the right has to be enforced, and that in turn will depend to a great extent upon the identity of the shipper and the place of shipment.

Surveyor
204. The shipowner or its P&I club may decide to have a surveyor attend at loading who is familiar with the cargo and with the correct technical language to be used. A surveyor may also be more familiar with the shippers' practices. The surveyor will be able, therefore, to supply the master with guidance in the event that clausing of the bill of lading is necessary. Any clausing prepared by the surveyor for the master should be inserted on, or if lengthy appended to, the mate's receipt and bill of lading. A typical example of where this procedure is followed by shipowners and P&I clubs is with regard to steel cargoes where a number of P&I clubs encourage shipowners to appoint a surveyor on all occasions when loading steel.

Certificate of origin / quality / quantity
205. There are other sources of information available to the buyer of the goods other than simply the bill of lading. For example, a buyer of a cargo may stipulate in the sale contract for a certificate to be issued by the seller (or, more probably, an independent organisation within the seller's country) confirming the country of origin of the cargo; and the buyer may also stipulate in the sale contract for the provision by the seller (or a recognised independent organisation) of a certificate as to the quality, grade and quantity of cargo which is being shipped. These are not documents which are likely to come into the master's possession, but they are mentioned as they illustrate that the full burden of describing the cargo in terms of its quality and origin, as well as its more general description of weight and condition, is not borne solely by the bill of lading. There may be occasions when this independent organisation is asked by the seller to bring pressure to bear on the master to include a slightly more detailed (and perhaps more favourable) description of the cargo or its quantity or condition than he would wish to do. Such pressure should be resisted on the basis that it is the role of the independent organisation to issue certificates to the cargo interests, and not to advise or coerce the master.

Inspector

206. Sometimes there may be a pre-shipment inspection by the buyer of the cargo. The purpose of this inspection is for the buyer to check issues of quality and packaging and should not be of concern to the master. If the inspector raises questions as to the condition of the cargo, or requires certain statements as to quality to be inserted in the bill of lading, and if the master is uncertain as to the accuracy, veracity or purpose of these requests, then the master should consult the local P&I correspondent, or P&I surveyor for advice. In the absence of such advice the master's obligation is limited to describing the cargo in purely generic terms, such as 'sugar', 'coal', 'grain' ⚖.

Draught surveys

207. The draught survey, if carried out properly, is a useful check of the accuracy of the shipper's figures for quantity to be loaded on board. The North of England P&I Association has produced a loss prevention guide which deals in detail with the practical aspects of draught surveys.

208. In the event that a draught survey shows figures which are different from the shipper's figures, the master is referred to paragraphs 1 – 21 for practical guidance and to paragraphs 115 – 168 for the underlying legal and commercial principles.

Ullages

209. The North of England P&I Association has produced a loss prevention guide dealing with shipboard petroleum surveys and all practical aspects thereof. The comments in paragraphs 207 and 208 (draught surveys) relating to the usefulness of such surveys also apply here.

210. Where ullages show a loaded figure which differs from that provided by the shipper (whether from a shore terminal or from a floating storage) it is important to record the difference between the shipper's figures and the ship's (ullage) figures. See paragraph 4 and paragraphs 141 – 154.

Mate's receipt

211. When a shipper puts goods on board, the ship will issue a written receipt for the goods which have been received on board. This receipt is usually drafted by the shipper or the charterer and will probably contain the shipper's or charterer's chosen description of the goods, and possibly their calculation of the quantity put on board. Both the description and the quantity must be carefully checked before the receipt is issued – see paragraph 214. When the shipper collects the bills of lading it will return the mate's receipt to the shipowner (or, more accurately, its agent, master or loading broker).

212. When a mate's receipt is issued it is prima facie evidence of receipt of the goods in the order and condition marked on the mate's receipt ⚖.

213. Sometimes instead of a mate's receipt a shipping note will have been prepared by the shipper. This will contain all of the details that the mate's receipt would contain; the name of the shipper, the name of the ship, the port of departure, the port of destination, the description of the cargo (including size, weight and quantity of packages), and other relevant details identifying the shipment. The shipper prepares the shipping note which is checked and signed when the goods are received for shipment by the freight forwarder, port authority or shipping agent of the vessel. The receipted copy is exchanged for the shipped bill of lading signed by or on behalf of the ship after loading has been completed.

214. It is important to ensure that mate's receipts are as accurate as possible. Not only will the mate's receipt then be the best available contemporaneous evidence as to the condition, quantity and nature of the cargo shipped, and the date and place of shipment, but it will also be the 'benchmark' which defines the conditions on which the charterer or shipper or its agent are empowered and authorised to issue bills of lading. Their failure to issue bills of lading in accordance with the mate's receipts may not prevent the bills of lading from being relied upon by third parties against owners ⚖️, but it may allow the shipowner to claim an indemnity from the party drawing up and issuing the bill of lading ⚖️.

MOVEMENT OF THE BILL OF LADING UNDER THE SALE CONTRACT

215. The goods are on board and the bill of lading has been signed. What happens next in the sales transaction, and in particular, what happens to the bill of lading?

What happens to the bill of lading?

216. The answer is that now the goods are on the move, it is time for the documents to move.

217. The bill of lading will go with other documents to form a complete set of shipping documents. The shipping documents will usually comprise

- the bill of lading issued by the master or the master's agent as discussed earlier
- the marine insurance policy insuring the goods against loss or damage on the voyage
- the commercial invoice.

    These are the main documents. Others may include

- a certificate of quality / quantity
- a certificate of origin.

218. None of these documents, save for the bill of lading, is issued by the master and none should concern him ⚖️.

219. Once the shipper has the shipping documents, it may do the following.

(a) Pass them to its buyer. This would usually be done where money changes hands independently of the bill of lading arrangements (under an entirely separate credit or cash payment arrangement) or where there is no cash transaction between shipper and buyer (for example, where the buyer is a subsidiary of the shipper).

(b) More usually, the shipper will deliver the documents to the shipper's bank. This will trigger payment under the letter of credit arrangement which usually underlies an international sales transaction.

220. To explain the letter of credit system very briefly, where the contract of sale provides for payment by letter of credit the buyer will arrange for its bank to open a credit (a promise to pay) in favour of the seller for the price of the goods. This bank is called the issuing bank. The issuing bank will then contact its correspondent bank in the country where the seller is based and this bank will either 'advise' the seller that the letter of credit has been opened and that the issuing bank will pay upon receipt of the shipping documents, or it will 'confirm' the issuing bank's letter of credit. This bank in the country of the seller is, in the first instance, acting as an 'advising bank', and in the second instance as a 'confirming bank', in which case it is confirming to the seller that it, the confirming bank, will pay upon receipt by it of the shipping documents. Each of these banks will have received from the buyer instructions which show the documents required by the sale contract. When the shipping documents are delivered to the advising or confirming bank, they will be examined to make sure that they comply with the instructions under the sale contract, and the seller will be paid either directly by the confirming bank or in due course by the issuing bank (via the advising bank).

221. As the bill of lading passes through the hands of these banks it represents security for any money they may have advanced on the goods and can be held by them until the buyer has satisfied its obligations to the issuing bank.

222. When the bill of lading is in the hands of the buyer, it will contact the shipowner's or charterer's agent at the discharge port and demand delivery of the goods. Alternatively, it may wish to sell the cargo to another party in which case the bill of lading will again be used in this next transaction as a receipt (showing what the new buyer is buying), as a document of title (giving to the new buyer in return for payment the right to demand possession of the goods at the discharge port) and as a contract of carriage with the new buyer who will acquire legal rights against the shipowner (under English law this would be under COGSA 1992 as discussed at paragraphs 98 – 100).

223. The master must deliver the cargo to the person holding the bill of lading at the named discharge port. The carrier can deliver the cargo to the holder of a 'bearer' bill of lading (see paragraph 224(e)). If a bill of lading requires endorsement in order to be properly transferred it is important to check that the bill of lading has been properly endorsed ⚖. If a bill of lading shows a consignee or named endorsee (see paragraphs 224 (a) – (d)) the person demanding delivery of the cargo must provide some evidence that it is the person identified in the bill of lading. As the bill of lading would usually be presented through the shipowner or time charterer's agents which are local to and familiar with the discharge port, the master probably need only be worried about identification of the person demanding delivery if he has actual reason for believing there has been fraud or that the bill of lading may have been stolen or that there is some reasonable ground for suspecting that the person is not entitled to claim the goods, or if the master has been notified of a competing claim for the goods ⚖.

224. By way of background information, it may be useful briefly to explain the legal and commercial mechanism by which the bill of lading, and therefore the right to receive or control receipt of the goods, passes from person to person.

(a) If the bill of lading shows

> shipper: X
> consignee: to order

then the shipper has the power to endorse the bill of lading and give orders as to whom the cargo should be delivered. An endorsement is simply the signature of the shipper on the back of the bill of lading ⚖. An endorsement in blank is the signature of the shipper alone. This means that any person to whom the bill of lading is intentionally passed can claim to be the proper holder of the bill of lading. A special endorsement is where the shipper wishes to direct the shipowner to deliver to a particular person. In that case, the shipper puts its signature and the name of the intended recipient on the bill of lading.

(b) If the bill of lading shows

> shipper: X
> consignee: Y

then the bill of lading can be consigned (that is physically passed) to Y who then becomes the proper holder of the bill of lading. However, because the bill of lading gives no express power to 'order' delivery, neither X nor Y can endorse the bill of lading to any other party, either by blank endorsement or by special endorsement. This kind of bill is sometimes called a 'straight' or 'non-negotiable' bill of lading and in many respects is similar to a sea waybill (the similarities are discussed at paragraph 286 and 287 below).

(c) If the bill of lading shows

> shipper: X
> consignee: Y or to order

then the bill of lading can be consigned to Y as in (b) above. However if Y wishes it can then endorse it, in blank or by special endorsement, to any other party who will then become the proper holder. That party cannot then endorse it further.

(d) If in situation (c) above, a special endorsement on the bill of lading shows 'Z or order', then that endorsee can further endorse the bill of lading.

(e) If the bill of lading shows

> shipper: X
> consignee: bearer [or left blank]

then the holder of this bill of lading is the person to whom cargo is to be delivered. The bill of lading can move from person to person by simple consignment (that is, by being physically passed from person to person).

225. All of the above are general rules and are determined by what is written in the 'consignee' box in the bill of lading. These general rules may be varied by express terms on the bill of lading stipulating how it is to be transferred.

THE VOYAGE – DEVIATION, DELIVERY, LOSS AND DAMAGE TO CARGO

226. The ship has been loaded and bills of lading issued. The shipping documents should now be working their way through the sale and accompanying finance transactions. The master is now under a duty to carry the cargo safely to destination by the usual geographical route, to care for the cargo en route, and to deliver the cargo in the same condition as when loaded to the person rightfully entitled to receive the cargo.

227. These obligations are essentially contractual in nature – the master by receiving the shipper's goods on board agrees to carry them safely to their destination. To be precise, the bill of lading is not the contract of carriage. The agreement to carry the goods has usually been made before the goods have been taken on board ⚖. However, it is usually the document which provides the best evidence of the terms of the contract of carriage. But it must be remembered that the terms of the bill of lading may be modified by one or more of the various sources of obligations discussed in paragraphs 65 – 68.

The duty to carry

228. The master is expected to proceed from the load port to the discharge port without delay and without departure from the usual geographical route. If the master fails to do so then this may amount to a deviation from the contractual voyage. The word 'deviation' is a legal expression which requires further explanation.

Deviation

229. Deviation in its legal sense is an unjustified departure from the contractual voyage. The general rule is that the contractual voyage will follow the usual geographical route. This general rule may not apply

- if it can be shown that there is a universal custom to follow another route
- that the circumstances surrounding the voyage made it clear that the intention of the parties was that some other route should be taken
- if the bill of lading expressly describes what route is to be taken or gives the shipowner liberty to select alternative routes even if this means departing from the usual geographical route
- if it is necessary for the ship to leave the contractual route for reasons of the safety of the venture
- if one of the sources of obligation listed in paragraph 67 permits departure from the contractual voyage, for example the Hague-Visby Rules permit deviation to save life or property or 'any reasonable deviation'
- if a change in destination has been agreed (see paragraph 232).

230. Where the ship departs from the contractual voyage without justification, the consequences of this deviation in legal terms are very drastic. In very broad terms, the shipowner will be deprived of its contractual rights (for example, to receive freight and to enjoy defences expressly given to it by the contract) and in addition may prejudice its insurance cover. (See paragraphs 101 – 104).

231. It is therefore important to realise that instructions to take the cargo to any destination other than that named in the bill of lading, even when those instructions are given by charterers or shippers who may appear to have very good reason for giving those instructions, should be treated with the utmost caution. In every circumstance where such instruction is given, the shipowner or the P&I club should be consulted.

Change of destination (and see paragraph 322(b) for electronic bills of lading)

232. Sometimes a change of destination can be agreed. The essential ingredient of such agreement is that the party giving the order for change of destination must be in a position to return the complete set of original bills of lading at the discharge port. This is essential because if one or more of those originals is now in the hands of another holder then that person may call upon the shipowner to discharge at the destination named in the original bill. If the shipowner changes destination and discharges the cargo at a new destination without collecting in all of the bills, then at some time in the future any uncollected bill may form the basis of a claim by its holder for mis-delivery. This is why in the standard recommended wording for the letter of indemnity to be given by a charterer or the bill of lading holder for change of destination, there is an absolute undertaking to return all sets of the original bills of lading. See appendix IV and paragraphs 249, 250, 254 and 265.

With dry bulk chemical cargo it is important to note any obvious contaminants or lumpy cargo

233. Some bills of lading, for example, the Congenbill, provide that the vessel shall proceed to a port or 'so near thereto as she may safely get'. This may ultimately give the master the right to carry the cargo to another discharge port if the vessel is prevented from reaching the named discharge port. However, the master is bound to wait a reasonable time before being entitled to proceed to an alternative place of discharge and that reasonable time will depend upon the nature of the voyage. It is a matter to be decided between the shipowner and the charterer or shipper after careful consultation.

Delay

234. Delay in proceeding to the discharge port may cause loss to the buyer of the goods. Delay may also amount to a deviation in the legal sense. However, simple failure to commence the loaded voyage and proceed as quickly as possible is not a deviation in the legal sense. To amount to a deviation in the legal sense delay which makes the voyage performed entirely different from that which the parties envisaged, would have to occur.

235. It is not the function of this guide to set out a detailed analysis on the complex law of deviation. The purpose of this short section is to emphasise the importance of proceeding directly from the load port to the discharge port as named in the bill of lading, unless there is very good reason, by reason of contract, custom, safety or agreement, to do otherwise.

236. One final note on delay. The Hamburg Rules, if applicable, have express provisions dealing with delay. (See paragraph 92 and appendix VII, Article 5).

Caring for the cargo

237. At common law the shipowner is under an absolute obligation to provide a seaworthy ship. A seaworthy ship is one in which her hull and machinery, equipment and crew are fit to take the cargo to sea and come safely through the kind of weather that she should expect to meet. If the shipowner fails in this obligation and the failure causes damage to the cargo then the cargo owner has a justified claim against the shipowner in respect of that cargo. Under the Hague and Hague-Visby Rules this absolute obligation is reduced to an obligation to exercise due diligence to make the vessel seaworthy. Due diligence means taking care to ensure a proper, efficient and effective system to maintain, equip, and repair the ship, hull and equipment and the proper training and competence of her master and crew. If a proper and careful check would reveal, or if a proper system of maintenance and repair would prevent, a defect which a normal careful shipowner would repair, but the defect is not repaired or timeously prevented, then there has been a failure by that shipowner to exercise due diligence to make its ship seaworthy.

238. In addition to the seaworthiness obligations, the shipowner must care for the cargo from the time of its receipt into the shipowner's care until the time of its delivery at the discharge port. Essentially this means taking care to ensure that what has been put on board the vessel at the load port can be delivered at the discharge port. It is a duty to ensure that the cargo is not lost, damaged, contaminated or changed in character in any way.

239. As between the shipowner and the cargo owner the bill of lading may set out a period for which the shipowner is responsible for caring for the cargo and identify who is to be responsible

and pay for loading and discharge operations. These are of course matters of great concern to the shipowner and cargo owner alike. They are often dealt with by phrases such as FIOST ('free in and out stowed and trimmed') FIOS and FIO (shorter versions of FIOST and of diminishing scope) and by expressions such as 'liner in liner out' or 'free in free out'. All of these expressions are of considerable significance. It is not within the scope of this guide to consider the detailed case law which has gone into the apportionment of responsibilities by these expressions. It is important, however, for the master to be aware of expressions or abbreviations such as these. If any such abbreviation is used which clearly goes to the allocation of loading and discharging responsibility (or indeed any abbreviation which is unknown to the master) then these are matters which he should report and discuss with the shipowner as soon as possible.

Cargo claims

240. The law recognises that goods, wherever and however they are handled, stored or transported can come to harm. Where the goods have been physically lost or damaged during the voyage the contract of carriage, and the laws and conventions within which it operates, allocate risk and liability between the shipowner and the cargo owner. (The shipowner's risk and liability may also have been allocated between it and its charterer, but that is not a matter for this guide).

The shipowner's defences

241. Where there is proof of loss or damage on the ship, then at common law the shipowner has a limited number of defences. It will not be excused from liability if it failed to make the ship seaworthy and this caused the loss or damage. It will be excused from liability at common law if damage to the cargo was directly caused by act of God, act of Queen's enemies, inherent vice of the goods themselves, negligence of the cargo owner or general average sacrifice. The modification of these common law obligations and defences by the Hague, Hague-Visby or Hamburg Rules is considered at paragraphs 82 – 93.

Evidence of damage or loss — the bill of lading

242. One very difficult question when cargo claims arise is whether the loss or damage complained of by the cargo owner happened on the ship, if it happened at all. For example, shortage claims can arise simply because of differences between recorded measurements at the load and discharge ports; damage claims can arise where the cargo discharged is the same as that loaded, but the description of the cargo in the bill of lading failed to draw the buyer's attention to existing defects in the cargo.

243. Both of these examples, shortage and damage claims, can be directly affected by the care which has been taken when issuing the bill of lading. Care in measuring and observing the cargo, and care in describing its quantity and condition on the bill of lading, can avoid or reduce the size of these claims.

244. The bill of lading contains important evidence of these facts and figures. If a bill of lading is issued which contains inaccurate information there is little opportunity for the carrier to say the information is not true. As a matter of law all of the descriptions stated in the bill of lading will be evidence in the hands of any cargo owner who says its goods have been damaged. In particular note the following.

(a) Under the Hague Rules, and probably as a matter of common law, the bill of lading represents 'prima facie evidence' of the facts stated in the bill of lading. The cargo owner can use this evidence to prove its claim against the carrier.
(b) The Hague-Visby Rules add more weight to this evidence by adding that in the hands of a transferee or endorsee of the bill of lading (usually the buyer of the cargo) it is 'conclusive evidence' of the fact that shipment has taken place, the time and place of that shipment, and the number, quantity, weight, marks and apparent order and condition of the goods.
(c) The Hamburg Rules, if they apply, take a similar position to (a) and (b) above.
(d) Section 4 COGSA 1992 has further increased the evidential effect of the bill of lading. It is now 'conclusive evidence' that the cargo owner can use against the carrier to prove shipment or receipt for shipment of goods which have been signed for in the bill of lading ⚖.
(e) '*Prima facie* evidence' is evidence which can be disproved by the carrier producing better proof that, for example, despite its best efforts the bill of lading is inaccurate. 'Conclusive evidence', however, cannot be overturned. The carrier is bound by and must live with it.

245. A third category of loss is where the cargo has been safely carried to its destination but then delivered to the wrong person. This question of delivery is a separate and important issue and is dealt with in the next section of this guide.

DELIVERY OF THE CARGO

246. The bill of lading is often referred to as a document of title. In fact the movement of title (the right of ownership of the cargo) is decided by the sale contract. However, if the parties to the sale contract require a bill of lading to be issued they are using it as a moveable (or negotiable) and tangible symbol of title to the cargo, or, more accurately, the right to demand possession of the cargo at its destination.

247. The master must deliver the cargo to the person holding the bill of lading at the named discharge port. The carrier can deliver the cargo to the holder of a 'bearer' bill of lading (see paragraph 224(e)). If a bill of lading requires endorsement in order to be properly transferred it is important to check that the bill of lading has been properly endorsed ⚖. If a bill of lading shows a consignee or named endorsee (see paragraphs 224(a) – (d)) the person demanding delivery of the cargo must provide some evidence to the carrier that they are the person identified in the bill of lading. As the bill of lading would usually be presented through the shipowner's or time charterer's agents which are local to and familiar with the discharge port, the master probably need only be worried about identification of the person demanding delivery if he has actual reason for believing there has been fraud or that the bill of lading may have been stolen or that the person is not entitled to claim the goods, or if he has been notified of a competing claim for the goods ⚖.

248. Upon delivery, the bill is said to be accomplished and the other bills of lading become worthless (except as evidence in the event of a dispute, for which reason they should be

retained carefully). 'Accomplished' is a reference to the bill of lading having completed its work, and that upon delivery of the cargo and the surrender of the bill of lading, it has become void. (See paragraph 322(c) for electronic bills of lading).

249. Problems which sometimes arise are where

(a) no bill of lading is available at the discharge port
(b) delivery of cargo is requested at a port which is not the named discharge port.
(c) the shipper or charterer insists that the 'bill of lading' is the same as a sea waybill and that the master cannot insist on requiring its production before commencing discharge. This problem is discussed at paragraphs 286 and 287 below.

Delivery of cargo without production of the bill of lading or at the wrong port (see paragraph 318(c) for electronic bills of lading)

250. Delivery of the cargo to a person who does not hold a bill of lading is a breach of the bill of lading contract itself and the holder of the bill of lading can bring a claim against the shipowner. Such delivery is also an infringement of the cargo owner's rights of ownership and the cargo owner can bring an action against the shipowner for infringing those rights. (The cargo owner can also, of course, bring a claim against the party who has wrongfully demanded delivery of the cargo). Similarly, delivery at the wrong port is not only a deviation under the contract of carriage (see paragraph 190) but is also an infringement of the true cargo owner's rights if this is done in circumstances where the agreement to change destination has not been accompanied by the return of all of the original bills of lading (see paragraph 232).

251. Some of the comments that follow appear in the practical guidance section of this guide. Those comments are here augmented by further explanation and legal notes.

252. In the absence of clear guidance from the owner or the P&I club correspondent the master should take note of the following points.

(a) The unavailability of a bill of lading at the discharge port is a problem for the buyers and sellers of the cargo to resolve ⚖.
(b) The master should not agree to discharge the cargo against a letter of indemnity (unless the shipowner has expressly agreed to this). The master does not have authority on behalf of the shipowner to vary the bill of lading contract in this way without the shipowner's consent.
(c) Delay to the vessel while waiting for the bill of lading will usually be paid for under the charterparty in the form of hire or demurrage (or as part of the laytime which has been paid for in the freight payment). Even if the vessel is threatened with the cost of the delay, that threat should not justify delivery of the cargo without production of the bill of lading or at the wrong port.
(d) Delivery without production of the bill of lading, or at the wrong port, will be a breach of the terms of the shipowner's P&I insurance and there may be no protection for the shipowner if in consequence a claim is subsequently brought by the 'true' cargo owner (see paragraphs 101 – 104).

(e) Sometimes the shipowner has agreed in a charterparty that it will discharge and deliver the cargo in return for a letter of indemnity from the charterer – see paragraphs 254 – 256.
(f) In some places the cargo can be discharged (at the named discharge port) into the custody of the port or a private warehouse where it will remain under the legal control of the master until the bill of lading has been produced. The master should investigate this, if possible through the P&I club correspondents.

253. Sometimes a person will claim to be entitled to possession of the cargo and will provide a plausible explanation that the bills of lading have been lost or destroyed. Sometimes the offer of a letter of indemnity (see below) accompanies the explanation. This is both a legal and a commercial problem for the shipowner and its advisors to resolve and the master should not agree to deliver the cargo (unless the shipowner expressly instructs the master to do so) ⚖.

Specific issues

254. *Letters of indemnity (and see paragraph 322(c) for electronic bills of lading)*
Unlike letters of indemnity given in return for issuing clean bills of lading (which are unenforceable as the bill of lading will deceive its holders), the giving of letters of indemnity in return for delivery of cargo at the wrong discharge port or without production of the original bill of lading is not wrong ⚖, nor is it unusual. It is, however, a matter for the shipowner to decide upon. It is a commercial decision for it to make. The desire to satisfy a charterer or receiver, and to free the vessel of cargo, must be balanced against the loss of P&I cover and the risk that the cargo may have been sold twice or not paid for.

255. If the letter of indemnity identifies a specific party to whom the cargo is to be delivered, it is important to ensure that delivery is given to that party and that steps are taken to check their true identity, with the assistance of the ships' agent or P&I correspondent, or by asking the charterer (who will usually be the party making such request) to confirm that the party making the demand is the party named in the letter of indemnity ⚖.

256. Standard letters of indemnity for these situations appear at appendix IV and the background to these letters is explained in the circulars at appendix III. These standard forms include counter-signature by a bank. Banks are rarely prepared to sign an indemnity for unquantified amounts. Frequently, therefore, the letter is accepted without a bank's countersignature. Alternatively a limit (e.g. 200% of the value of the cargo) is placed on the bank's liability under the letter. Again, these are commercial decisions for the shipowner to take.

257. *Photocopy or faxed bills of lading*
Sometimes the master is asked to deliver against a copy or faxed bill of lading, the original being unavailable. Unless special arrangements have been made in writing by the shipowner to accept such a bill of lading, delivery should be refused. The usual rule is that delivery shall be given against presentation of at least one original bill of lading.

258. Multiple originals
Bills of lading are often issued in sets of three or four originals. The bill of lading will usually provide on its face that production of any one of those originals will be acceptable. At the same time, the other originals are considered to be void and cancelled even if they have not been collected in by the master or ship's agent.

259. Retention of the original bill of lading
The master should retain the original bill of lading against which cargo has been delivered. The receivers should have no need to retain it; as a contract of carriage it is merely evidence and a copy will suffice, as a document controlling possession its function is now complete, as a receipt for the goods it makes sense that it should be returned to the master when the goods are delivered. (If multiple bills have been issued then, of course, it is probable that the receiver has retained one of the duplicates).

260. Originals are sometimes required by local officials or customs and in those circumstances the master should ensure that he (or the master's agent) is allowed to see the original bill of lading and that if he is not allowed to retain the original then he should be allowed to retain a photocopy of the front and reverse of the original. This should, if possible, be certified by the receiver or its agent as follows: 'This is certified to be a true copy of this original bill of lading which is now accomplished'.

261. More than one person demanding delivery of the cargo (for electronic bills of lading see paragraph 270(d))
This situation may arise where

(a) no bills of lading are available at the discharge port
(b) more than one set of bills of lading has been placed in circulation, all or some of which are unauthorised
(c) the originals from a single set have found their way in to the hands of a number of holders
(d) the original shipper (seller) has parted with the bills of lading and is asserting that the holder has not complied with its obligations under the sale contract (e.g. that it has somehow acquired the bills of lading without making payment).

262. Each of these situations places the master (and the shipowner) in a very difficult position. The master is now on notice that one or more of the bills of lading may not be valid, and that one or more of the holders may have acquired possession of the bills of lading in circumstances where the transfer of the bills of lading into their possession was not intended to transfer the right to demand delivery ⚖.

263. The situations can give rise to complex legal issues ⚖ and may involve complex commercial solutions ⚖ and legal solutions ⚖.

264. The best advice that can be given to the master, if he cannot obtain guidance from the owner, is as set out in paragraph 24.

265. Change of destination during voyage
Sometimes the master may be asked to change destination during the voyage and to proceed to a discharge port other than that named in the bill of lading. The master has no authority on the owner's behalf to vary the contract of carriage in this way. The shipowner may choose to accept a letter of indemnity in return for such a variation. These are matters for the shipowner to decide.

OTHER MATTERS
Blending/co-mingling of oil cargoes
266. There appears to be an increasing practice for oil traders to blend or co-mingle cargoes from different ports shipped on different dates and often with different specifications. This can create difficulties in the context of issuing bills of lading. These difficulties derive from three points.

(a) When goods which essentially are of the same specification are shipped by more than one shipper, and the goods are co-mingled on board the carrying ship, then the shippers share ownership in the whole of the mixed goods.

(b) Where the goods are of different specification then not only do questions of shared ownership arise, but also all the goods shipped may by reason of comingling have changed in nature or specification – perhaps more accurately described as blending. For example, if a bill of lading records the receipt on board in apparent good order and condition of a parcel of cargo which is subsequently mixed with a later cargo of different specification, then there is no basis for clausing the bills of lading (because that cargo was received on board in good order and condition), and there may be no opportunity to clause the bill of lading (because it is in the sale and purchase in the chain); but there is a possibility of a claim or claims at the discharge port from disappointed consignees who have not received what is described in the original bill of lading.

(c) If the goods have been shipped on different dates from different ports, then each bill of lading must accurately show the ports of shipment and the dates of shipment for the reasons given at paragraphs 188 and 189. A single bill of lading for the co-mingled cargo could not accurately describe these details.

267. To the oil trader none of these points may be of great significant because it will be its intention to control ownership of the cargo at some stage, and then to sell it in different parcels and with its newly acquired specification. None of this is within the shipowner's knowledge, however, and so it must fall back on basic principles so that it can ensure that in respect of each parcel shipped a bill of lading is issued showing the time and place of that shipment, and the quantity, and apparent condition of the goods; and that the ship will be able to deliver goods at destination complying with that description. The master must also proceed on the assumption that each shipper will require an individual bill of lading for each parcel. Practical guidance is given at paragraph 16.

268. Whether the master can properly be instructed to blend or co-mingle one cargo with another is a matter of contract between the owner and, usually, the charterer (often the oil trader). Often there is provision in charterparties for blending or co-mingling to take place.

Oil trader charterers may also include in such charterparty the right to call on the master to deliver the cargo at a different destination and without production of the bill of lading. They will often manipulate these rights to enable them to co-mingle or blend cargoes, sometimes by discharge and pumping ashore and then re-loading the new mixture or blend.

269. The problems which will undoubtedly arise with the issue of bills of lading in circumstances where cargoes are blended or co-mingled, and the problems arising from the owner making a contractual commitment to blend or co-mingle cargoes received on board, can all be resolved by proper negotiation of the governing charterparty, return of original bills of lading, and letters of indemnity. These are matters for the shipowner to decide. It is important when faced with these situations, for the master to carefully adhere to the principles set out in paragraph 267.

Mixing of dry cargoes
270. The fundamental issues here are the same as identified in paragraphs 266 – 269. However, in practical terms the mixing of dry cargoes will usually involve goods of one description loaded at one port and so many of the difficulties in issuing an accurate bill of lading will not arise. The point at paragraph 266(a) does arise but will not be of practical importance. The individual buyers will draw their share of the cargo from the bulk cargo. If separate bills of lading for each parcel loaded were not issued delivery may be given against presentation of the original bill of lading together with ship's delivery orders (see paragraph 288) or non-negotiable bills of lading for the separate parcels, sometimes known as 'split' bills of lading (see paragraph 293).

Charterparties and charterer's bills of lading
271. The ship will often be operating under a charterparty. The question then arises whether the bill of lading is a contract between the charterer and the shipper or between the shipowner and the shipper. Although this is a complex issue under English law, it is probably correct to say that in most instances a bill of lading will represent a contract between the shipowner and the holder of the bill of lading, because the master is employed by and is the agent of the shipowner ⚖. The exception to the rule is where the ship is operating under a demise or bareboat charterparty so that the master is the employee of the demise or bareboat charterer and not of the shipowner and any bill of lading signed by the master is done so by the master as the charterer's agent. More complex and unusual examples of a charterer's bill may be where the master has been given express authority by the shipowner and charterer to sign on the charterer's behalf, or where the charterer has signed the bill of lading in its own name, or where the bill of lading attempts to define who is the carrier ⚖. The master will not necessarily be aware of all of these arrangements.

272. The significance of the distinction between an owner's bill and a charterer's bill is, of course, that if the contract is between the charterer and the shipper (and subsequent holders of the bill of lading) then any promises made in that bill of lading (for example, to carry to the destination, and to care for the goods) and any representations made in the bill of lading (for example, as to condition or quantity of cargo), are matters between the charterer and the cargo owner. That said, the shipowner may, of course, continue to have duties of care because the cargo is in its physical possession.

273. The ability of a charterer to bind a shipowner to a bill of lading which has been issued without authority being conferred upon the charterer or its agent, is a complex legal question and much will depend upon unusual or unique factual situations. However, because the problem of charterers or their agents issuing bills of lading without authority, or not in accordance with mate's receipts, has been identified as a problem area for shipowners, a brief summary of the guiding principles may be useful.

(a) In any time charterparty where the master is obliged to follow the orders of the charterer as to the employment of the vessel then unless there is an express prohibition, the charterer or its agent will have actual authority to issue and sign bills of lading on the owner's behalf. A sub-time-charterer may also have such authority in some circumstances ⚖.

(b) If charterers or their agents issue bills of lading in breach of charterparty terms they will still have ostensible (that is, apparent) authority to issue and sign bills of lading on the shipowner's behalf, unless the shipowner has been able to advise cargo interests of the lack of actual authority before the bills have been signed, or unless the bills contain extraordinary terms, or unless the cargo interests had reason to know of the lack of authority ⚖.

(c) The master and shipowner may be entitled to refuse to issue clean bills of lading for unsound cargo and this will cause problems for the shipper and charterer but in practice, if the charterer or its agent decide that it will, without notifying the master, abuse the authority identified at (a) and (b) above so as to issue clean bills for unsound cargo itself, there is a strong possibility that the shipowner will be found to be bound by these bills of lading. The shipowner's remedy is against the charterer or its agent ⚖.

274. *What dates should be inserted in a bill of lading which refers to a charterparty?*
Many standard form bills of lading make printed reference to a charterparty, sometimes in the context of freight (see, for example, the Congenbill as discussed at paragraph 45) and sometimes in wider terms, such as governing law and choice, forum for resolving disputes (see the example at paragraph 51.1) and responsibility for loading and stowage ⚖.

275. The importance of inserting the date in the charterparty is that many of the protective clauses in the charterparty which are designed to protect the shipowner may in many legal systems be considered to be incorporated into the bill of lading only if the date of the charterparty is shown on the bill of lading (see paragraph 51.1) ⚖.

276. If the ship is operating under a chain of charterparties, the question arises as to which charterparty date should be shown on the bill of lading. If the matter is left to the master, then in the absence of guidance or direction from any other source, it is recommended that the master should insert the date of the head charterparty. This is the contract with which the shipowner is most familiar ⚖.

277. Sometimes shippers or charterers wish to insert a date other than that of the head charterparty into the bill of lading, and the question arises as to whether they are entitled to do so. As a matter of general principle, the lowest time charterer in the chain will have authority to issue bills of lading on the master's behalf – see paragraph 273(a) – therefore it should have the power to direct that the terms of its own voyage charterparty or contract of affreightment are to be incorporated. The master should seek guidance from the shipowner or its P&I club whenever such a matter arises. If the master cannot obtain guidance then it would be prudent to follow that time-charterer's instruction, as to do otherwise might be seen as overriding its right to have certain forms or content of bills of lading in certain trades. This would also be consistent with the principle that the voyage charterparty in the chain is most germane to the bill of lading voyage ⚖.

Freight

278. Freight terms on a bill of lading are of great importance to the shipper and consignee of the cargo as they will show either that the shipowner has received the freight (for example 'freight prepaid') and therefore that the shipowner will not be exercising a lien over the goods at the discharge port, or that all or some of the freight remains payable (e.g. 'payable at destination'). If there is no charterparty involved, then any freight terms recorded on the face of the bill of lading, for example, that freight has been prepaid, or that a certain amount has been paid in advance, will operate as a receipt issued by the master on behalf of the shipowner confirming that the money has been paid to the shipowner. If the vessel is operating under a charterparty, the charterer will usually receive the freight for the shipment (for example, where it is a time-charterer receiving freight from a voyage charterer, or a CIF seller receiving freight from the buyer within the sale price of the goods). In those circumstances it would not seem to be sensible for the shipowner to issue a receipt for something which it has not received.

279. Despite this, it can be dangerous for a shipowner to refuse to sign a bill of lading which includes terms as to payment of freight, particularly if those terms are standard within the charterer's trade. So, for example, when a ship is operating under a time-charterparty and the obligation on the master is to sign bills of lading 'as presented', he should not generally refuse to issue bills of lading simply because they are marked 'freight prepaid' and a shipowner should be very careful to take detailed legal advice before it instructs the master not to sign such a bill ⚖. Voyage charterparties usually contain terms that are more precise about the issue and release of bills of lading marked 'freight pre-paid', or will expressly state the freight terms that are to be included in any bills of lading issued under the charterparty, for example that freight is 'payable at destination'. If no provision has been made in the voyage charterparty for the issue of freight pre-paid bills of lading the master should seek clear instructions from the shipowner. If the master cannot obtain instructions then he should advise the shippers and charterers that he is awaiting clear instructions from the shipowner that the bill of lading can be marked 'freight pre-paid' and that he will not sign until he receives that authority, or that he will sign and leave the bills of lading in the hands of the owner's agent to be released only with the shipowner's consent ⚖.

OTHER DOCUMENTS AND VARIATIONS
Sea waybills
280. A sea waybill, like a bill of lading, is a document which functions as a receipt for the goods and as evidence of the contract of carriage. Unlike a bill of lading, however, it does not operate as a documentary '*key*' the holder of which is entitled to possession of the goods. Instead, the carrier is to deliver the goods to the person named in the sea waybill as the person to whom the goods are to be delivered, whether or not that person can produce the sea waybill at the discharge port.

281. Recognition of sea waybills is given by COGSA 1992 (see paragraphs 98 – 100 and appendix IX) which recognises the two functions referred to above, namely that it is a receipt for goods and it contains or evidences the contract of carriage, and it identifies the person to whom delivery of the goods is to be made by the carrier in accordance with that contract.

282. Sea waybills are usually used where it is commercially impractical for the goods to be sold when afloat or where there is no need for the goods to be sold afloat (and so they are sold before loading or after discharge) or where there is no sale of the goods at all (for example in carriage of personal effects or between two branches of one company).

283. For these reasons, sea waybills may be familiar and frequently used in some trades, for example ferry and liner operations, but rarely seen or used on other trades, such as bulk shipments of dry cargo or oil or the tramping trade generally. The important practical guidance which can be given to a master, therefore, is that if he is requested to issue or becomes aware of the intended issue of sea waybills in circumstances where, on the basis of the guidance given above, the master feels they may be inappropriate, or if the master is simply unfamiliar with them, then the master should bring this to the attention of the local P&I correspondent and the shipowner.

284. Practical problems which may arise from the issue of sea waybills where they have not been carefully thought about by the shipowners (or indeed by the charterers or shippers are):

(a) The proper identification of the person who has the right to receive the goods. This is a practical matter for the shipowner or its agents to arrange and attend to. It is made difficult because that person does not have to produce the sea waybill. Usually the agents will be local to and familiar with the discharge port. Furthermore, waybills are common to liner business, ferry operations and repeat trade. Therefore there is likely to be an element of familiarity between the agent handling the ship's discharge and the person named in the sea waybill. However, identification is a matter for care and caution.

(b) The failure properly to incorporate the Hague or Hague-Visby Rules. While bills of lading attract the compulsory application of the Hague or Hague-Visby Rules, sea waybills do not. The Hague or Hague-Visby Rules will apply to sea waybills only where they are, by the terms of the sea waybill, contractually incorporated ⚖. The P&I associations expect the shipowner to carry goods, wherever possible, subject to the Hague or Hague-Visby Rules and will expect sea waybills to incorporate the rules accordingly. It is therefore important to the shipowner's P&I cover that the sea waybill effectively incorporates these Rules.

(c) The risk that the receiver of the goods and/or the local authorities (e.g. customs) at the discharge port, may be unfamiliar with the sea waybill and in particular with the concept that it is not a document which has to be produced in return for delivery of the goods ⚖.

These are all issues which need to be addressed by the shipowner and its advisors, particularly if the charterparty under which the ship is operating neither refers to nor contemplates the issue of sea waybills.

285. The sea waybill as a receipt

On the basis that the sea waybill has incorporated the Hague or Hague-Visby Rules, the information which the shipper can call upon to be inserted in the sea waybill is the same as that described earlier in this guide in relation to bills of lading. The standard of care to be exercised by the master is also the same. The guidance given at paragraphs 133 – 192 should be followed.

'Straight' bills of lading

286. This is the name commonly given to bills of lading which, by their nature, are not negotiable – usually because there is a named consignee and there is no facility for the negotiations of bill of lading by consignment or endorsement, that is the words '*to order*' do not appear on the bill and there is no other wording making the document transferable. In some countries these bills of lading may be treated as sea waybills, giving rise to the problems discussed at paragraph 284 ⚖.

287. The legal issues which arise from the overlapping concepts of '*straight*' bills of lading and sea waybills are not of concern to the master, but practical issues may arise, in particular whether he should insist on production of a '*straight*' bill of lading at the discharge port in the face of assertions by the receiver or the charterer that it is to be treated as a sea waybill and therefore its production is not required. The best practical advice that can be given to the master is that, wherever the document refers to itself as a bill of lading, or it contains an 'accomplishment' provision, such as that which is discussed at paragraph 51, then he should call for the production of the bill of lading at the discharge port unless he is clearly advised by the shipowner or its P&I correspondent that the master is not entitled to call for its production. It is essential to seek such advice from the shipowner or its P&I correspondent as soon as possible, and preferably before arrival at the discharge port, as a dispute may arise between the owner and charterer/receiver about time lost as a result of refusing to discharge ⚖.

Delivery orders

288. The use of delivery orders in relation to carriage of goods by sea is to enable bulk cargoes to be split into separate parcels and sold to separate buyers during the course of the sea voyage. The separate buyers acquire, through the delivery order, the right to demand possession of the goods and the right to sue the shipowner if the goods are lost or damaged. This legal mechanism is created by COGSA 1992, see paragraphs 98 – 100 and appendix IX.

289. In essence, a ship's delivery order must contain a promise by or on behalf of the shipowner to the person to whom it is issued, to deliver the parcel of cargo to that person or to whom they may direct. Whilst in practice the master may sign this document at the request of the shipowner or its agent, it is not a document which the master is expected to prepare, and all requests by charterers, shippers or receivers for delivery orders to be issued should be referred to the shipowner.

290. Unlike bills of lading and sea waybills, a delivery order is neither a receipt nor a contract of carriage. It plays a subordinate or supporting role to the actual contract of carriage, which will typically be the bill of lading. So by way of example, if A ships goods on B's ship, B will issue a bill of lading for the entire cargo to A. If A then decides to sell individual parcels to C, D, E and F, A can ask B to issue a delivery order to each of C, D, E and F in which B undertakes to C, D, E and F that it will deliver the cargo to them.

291. If the ship's delivery order complies with the ingredients described in COGSA 1992 section 1(4), this is, in theory at least, a proper way to divide a bulk cargo into parcels for separate receivers. However, it is not clear how frequently such delivery orders are used in practice. Furthermore, one possible difficulty is that the issue of a delivery order does not extinguish the rights of the original bill of lading holder, so that in theory, the shipowner may owe inconsistent obligations under the bill of lading and under the delivery order ⚖. Therefore, a shipowner would be well advised to issue delivery orders only against surrender of the original bill of lading or by marking the bill of lading with a clear reference to the existence and amount of the delivery order(s) that has been issued; or by using split bills of lading subject to the comments at paragraph 293 ⚖.

292. See also the comment on 'parcels of cargo' at paragraph 15 and 191.

'Split' or 'switch' bills of lading

293. There are occasions when a buyer of goods, having taken up the bills of lading from its seller, will wish to have new bills issued showing itself as shipper in place of the original shipper. This is usually done for commercial reasons. Such bills are sometimes referred to as '*switch*' bills of lading. On other occasions, a shipper of bulk cargo may wish to sell the cargo to individual buyers all of whom, for commercial reasons '*need*' a bill of lading, as distinct from a ship's delivery order as described above. Such bills of lading are sometimes referred to as '*split*' bills of lading. Each of these arrangements ('*switch*' and '*split*' bills) may or may not be accompanied by problems, largely depending on whether the original bill of lading is surrendered in return for the issue of such new bills of lading. The only practical guidance that can be given is that masters should not involve themselves in the issue of such bills of lading, or in negotiating for the surrender of the original bill, other than in consultation with the shipowner ⚖.

294. See also the comments on 'parcels of cargo' at 15 and 191.

SECURITY ISSUES

295. Recent legislation and regulation has considerably increased the burden on shipowners and charterers with regard to security and documentation. The United States has issued extensive legislative and regulatory responses to terrorism in the form of the Homeland Security Act, Maritime Transportation Security Act of 2002, USA Patriot Act of 2001 and various others. Globally, the International Ship and Port Facility Security Code (ISPS Code) came into force in relation to most cargo carrying ships in 2004. However, the bill of lading does not occupy a front-line position with regard to such regulations. By way of example, the destination of a loaded voyage, both in terms of the destination port and the destination facility, will be of considerable importance to the shipowner's company security officer. Therefore the insertion of that destination in the bill of lading, thus making it a contractual destination (subject to legality and safety), will also be of considerable importance to the shipowner. However, the need for care and diligence in ascertaining the security status of that port or facility is vested in the company security officer rather than the master.

296. United States customs authorities forbid the use of generic cargo descriptions such as '*said to contain*' in the vessel cargo manifest required to be submitted in advance to the customs authorities. Although the customs regulations do not prevent the use of such descriptions in the bill of lading itself, the master may, out of caution, wish to discuss with the shipowner or the P&I club or its correspondent at destination, where a vague description such as '*said to contain*' is inserted by the shipper in a bill of lading destined for the United States.

SANCTIONS

297. Sanctions are seen as a useful and successful tool by national and supranational authorities and now appear to be a permanent feature within the international community.

298. The master should be aware of the far-reaching effect of sanctions legislation, but the very nature of the different sanctions regimes that have been and are in place now makes it difficult to offer any specific guidance. North of England P&I Association provides regular updates on sanctions through its industry news service and by way of loss prevention briefings, which can be accessed on the club's website. Other organisations will provide similar updated advice.

ELECTRONIC BILLS OF LADING

BACKGROUND

299. The concept of an electronic version of the traditional paper bill of lading is readily understandable, the most obvious attraction being the almost instantaneous transfer of an electronic 'document' instead of the administrative burden of moving a paper document from place to place.

300. However, a traditional paper bill of lading performs a number of legal functions – as a receipt, as a document of title and as a contract of carriage. The functions are only made effective by operation of law, be it by statute (for example Carriage of Goods by Sea Act 1992) (see paragraphs 98 – 100) or by recognition of long-established custom and practice.

301. An electronic bill of lading is not, as the law currently stands, treated in the same way. It cannot rely on the statutory support of COGSA 1992 ⚖, nor is there any established custom or practice surrounding this relatively new concept. In the eyes of the law, therefore, an electronic bill of lading may be capable of performing its function as a receipt (the simple recording and transfer of information) but it does not have the ability to transfer liabilities or rights under the contract of carriage, or to operate as a key to the possession of the goods. Until electronic bills of lading are afforded the same legal status and support as paper bills of lading with regard to these two functions, their operational effectiveness may have to depend on legal devices such as contractual groupings, deeming provisions or notional agency arrangements.

302. The more successful attempts at creating an effective electronic bill of lading system, capable of performing the three vital legal functions described above, have taken the form of multi-party contracts in which the key parties to the transaction (seller/shipper, buyer/receiver, carrier and, where appropriate, banks) all agree in advance that the electronic bill of lading will take a certain form and will perform certain functions. It is a bill of lading in the eyes of those parties. It is not a bill of lading in the eyes of the law. Such systems are often referred to as 'closed systems' because they are only available to an identifiable or closed group of contractual parties, often referred to as 'users' within the contract ⚖.

303. Other systems approach the need to perform the three legal functions described above, by 'deeming' the transfer of the electronic bill of lading to equate to the transfer of a paper bill of lading thereby attempting (so far as English law is concerned) to invoke a 'deemed' operation of COGSA 1992 (see paragraph 98).

304. Some of these systems provide a web-based or cloud-based secure system, or provide patented hardware enabling the creation and transfer of electronic documents, and some also facilitate the electronic transfer of other documents relevant to the sale and finance transaction.

305. There are also some trade organisations which have drafted a putative set of standard terms and conditions which could be adopted for the purpose of electronic trading again on a multi-party contract basis), by the parties adopting the recommended terms as the template for an agreed transaction, but do not provide the electronic trading system ⚖.

Advantages

306. Despite the need for the technical legal devices described above, the advantages claimed for electronic bills of lading are many and may include:

- reduction or avoidance of use of paper
- reduction of number of personnel handling documentation
- efficiency and speed of transfer
- reduced credit time for financial transactions
- avoidance of 'delivery of cargo without production of (paper) bill of lading' problems
- corresponding reduction in use of letters of indemnity
- traceability of the bill of lading at all times
- ability of the shipowner to check content of the bill of lading instantaneously (thus avoiding issue of unauthorised content by agents)
- ease of amendment including change of destination
- avoidance of risks caused by multiple originals (see paragraph 258).

Perceived risks and disadvantages

307. Electronic bills of lading and electronic trading systems are, in comparison with their long-established paper relatives, still in their early stages in terms of development and user experience. These will no doubt be overcome, but the risks and disadvantages cannot yet be fully predicted. Those that have been identified include:

(a) legal functionality – the risk that a system, whether closed or not, may not achieve all of its intended legal functions or may not be recognised as achieving them in any particular jurisdiction; or may not attract the statutory application of key conventions such as the Hague-Visby Rules (although a closed system will endeavour to achieve this contractually rather than by force of statute).

(b) technical functionality – that is

- failure of the electronic trading system's own hardware or software
- consequential delay
- consequential loss of data
- consequential unintended distribution of data
- failure of one of the user's systems resulting in the same problems as above
- security issues – that is identifying who is sending a message, whether it has been altered, its veracity and authenticity
- whether legal requirements in any particular jurisdiction are satisfied, such as being in writing, effective electronic signature (see paragraph 319 below), production of originals and admissibility in evidence.

Electronic signature

308. Under English law an electronic signature (that is, a scanned signature appearing on a paper document – for example, sent by fax) is a valid signature, and this applies both to a bill of lading and to its acceptability under UCP600 (subject to the terms of the particular credit). But if a document is to remain in a purely electronic form, then it is for the electronic trading system to ensure

(a) that the 'electronic signature' is an effective means of showing the veracity, authenticity and provenance of a document
(b) that it is acceptable to whichever legal system governs the underlying transaction.

P&I COVER

309. Given the risks and uncertainties referred to above, the initial response of the International Group of P&I Clubs to electronic bills of lading was to place the risk of their use on the individual members using them, and not on the mutual membership. As the risks were unpredictable, it was felt inappropriate when electronic bills first came into early use, albeit in small numbers, to regard such risks as mutual risks.

310. This was achieved by a 'paperless trading' exclusion of cover, the effect of which was to bar any recovery from a P&I club for any liability, cost or expense arising from the use of any electronic trading system. A discretionary claim would be allowed if the P&I club considered that the liability cost or expense would also have arisen under a paper trading system.

311. In due course, a number of electronic trading systems were developed and gained increasing use and experience. These were assessed carefully by the International Group of P&I Clubs and it was decided that if, after very careful consideration and legal review, they could reasonably be expected to replicate the legal requirements and functions of a paper bill of lading, then their use could be regarded as a mutual risk. The paper trading exclusion was relaxed in favour of two trading systems which were designated as 'approved' by the International Group of P&I Clubs.

312. Systems which had not or have not yet been designated as approved can of course be used by whoever wishes to use them. However, in the event of claims arising which would not have arisen had a paper bill of lading been issued, those claims – insofar as they may give rise to a P&I type of liability – would be subject to the paperless trading exclusion and may be subject to reimbursement solely at the discretion of the P&I club.

313. The position with regard to P&I cover in general for liabilities arising under any electronic bills of lading is summarised below.

(a) Cover is available for typical P&I liabilities arising under any electronic bills of lading to the extent these liabilities would also have arisen under paper bills of lading.
(b) But, to the extent these liabilities would have arisen because an electronic bill of lading has been used instead of a paper bill of lading, cover is discretionary unless the electronic trading system has been approved by the International Group of P&I Clubs.

314. The two systems designated as 'approved' are

(a) Electronic Shipping Solutions DSUA 2009.3 and DSUA 2013.1 ('ESS') (www.essdocs.com)
(b) Bolero International Ltd Rulebook/Operating Procedure 1999 ('Bolero') (www.bolero.net).

315. It follows that, so far as P&I cover is concerned, a shipowner's position is better when using one of the approved systems, than another electronic system which has not been approved. The shipowner will have cover for all normal P&I liabilities arising out of the use of one of the approved systems (though not for liabilities which are of a non-traditional P&I nature – see paragraph 318) and thereby avoid exposure to the risks connected with the use of non-approved systems as described in paragraph 317.

316. However, it is important to note that all exceptions and exclusions under typical P&I club rules continue to apply (as they would with a paper bill of lading). This includes the traditional exclusions of cover relating to the carriage of goods, such as

- the issue or creation of an electronic document/record with a description of the cargo or its condition known to be incorrect
- short delivery where an electronic document/record is issued or created for an amount of cargo greater than that known to have been loaded
- discharge at a port or place other than the port or place provided for in the contract of carriage
- the issue or creation of an ante or post-dated electronic document/record
- delivery of the cargo without production of the negotiable electronic document/record.

317. In contrast with carriage under an 'approved' system, the risk and limitation of P&I cover which a shipowner may face when carrying under an 'unapproved' system is that it is not recognised as performing all the functions that a paper bill of lading would have performed. This is the risk identified at paragraph 307(a). One example could be that an unapproved system is found, when challenged legally, not to transfer rights in goods in the manner that the creators of the system intended. This may give rise to a dispute about ownership and mis-delivery of the cargo. Another example could be if the Hague or Hague-Visby Rules have not been effectively incorporated into the electronic bill of lading. If it is found that in each case the liability has arisen because of the use of the (unapproved) electronic system, then that will not be covered within normal P&I cover. It may be covered at the discretion of the board of directors of P&I clubs.

318. It must also be recognised that using an electronic bill of lading may expose a shipowner to additional types of risks which are not in the nature of traditional carriage risks; for example the risk of viruses, 'hacking', or the accidental release or theft of information. Simply put, it is the risk of using computers. In this context, such liabilities may include, for example, those which arise under the contractual arrangements with the system operator such as obligations to maintain computer links, or the introduction of a

virus within the operator's or a user's system. The user agreements for these systems may also contain undertakings of confidentiality and could give rise to liabilities if broken. These are not in the nature of P&I risks. In insurance terms, they may be described as 'cyber-risks' or business risks.

319. The history of these changes is set out in the circulars approved by the International Group of P&I Clubs and, in North of England P&I Association's case, dated 13 September 2010 and 9 April 2013 and which appear at appendix X in this guide. A more detailed explanation of the risks perceived with electronic bills of lading, the distinction between 'approved' and 'non-approved' systems (together with examples) and the role of the clubs with regard to 'risks not of a traditional P&I nature' are dealt with in more detail in the 'frequently asked questions' circulated by each of the clubs in the International Group of P&I Clubs in 2013, and which also appears at appendix XI.

THE MASTER'S ROLE

320. The creation and transfer of an electronic bill of lading is far more likely to take place in an office than on board the ship. The master's role as the issuer of a bill of lading is therefore likely to be further diminished with the increase in use of electronic bills of lading. Nevertheless, the master remains the eyes and ears of the shipowner, and his function in checking the condition of the cargo and providing accurate information to the shipowner to enable an electronic bill of lading to be issued is as crucial as with a paper bill of lading or a mate's receipt. All of the practical and theoretical guidance given in the practical and theory sections regarding the quantity and condition of the cargo, the date of loading and whether or not it is stowed on deck, remains as vital a task with the electronic bill as it does with the paper bill of lading.

321. Changes to the bill of lading or information contained within it are likely to be made during the course of the voyage and, as with a paper bill of lading, the master is unlikely to be involved in such activities.

322. No physical bill of lading will be produced at the discharge port. The traditional role of the master delivering the cargo to the person who 'surrenders' the paper bill of lading is replaced by an electronic confirmation, probably to the shipowner's office itself, and in turn to the shipowner's agent at the discharge port, that the bill of lading has been successfully negotiated and endorsed (or the electronic equivalent of these terms, which will usually be defined by the relevant electronic trading system in use). The key issue for the master, therefore, is to ensure that delivery is given to the person who has been designated as the proper receiver of the cargo. Clearly this can give rise to problems as to the proper identification of that person. This is a practical matter for the shipowner or its agents to arrange and attend to. Usually, the agents will be local to and familiar with the discharge port and there is likely to be an element of familiarity between the agent handling the ship's discharge and the person named in the order to discharge. However, identification is a matter for care and caution in which the master must exercise both prudence and vigilance and, if in any doubt, liaise closely with the shipowner or the local agent.

323. The following is a list of issues which frequently arise with paper bills of lading, with corresponding comments relating to electronic bills of lading.

(a) *Who is to sign the bill of lading?*
Some electronic trading systems will use a paper bill of lading, issued in the usual way, which is then scanned electronically and introduced to the electronic transfer system. The master will be involved to the same extent as with a paper bill of lading. Other systems will create the document in electronic form from the outset. The authority to issue this will come from whoever is defined as the carrier under the particular electronic trading system. Save as set out at paragraph 320, the master is unlikely to be involved in its issue. (For paper bills of lading, see paragraph 125.)

(b) *Correcting bills of lading after signature*
The usual problem with paper bills of lading, even where all parties agree, is that the bills of lading are in transit and not available for physical amendment. Most electronic trading systems will permit immediate access to the electronic document and will permit consensual amendment (for paper bills of lading, see paragraph 130). This may include, for example, change of destination (paragraph 232).

(c) *Bill of lading not available at the discharge port (for paper bills of lading, see paragraph 250)*
This should not be a problem with an electronic bill of lading as the electronic trading system should facilitate immediate access, confirmation of 'accomplishment' (paragraph 248) and clear guidance as to whom delivery of the cargo should be given. The use of letters of indemnity (paragraph 254) is therefore likely to be greatly reduced.

(d) *More than one person demanding delivery of the cargo*
The electronic trading system will identify one final 'holder' of the bill of lading to whom delivery is to be given. This should avoid the possibility of competing demands. There remains the risk of identification, however, with the risk of more than one party claiming to be the party named in the order for delivery. As with delivery of goods carried under a seawaybill, or (in some jurisdictions) a straight bill of lading, or where a letter of indemnity is used in place of production of the bill of lading, proper systems for checking identification are essential.

CHARTERPARTY REQUIREMENTS

324. As stated at paragraph 307 the full range of risks or problems which may arise from the use of electronic bills of lading may not yet be fully apparent. In broad terms the use of electronic bills of lading is likely to be driven by major traders and operators, and it is they who will impose upon shipowners from whom they charter the requirement to use electronic bills of lading and, where necessary, to become a user of a particular electronic bill of lading system. The balancing of the risks of using such a system can be dealt with by a suitable charter party clause. Clauses will vary according to market forces and development of (and trust in) electronic trading systems, but examples of model clauses should be available from time to time from BIMCO (www.Bimco.org) and the P&I clubs.

LEGAL NOTES

These legal notes refer to paragraphs in the practical guidance, theory and electronic bills of lading sections. They are denoted in the text by the ⚖ symbol. The law is stated as understood at 1 January 2014. For full textbook references see the Bibliography at appendix X.

Paragraph	Legal note
2	See *Derry v. Peek* (1889) 14 App.Cas 337. *'Fraud is proved when it is shown that a false representation has been made (i) knowingly, or (ii) without belief in its truth, or (iii) recklessly, careless whether it is true or false.'*
4(b)(ii)	See *The Boukadoura* [1989] 1 Lloyd's Rep. 393 at 399.
4(b)(v)	This complies with the Hague and Hague-Visby Rules obligation to issue a bill which shows the apparent order and condition of the cargo. In the case of perishable goods, apparent good order and condition includes the apparent ability of the goods to withstand ordinary methods of transport. If the words 'shipped in good order and condition' do not appear at all on the bill of lading then the cases suggest that the bill of lading then ceases to be prima facie evidence of the condition of the goods on shipment. Except where the Hamburg Rules apply (see appendix VIII) omission of the phrase does not infer that the goods were shipped in good condition. See Scrutton on Charterparties and Bills of Lading, 22nd edition, page 140.
4(c)	This warning is given because there has been a case where affixing the ship's stamp next to the shipper's figures has been construed as an acceptance of those figures as correct. See *The Herroe and Askoe* [1986] 2 Lloyd's Rep. 281 and Scrutton on Charterparties and Bills of Lading, 22nd edition, page 142.
10	According to BIMCO, there have been cases where such a bill of lading has been construed as an *ad valorem* bill of lading. An *ad valorem* bill of lading is described in the glossary in appendix I.
14	The custom has been to issue three bills of lading, one of them to go with the ship, one to find its way through the documentary credit system to the consignee, and one to stay with the shipper to prove that the goods were actually shipped, should this ever become disputed. There is a brief commentary on this in Scrutton on Charterparties and Bills of Lading, 22nd edition, page 86.
15	Problems may arise where a homogeneous parcel is damaged and the shipper or charterer require separate bills of lading for individual parcels to be signed. This may result in one parcel being heavily claused with the other parcels bearing no clausing; which could give rise to difficulties at the discharge port in ensuring that good cargo is discharged against unclaused bills, with the remaining *'dirty'* being discharged against the dirty bill of lading. In this situation there would be justification for the master either saying that he simply will not issue parcel bills but only a single bill of lading for the entire cargo (see paragraph 6.22-24, page 139 in Bills of Lading in Export Trade, 3rd edition) or to insist that the clausing has to go on each of the sets of bills of lading for each parcel. The master would have to be careful with the wording of the clausing and the shipowner or the P&I correspondent or surveyor would have to help with that.
17	Such a letter of indemnity is unenforceable because the issuing of a bill of lading containing representations which the master knows to be false is fraudulent, (*Brown Jenkinson v. Percy Dalton* [1957] 2 Lloyd's Rep. 1.). It is sometimes possible to identify a genuine doubt about the condition of the goods and a genuine dispute between the shipowner and the shipper as to what should be written in the bill of lading. In those circumstances a letter of indemnity which recites the fact of a genuine dispute and identifies how the genuine dispute has arisen may be enforceable. However the

	borderline is fine and the acceptance of such a letter of indemnity is a matter for the shipowner rather than the master to decide. See also paragraphs 181 to 183 for a more detailed discussion.
22(1st)	Scrutton on Charterparties and Bills of Lading, 22nd edition, page 296.
22(2nd)	This is because the person holding and presenting the bill and calling for delivery must also be legally entitled to receive the goods in accordance with the terms of the bill of lading; and if the bill requires endorsement, this must be done. See *Sze Hai Tong Bank Ltd v. Rambler Cycle Co Ltd.* [1959] 2 Lloyd's Rep. 114; and *Carewins Development (China) Limited v. Bright Fortune Shipping Limite*d [2009] 3HKLRD 409; and *Charmax Trading v. Wt Sea Air Limited* (LMLN 28/1/10).
24(a)	Recent cases have re-affirmed the principle that the master is obliged to deliver goods upon production of the original bill of lading and, indeed, that delivery without production of the bill of lading constitutes a breach of contract even when made to the person entitled to possession. The master cannot know if the person seeking delivery of the cargo is entitled to possession unless that person has produced an original bill of lading. *The Houda* [1994] 2 Lloyd's Rep. 541; *East West Corp. v. DKBS 1912* [2003] 1 Lloyd's Rep. 239 (CA).
25	See *The Somorvskiy 3068* [1994] 21 Lloyd's Rep. 262 at page 272 but also see *The Houda* [1994] 2 Lloyd's Rep. 541 and *Motis Exports Limited v. Dampskibsselskabet AF 1912* [1999] 1 Lloyd's Rep. 837 at 841 upheld at [2000] 1 Lloyd's Rep. 211 (CA) which together suggest that a '*reasonable explanation*' may not be sufficient to justify delivery of the cargo, but that a court order may be required.
27	The promises by the issuer of the letter of indemnity will not be engaged if delivery is not given to the person named. If the charterer confirms that the person calling for delivery is the person named in the letter of indemnity, then the charterer will be estopped from relying upon this argument. See *The Bremen Max* [2009] 1 Lloyd's Rep. 81.
38	If there is a notify party or address entered on the bill of lading (and it will be the shipper who supplies this information when drawing up the bill of lading) then the master must take care to contact this party, usually through the ship's agent at the discharge port, on arrival. See *Clemens Horst v. Norfolk and North Western American S.N. Co. Ltd.* (1906) 22 TLR 403).
39	The implication from Article 3 rule 3 and Article 3 rule 7 of the Hague-Visby Rules is that the bill of lading which the shipper can demand once the bills have been 'shipped' should show the name of the ship concerned.
41	The reasoning is this. Once the charterer has required the shipowner to issue a bill of lading naming a discharge port, then the shipowner is bound under the bill of lading to proceed to the discharge port and to do otherwise may amount to a deviation. In that situation the charterer, as a matter of general principle, cannot then order the shipowner to be in breach of that bill of lading obligation. By analogy see the principles enunciated in *The Houda* [1994] 2 Lloyd's Rep. 541 where it was held that a charterer could not lawfully order a shipowner to discharge without production of the bill of lading as to do so would be a breach of the bill of lading contract. For a typical example see LMLN 59, 4 February 1982, London arbitration number 2/820.
45	See *The San Nicholas* [1976] 1 Lloyd's Rep. 8, *The Sevonia Team* [1983] 2 Lloyd's Rep. 640, 644, and *The Nai Matteini* [1988] 1 Lloyd's Rep. 452, 459; and the discussion in Voyage Charters, 3rd edition, paragraphs 18.59–18.63 and in Scrutton on Charterparties and Bills of Lading, 22nd edition, pages 97–98, 100 and 463.Under English law the failure to insert a date in the blank form on the bill of lading will probably not prevent the incorporation of the terms of the selected charterparty into the bill of lading. See Roskill L.J. in *The San Nicholas* (above) where he stated: '*I would hesitate long before holding that the mere omission to include the date of a charterparty in a bill of lading negatives an intention to incorporate the terms of that charterparty into the bill of lading ...*'. See also *The Ikariada* [1999] 2 Lloyd's Rep. 365.

61	More accurately, it became a document giving the right to demand possession of the cargo at its destination. See also paragraph 245 and the discussion in Bills of Lading in Export Trade, 3rd edition, page 25, paragraph 2.2.
75	See Bills of Lading in Export Trade, 3rd edition, Chapter 2.
78	For guidance on the Incoterms and UCP600 and the common law requirements for a bill of lading to be acceptable to the seller, see the International Chamber of Commerce publications on UCP600 and Incoterms 2010.
85	The variations in precise application are too many to mention but a useful analysis appears in the International Journal of Shipping Law, June 1998.
94	The full title is the United Nations Convention on Contracts for the International Carriage of Goods Wholly or Partly by Sea.
98	For a more detailed discussion see Bills of Lading in Export Trade, 3rd edition, page 130 2.8.
99	The Act distinguishes between bills of lading, sea waybills and delivery orders. For more detail see paragraphs 280 et seq.
100	See *Grant v. Norway* (1851) and Section 4 COGSA 92 at appendix IX.
108	See *The Arctic Trader* [1996] 2 Lloyd's Rep. 449 (CA).
109(1st)	See the *David Agmashanebeli* [2003] 1 Lloyd's Rep. 92 at 103.
109(2nd)	For example where inspection before loading is standard practice for the type of cargo, or where the master has an obligation to reject the cargo if it would, if loaded, be subject to the need for clausing. See *The Sea Success* [2005] 2 Lloyd's Rep. 692.
111	See Bills of Lading in Export Trade, 3rd edition, pages 130-132, paragraphs 6.10-6.12, and *Vita Food Products v. Unus Shipping Co.* [1939] AC 277. and *Canadian and Dominion Sugar v. Canadian National (West Indian) Steamships Ltd* [1947] AC46.
113	For a little more detail on a typical process for preparing and issuing bills of lading see *The Sea Success* [2005] 2 Lloyd's Rep. 692 paragraphs 21–26.
114	If the master knowingly signs a bill of lading which inaccurately records, for example, the date of shipment, or the nature, quantity or condition of the cargo, the shipowner will not be entitled to an implied right of indemnity, and even if he has an express indemnity it may be rendered unenforceable. The master is under an obligation to take reasonable steps to inspect the cargo before signing the bills of lading and the shipowner will not be entitled to an indemnity from the cargo owner where the inaccuracies in the bill of lading, or the failure of the master to identify inaccuracies in the bill of lading, have arisen through the master's negligence. (*The Nogar Marin* [1987] 1 Lloyd's Rep. 456) and [1988] 1 Lloyd's Rep. 412. For a detailed discussion see Scrutton on Charterparties and Bills of Lading, 22nd edition, pages 106–109 and footnotes. As to the nature of the master's duty when noting the apparent condition of the cargo see paragraph 164 and its legal notes.
117(1st)	See *Jones v. Hough* (1879) and the general discussion in Time Charters, 6th edition, paragraph 21.31, page 398.
117(2nd)	See *The Almak*, [1985] 1 Lloyd's Rep. 557 a case concerning an ante-dated bill of lading where the judge said that '*the obligation to sign bills of lading as presented would not oblige the master to sign bills of lading which stated a falsehood*'. Furthermore, if for some reason damage to cargo has not been noted on the mate's receipts, the master cannot be required to sign clean bills of lading simply because the mate's receipts are 'clean' see Time Charterers, 6th edition, paragraph 21.51, page 405. In *The Boukadora* [1989] 1 Lloyd's Rep. 393 the judge held that the requirement of the master to sign bills of lading 'as presented' does not mean that the master is bound to sign, or that the charterer may issue, a bill of lading in whatever terms the charterer chooses. There is a basic and

	implied requirement that the bills as presented shall relate to goods actually shipped and that they shall not contain a misdescription of the goods which is known to be incorrect.
119(1st)	*Halcyon Steamship Co. v. Continental Grain Co.* [1943] 75Ll.L. Rep. 80.
119(2nd)	This should be contrasted with those clauses which only maintain their effect if they are incorporated in the bill of lading and where there is no express provision for them to be incorporated in the bill of lading. In those cases the master cannot insist that they are included. (See also the discussion in *The Nanfri* [1979] 1 Lloyd's Rep. 201).
119(3rd)	*The Almak* [1985] 1 Lloyd's Rep. 557.
119(4th)	See Time Charters, 6th edition, paragraph 21.53, page 406.
119(5th)	See Voyage Charters, 3rd edition, paragraph 18.213, page 527 and see *Reynolds v. Jex* (1865) 7B and S86.
120(1st)	Insofar as the bills of lading which have been presented to the master exceed the owner's obligations to the charterer under the charterparty.
120(2nd)	See Time Charters, 6th edition, paragraph 21.55, page 406.
120(3rd)	See Time Charters, 6th edition, paragraph 21.57, page 406
120(4th)	See Time Charters, 6th edition, paragraph 21.59, page 407.
122	See for example clause 8 of the NYPE charterparty and see Time Charter,s 6th edition, paragraph 21.35.
123	See *The Universe Sentinel* [1983] 1 AC 366 and *The Evia Luck* [1992] 2 AC 152, *The Alev* [1989] 1 Lloyd's Rep. 138, *Huyton v. Peter Cremer* [1999] 1 Lloyd's Rep. 620, and *The Cenk Kaptanoglu [2012]* EWHC 273 (Comm).
124	This right of indemnity will be lost if the master deliberately signs a bill of lading which is inaccurate, and may be lost if he is reckless or negligent as to its accuracy. See the commentary in Scrutton on Charterparties and Bills of Lading, 22nd edition, page 364.
125	For a little more detail on a typical process for preparing and issuing bills of lading see *The Sea Success* [2005] 2 Lloyd's Rep. 692 paragraphs 21–26.
127	See the cases referred to at 273(a) and (c).
128	See the cases referred to at 273(a) and (c).
130(1st)	*The Wiloma Tanana* [1993] 2 Lloyd's Rep. 41.
130(2nd)	See Scrutton on Charterparties and Bills of Lading, 22nd edition, p71.
131(1st)	See *The Lycaon* [1983] 2 Lloyd's Rep. 548 and *The Future Express* [1992] 2 Lloyd's Rep. 79 and *The Wiloma Tanana* [1993] 2 Lloyd's Rep. 41.
131(2nd)	See *Hansson v. Hamel* [1922] AC 36 and SIAT v. Tradax [1980] 1 Lloyd's Rep. page 53.
132	See the similar situation at paragraph 253 and the legal notes thereto.
133	See Scrutton on Charterparties and Bills of Lading, 22nd edition, page 71.
136	See *The Arctic Trader* [1996] 2 Lloyd's Rep. 449.
137	Indeed, in *The Arctic Trader* [1996] 2 Lloyd's Rep. 449 at 458 the Court of Appeal stated that the obligation under Article 3 rule 3 to issue on demand a bill of lading which states the apparent order and condition of the goods is '*an unqualified or absolute contractual undertaking and not merely one which the shipowner or the master must take reasonable care to perform*'. This is a practical book, however, and so it also worth noting that the Court of Appeal went on to say '*however, since making an accurate statement as to the apparent order and condition of goods may involve some degree of skill and expertise, though it does not necessarily do so,*

	then in such cases the distinction between a duty to exercise reasonable skill and care in making accurate statement, on the one hand, and a contractual duty to base the statement on the exercise of reasonable skill and care, is of no practical relevance. But, one should not, in our judgment lose sight of the fact that the duty is to make an accurate statement in the circumstance of the case'. Furthermore, the judge in *The David Agmashenebeli* [2003] 1 Lloyd's Rep. 92 held that the master is not required to act as an expert surveyor, but only as a reasonably careful and observant master. He considered the passages from *The Arctic Trader* referred to above and suggested that they were not a vital part of that judgment, and could not be correct if they suggested that the master was under any higher duty than one of being reasonably careful and observant. See also the discussion at paragraph 164 and its legal notes.
139(1st)	Scrutton on Charterparties and Bills of Lading, 22nd edition, pages 142 and 426 suggests that the requirement of Article 3 rule 3(b) that the bill must show '*either the number of packages or pieces, or the quantity, or weight, as the case may be..*' means that the obligation is alternative and therefore if the carrier issues a bill of lading showing both the number of pieces and the weight he may qualify the statement as to weight as, for example, by the words '*weight unknown*'. Scrutton says that such a bill of lading will then be prima facie evidence of the number of pieces but not of the weight.
139(2nd)	There has been some suggestion that the use of the expression '*weight and quantity unknown*' is somehow in contravention of Article 3 rule 3 of the Hague or Hague-Visby Rules. See *The Atlas* [1996] 1 Lloyd's Rep. 642 at 646 where the judge agreed that a bill of lading which provided '*weight..number..quantity unknown*' showed nothing at all about the number or weight of goods loaded but the shipowner could have been required to show it under Article 3 rule 3 if the shipper or charterer had so demanded. We would suggest that this disregards the proviso to Article 3 rule 3 and that in circumstances where the master has reasonable ground for suspecting the shipper's figures do not accurately represent the goods received, or where he has no reasonable means of checking, it is permissible for him to use the descriptive words which we have recommended. There is support for this in Voyage Charters, 3rd edition, paragraph 85.138, page 983, and the cases referred to therein.
140(1st)	One small but perhaps significant difference is that the Hamburg Rules require the bill of lading to state the number of packages or pieces and the quantity and weight of cargo. Contrast this with the 1st legal note on paragraph 139.
140(2nd)	Article 16 of the Hamburg Rules requires the carrier to specify '*any inaccuracies, grounds of suspicion or the absence of a reasonable means of checking*'. It seems that general printed clauses such as those which appear on the Congenbill (see paragraph 49) may not be sufficient and that if a master wishes to state that the quantity, condition or contents of the goods or packages is unknown to him, then he has to say in more express terms why.
144	See the legal note to paragraph 2.
145	See North of England P&I Association's loss prevention guide *Shipboard Petroleum Surveys*, page 15.
155	Article 31 UCP600 expressly states that banks will accept a transport document which '*bears a clause on the face thereof such as 'shippers load and count' or 'said by shipper to contain' or words of similar effect*'. Thus although UCP600 does not necessarily apply to all documentary credit requirements, there is a strong argument that this form of qualification of quantity loaded should be acceptable to the shipper.
156	See *The Boukadoura* [1989] 1 Lloyd's Rep. 393, *Noble Resources v. Cavalier Shipping (The Atlas)* [1996] 1 Lloyd's Rep. 642, *The River Gurara* [1998] 1 Lloyd's Rep. 225, 234 and Voyage Charters, 3rd edition, page 465.
157	See the cases referred to at the note to paragraph 156 above.
158	See *New Chinese Antimony v. Ocean Steamship* [1917] 2 K.B. 664; *The Herroehe and Askoe* [1986] 2 Lloyd's Rep. 281; and *The Atlas* [1996] 1 Lloyd's Rep. 642. Also see security implications at paragraph 296.

160	This complies with the Hague and Hague-Visby Rules obligation to issue a bill which shows the apparent order and condition of the cargo. In the case of perishable goods, apparent good order and condition includes the apparent ability of the goods to withstand ordinary methods of transport. If the words *'shipped in good order or condition'* do not appear at all on the bill of lading then the cases suggest that the bill of lading then ceases to be prima facie evidence of the condition of the goods on shipment. Except where the Hamburg Rules apply, the omission of the phrase does not infer that the goods were shipped in good condition. See Scrutton on Charterparties and Bills of Lading, 22nd edition, page 140.
163	A similar approach has been taken with containers. See *The Esmeralda 1* [1988] 1 Lloyd's Rep. 206.
165	These examples are drawn from the judgment of Aikens J in *The Sea Success* [2005] 2 Lloyd's Rep. 692, a case in which the master purported to reject a steel cargo because it was rusty, dented and buckled, and the charterparty required him to reject any cargo that would be 'subject to clausing the bills of lading'. The judge decided that the master's rejection was wrongful because the shippers intended to describe the cargo with these defectsand therefore the bill would not require any additional comments or 'clausing' by the master.
166(1st)	See *The David Agmashenebeli* [2003] 2 Lloyd's Rep. 9.
166(2nd)	See *The Sea Success* and the legal note to paragraph 165 above.
166(3rd)	See *The David Agmashenbeli* [2003] 2 Lloyd's Rep. 9.
167	See *Potts v. Union Steamship Company of New Zealand* [1946] NZLR 276.
170(a)	See *The Galatia* [1980] 1 Lloyd's Rep. 453.
171	Article 27 UCP600 . It has on occasion been argued that a bill of lading will not be clean if it contains a qualification of ***any*** of the representations made about the goods, including those about quantity. The preferred and authoritative view appears to be that whether or not a bill of lading is *'clean'* will be limited to qualifications of the cargo's apparent good order and condition and not qualifications as to quantity. (See in particular the discussion at footnote 68 paragraph 6.26, page 141, Bills of Lading in Export Trade, 3rd edition)
173	See *The Galatia* referred to in paragraph 170 (a) and legal note. The bill of lading will not be 'unclean' as it does not cast doubt on the condition of the goods as loaded.
177	These clauses will, however, always be construed restrictively against the shipowner so that, for example, a clause stating *'weight, contents and value when shipped unknown'* did not protect a shipowner from a buyer who is relying on a statement on the bill of lading as to the 'number' of bags of rice shipped. (*Att. – Gen (Ceylon) v. Scindia Steam Navigation* [1962] A.C. 60).
178	*The Galatia* [1979] 2 Lloyd's Rep. 450 and (C.A.) [1980] 1 Lloyd's Rep. 453 and Carver on Bills of Lading, paragraph 2-002.
181(1st)	See for example clause 16 of the Sugar Charterparty 1999.
181(2nd)	See for example LMLN 547 London Arbitration 16/00.
181(3rd)	As an example of the caution the master must exercise before rejecting cargo, even if it is clearly not in perfect condition, see *The Sea Success* referred to in the legal notes to paragraph 165.
182	See *Brown Jenkinson v. Percy Dalton* [1957] 2 Lloyd's Rep.1. Here, agents for the owners of the *Titania* signed clean bills of lading acknowledging shipment in apparent good order and condition of cargo which was in fact shipped in patently defective barrels. The clean bills of lading were issued against letters of indemnity from the shipper. Having paid claims by the consignee of the cargo, the owner sought to recover under

the letters of indemnity. The Court of Appeal held that the letters of indemnity were unenforceable against the shipper since the shipowner, through its agent, was a party with the shipper to a fraud. The bills of lading, containing false representations, had been issued with knowledge that those into whose hands the bills of lading might come, (namely receivers or bankers) would rely on the representations. So far as the master is concerned he should always proceed on the basis that a letter of indemnity given in return for issuing bills of lading which do not completely accurately describe the condition of the cargo, is an incorrect practice and one which he should not follow. From a legal point of view, however, there are subtleties in the *Brown Jenkinson v. Percy Dalton* decision. For example it may be possible legitimately to use indemnities where there is a bone fide dispute as to whether the goods are damaged or not, or where the defect is trivial, or the difficulty of ascertaining the precise nature of the defect is disproportionate to its potential importance. It is also worth noting that the Hamburg Rules at Article 17 say that an indemnity can be taken and enforced against a shipper (but not a third party) unless the carrier '*intends to defraud a third party, including a consignee..*'. If the Hamburg Rules gain wider use, then this provision may sometimes be used to argue that a master should accept a letter of indemnity. That is for the shipowner to decide. In any event this permissive part of Article 17 of the Hamburg Rules is perhaps of limited use. There must surely always be a strong possibility that intent to defraud will be imputed where a shipper has gone out of its way to persuade a master, by providing a letter of indemnity, not to include information. The obvious inference is that the information would be relevant to the consignee. The intention of the omission is therefore to deceive.

183   See paragraph 182 and legal note.

185   See the US cases of *Tokyo Marine and Fire Insurance Co. v. Retla Steamship Co.* [1970] 2 Lloyd's Rep. 91 where the wording was '*The terms 'apparent good order and condition' when used on this bill of Lading with reference to iron, steel or metal products does not mean that the Goods, when received, were free of visible rust or moisture. If the Merchant so requests a substitute bill of Lading will be issued omitting the above definition and setting forth any notations as to rust or moisture which may appear on the mate's or tally clerks' receipts*' and *GF Company v. Pan Ocean Shipping Company* (1992) AMC 2298 (a decision of the United States Courts); and see the commentary on that case, and the approach of English law to such a clause in *The Saga Explorer* [2013] 1 Lloyd's Rep. p. 401 to 407 where substantial clausing on a mates receipt referring to extensive rusting of a steel cargo, was not included on the bill of lading. The owners sought to defend this by reference to a clause very similar to that above. The decision recognised the usefulness of the RETLA clause, but pointed out that in the particular case in question, the key fact was that the load port report showed that the cargo was damaged; the master chose not to clause when he should have done, and instead tried to use the RETLA clause (at the shipper's behest) to avoid his duty in relation to the apparent good order and condition of the cargo. It was that decision that was unacceptable, not the use of the clause itself. It follows that a master who makes a decision in good faith without notice of the damage that justifies clausing ought still be able to rely on the RETLA clause, and the RETLA clause does have a function to perform as a 'shorthand' means of drawing to the bill of lading holder's attention that the cargo contains typical defects characteristic of that type of cargo.

187(1st)   For the scope and effectiveness of such deck carriage clauses see Baughen [2000] LMCLQ 295.

187(2nd)   The shipowner will still be entitled to rely on the time-bar and package limitation contained in the Hague or Hague-Visby Rules. See *The Kapitan Petko Voivoda* [2003] 2 Lloyd's Rep. 1.

187(3rd)   See *The Antares* [1987] 1 Lloyd's Rep. 424; *The Sara D* [1989] 2 Lloyd's Rep. 277; *The Chandla* [1989] 2 Lloyd's Rep. 494 and *The Fantasy* [1992] 1 Lloyd's Rep. 235, and *The Kapitan Petko Voivoda* [2003] 2 Lloyd's Rep. 1; and for an illustration of the need for clarity when stating that the cargo is being (rather than may be) carried on deck, see *The BBC Greenland* [2012] 1 Lloyd's Rep. 230.

188(1st)	See for a striking example *The Ulyanovsk* [1990] 1 Lloyd's Rep. 425 where a difference of a few days on the date of a bill of lading (brought about by the vessel berthing and completing loading earlier than ordered by the charterers) involved a fluctuation in the commodity price of the cargo of several hundred thousand dollars.
188(2nd)	The bill of lading should only be issued and dated when all of the cargo covered by the bill of lading has been loaded. *The Wilomi Tanana* [1993] 2 Lloyd's Rep. 41.
190	This may be even before the laydays have expired. See Scrutton on Charterparties and Bills of Lading, 22nd edition, page 179.
191	Problems may arise were a homogeneous parcel is damaged and the shipper or charterer require separate bills of lading for individual parcels to be signed. This may result in one parcel being heavily claused with the other parcels bearing no clausing; which could give rise to difficulties at the discharge port in ensuring that good cargo is discharged against unclaused bills, with the remaining '*dirty*' being discharged against the dirty bill of lading. In this situation there would be justification for the master either saying that he simply will not issue parcel bills but only a single bill of lading for the entire cargo (see Bills of Lading in Export Trade, 3rd edition, 6.22–6.24, page 139) or to insist that the clausing has to go on each of the sets of bills of lading for each parcel. The master would have to be careful with the wording of the clausing and the shipowner or the P&I correspondent or surveyor would have to help with that.
192	See Scrutton on Charterparties and Bills of Lading, 22nd edition, page 179.
193	See, Scrutton on Charterparties and Bills of Lading, 22nd edition, page 193.
196	According to the BIMCO publication Check Before Fixing 09-10, page 57, there have been cases where such a bill of lading has been construed as an *ad valorem* bill of lading. An *ad valorem* bill of lading is described in the glossary at appendix I.
206	The Hague and Hague-Visby Rules make no requirement for a description of quantity, (see paragraph 134), the Hamburg Rules require the bills to show 'the general nature of goods' (paragraph 140) and, where none of the Rules applies, the master's position is set out in paragraphs 111 and 112.
212	*The Nogar Marin* [1988] 1 Lloyd's Rep. 412. While a receiver may be able to rely upon this evidence, a shipper or charterer is expected to know, or is deemed to know, the apparent condition of the cargo it has shipped. See *The Arctic Trader* [1996] 2 Lloyd's Rep. 449 9CA.
214(1st)	See Time Charters, 6th edition, page 404, 21.48 to 21.50 and *Alimport v. Subert Shipping* [2000] 2 Lloyd's Rep. 447 agreeing with *The Starsin* [2000] 1 Lloyd's Rep. 85, page 97, agreeing with *The Nea Tyhi* [1982] 1 Lloyd's Rep. 606 and with *The Saudi Crown* [1986] 1 Lloyd's Rep. 261.
214(2nd)	See *The Nogar Marin* [1988] 1 Lloyd's Rep. 412 and *The Arctic Trader* [1996] 2 Lloyds Rep. 449. For a discussion on unauthorised issue of bills of lading generally see *The Berkshire* [1974] 1 Lloyd's Rep. 185 and *The Nea Tyhi* [1982] Lloyd's Rep. 606 and the references at legal note 273(c).
218	For a further and much more detailed discussion of these documents see Goode on Commercial Law, 4th edition, paragraphs 896 to 903.
223(1st)	This is because the person holding and presenting the bill and calling for delivery must also be legally entitled to receive the goods in accordance with the terms of the bill of lading; and if the bill requires endorsement, this must be done. See *Sze Hai Tong Bank Ltd v. Rambler Cycle Co Ltd.* [1959] 2 Lloyd's Rep. 114; and *Carewins Development (China) Limited v. Bright Fortune Shipping Limited* [2009] 3HKLRD 409; and *Charmax Trading v. Wt Sea Air Limited* (LMLN 28/1/10).
223(2nd)	See Scrutton on Charterparties and Bills of Lading, 22nd edition, page 296.
224(a)	The use of the word 'endorsement' in this guide is limited to legal movement of the bill

227	of lading and not to the noting of comments on the bill of lading or to the condition of the cargo. This guide uses the word 'clausing' to describe that function.
	English law approaches this problem on the basis that the shipper of goods will be aware that the carrier will issue a bill of lading which will contain the terms of carriage. For a more detailed discussions see Carver on Bills of Lading, 3rd edition, paragraphs 3.001 et seq. page 97.
244(d)	There is a reason for this. Section 4 COGSA 1992 displaces the previous position under English law based on an old case which said that a master who signs accidentally for, in that example, five bales of silk, when only one bale of silk was shipped, could not be bound by the representation that five bales of silk had been shipped, because he did not have authority to issue a bill of lading in respect of goods that had not been put on board *Grant v. Norway* (1851).
247(1st)	This is because the person holding and presenting the bill and calling for delivery must also be legally entitled to receive the goods in accordance with the terms of the bill of lading; and if the bill requires endorsement, this must be done. See *Sze Hai Tong Bank Ltd v. Rambler Cycle Co Ltd*. [1959] 2 Lloyd's Rep. 114; and *Carewins Development (China) Limited v. Bright Fortune Shipping Limited* [2009] 3HKLRD 409; and *Charmax Trading v. Wt Sea Air Limited* (LMLN 28/1/10).
247(2nd)	See Scrutton on Charterparties and Bills of Lading, 22nd edition, page 296
252(a)	The failure of the seller to get the document to the buyer will be a breach of the sale contract. Alternatively the buyer may not have paid for the goods. It is for the seller and buyer to resolve this problem. See Goode on Commerical Law, 4th edition, Commercial Law, p.1045. Recent cases have re-affirmed the principle that the master is obliged to deliver goods upon production of the original bill of lading and, indeed, that delivery without production of the bill of lading constitutes a breach of contract even when made to the person entitled to possession. The master cannot know if the person seeking delivery of the cargo is entitled to possession unless that person has produced an original bill of lading. *The Houda* [1994] 2 Lloyd's Rep. 541; *East West Corp. v. DKBS 1912* [2003] 1 Lloyd's Rep. 239 (CA).
253	See *The Somorvskiy 3068* [1994] 21 Lloyd's Rep. 262 at page 272 but also see *The Houda* [1994] 2 Lloyd's Rep. 541 and *Motis Exports Limited v. Dampskibsselskabet AF 1912* [1999] 1 Lloyd's Rep. 837 at 841 upheld at [2000] 1 Lloyd's Rep. 211 (CA) which together suggest that a '*reasonable explanation*' may not be sufficient to justify delivery of the cargo but that a court order may be required.
254	Taking of letters of indemnity in return for delivery of cargo at the wrong discharge port or without production of the original bill of lading is not wrong. This assumes, however, that all of the original bills of lading for the cancelled destination are collected in by the shipowner. Whilst it is not unlawful for the shipowner to agree to a change of destination without collecting in the bills of lading, it is extremely dangerous to do so as the exposure to claims is enormous, and there is unlikely to be P&I insurance in place to protect the shipowner in respect of such claims.
255	See the legal note to paragraph 27.
262	See the discussion by Diamond J in *The Future Express* [1992] 2 Lloyd's Rep. 79.
263(1st)	Such as whether the shipper has a right of stoppage in transit under the Sale of Goods Acts; and the intention of the parties to transfer title, (*The Future Express* [1992] 2 Lloyd's Rep. 79).
263(2nd)	For example, the acceptance of letters of indemnity with the accompanying commercial risks and loss of P&I cover.
263(3rd)	For example, the possibility of interpleader proceedings in the local court or in the courts whose law governs the contract of carriage.

271(1st)	See *Wehner v. Dene Steam Shipping* [1905] 2 KB 92 and the discussion in Time Charters, 6th edition, page 392, paragraph 21.11
271(2nd)	See the detailed discussion by the House of Lords in *The Starsin* [2003] 2 WLR 711. In essence the court decided that in determining who is carrier, the dominant ingredients are any clear and unambiguous identification of the carrier on the face of the bill of lading and the manner of signature of the bill. These will tend to override pre-printed terms, often in the form of an identity of carrier clause in small print on the reverse side of the bill of lading. See also the discussion in Time Charters, 6th edition, 21.2 to 21.10 page 389.
273(a)	See Time Charters, 6th edition,, paragraphs 21.13 to 21.28 at pages 393 to 398, and see *Tillmanns v. Knutsford* [1908] 2 KB 385, *The Berkshire* [1974] 1 Lloyd's Rep. 185 at page 188, and *The Ines* [1995] 2 Lloyd's Rep. 144 at 149. For the authority of a sub-charterer to sign see *The Vikfrost* [1980] 1 Lloyd's Rep. 560.
273(b)	See the cases referred to at legal note for paragraph 273(c).
273(c)	See Time Charters, 6th edition, paragraph 21.18 page 395 and *Alimport v. Subert Shipping* [2000] 2 Lloyd's Rep. 447 agreeing with *The Starsin* [2000] 1 Lloyd's Rep. 85, page 97, agreeing with *The Nea Tyhi* [1982] 1 Lloyd's Rep. 606 and with *The Saudi Crown* [1986] 1 Lloyd's Rep. 261.
274	See *The Eems Solar* (QBD Admiralty Registrat, 5 June 2013) and *The Jordan II* [2003] 2 Lloyd's Rep. 87.
275	Under English law the failure to insert a date in the blank form on the bill of lading will probably not prevent the incorporation of the terms of the selected charterparty into the bill of lading. See Roskill L.J. in *The San Nicholas* (above) where he stated: '*I would hesitate long before holding that the mere omission to include the date of a charterparty in a bill of lading negatives an intention to incorporate the terms of that charterparty into the bill of lading …*'. See also *The Ikariada* [1999] 2 Lloyd's Rep. 365. But an oral charterparty not reduced to writing will not be incorporated. See *The Heidberg (No.2)* [1994] 2 Lloyds Rep. 287.
276	See *The San Nicholas* [1976] 1 Lloyd's Rep. 8, *The Sevonia Team* [1983] 2 Lloyd's Rep. 640, 644, and *The Nai Matteini* [1988] 1 Lloyd's Rep. 452, 459; and the discussion in Voyage Charters, 2nd ed, paragraphs 18.59 – 18.63 and in Scrutton on Charterparties and Bills of Lading, 22nd edition, page 97 and, illustrating that there is no fixed rule, see *The Vinson* (2005) 677 LMLN 1.
277	See *The San Nicholas* [1976] 1 Lloyd's Rep. 8, *The Sevonia Team* [1983] 2 Lloyd's Rep. 640, 644, and *The Nai Matteini* [1988] 1 Lloyd's Rep. 452, 459; and the discussion in Voyage Charters, 3rd edition, paragraphs 18.59 – 18.63 and in Scrutton on Charterparties and Bills of Lading, 22nd edition, page 97 and, illustrating that there is no fixed rule, see *The Vinson* (2005) 677 LMLN 1.
279(1st)	For further discussion and for the leading case see *The Nanfri* [1979] 1 Lloyd's Rep. 201 and Time Charters, 6th edition, page 406, paragraph 21.57.
279(2nd)	The right of the master to refuse to sign is not clear as a matter of law. See Voyage Charters, 3rd edition, and 18.213 and 18.237.
284(b)	The BIMCO GENWAYBILL is an example of a seawaybill which expressly incorporates the Hague or Hague Visby Rules.
284(c)	See by way of example the difficulties discussed and resolved in *The Rafaela S* [2003] 2 Lloyd's Rep. 113 C.A. and [2005] 1 Lloyd's Rep. 347 H.L;and the Singapore case of *Voss v. APL* [2002] 2 Lloyd's Rep. 707. And see the cases referred to at the note to paragraph 287 below.
286	In *The Rafaela S* (HL); (references at 284(c) above) two of the judges sought to explore the difference between a 'straight' and a 'waybill'. They drew attention to the absence of detailed contractual terms in a seawaybill, and to the fact that straight bills are issued

	in 'sets' and often will have a clause indicating that upon one being surrendered the others will be void – which they say would be meaningless if the document was a mere receipt or seawaybill. The significance of the difference relates to the fact that in most jurisdictions there appear to be different requirements with regard to whether the document must be surrendered in return for delivery of the cargo. See paragraph 287.
287	*The Rafaela S* referred to at the note to paragraph 284(c) above left the position unresolved. The straight bill of lading in that case expressly required presentation. Rix L.J. took the view that even when a straight bill of lading contained no such express requirement, the carrier should insist on presentation for delivery. However, this was not an essential part of the decision in that case. In *Voss v. APL* referred to above, it appears that the position in Singapore is that the master should insist on presentation of the straight bill of lading before giving delivery. A similar position is adopted in China according to the Thirteenth National Seminar on Maritime Adjudication in September 2004. Hong Kong follows *The Rafaela S* (see *Carewins Development (China) Ltd v. Bright Fortune Shipping Ltd* [2009] 3 HKLRD 409). In the USA production of a straight bill of lading is not required in order to take delivery of the goods. The preponderance of authority (other than in the USA) is that a straight bill of lading should be produced in return for delivery of the cargo. These examples highlight the problems faced by the carrier and the need for the master to be aware of the need to seek guidance.
291(1st)	For a detailed discussion on delivery orders, see Carver on Bills of Lading, 3rd edition, paragraph 8.028 to 8.066, pages 532–558 and Benjamin's Sale of Goods, 8th edition, paragraphs 18-209 to 18-237.
291(2nd)	Some doubts were expressed in the case of *SIAT v. Tradax* [1978] 2LL.L.Rep. page 470 at page 493 about the validity of split bills of lading issued well after the loading date, the judge in that case favouring the use of delivery orders.'
293	See *The Atlas* [1996] 1 Lloyd's Rep. 642–644.
301	COGSA 1992 applies to paper bills of lading and provision is made by Section 1(5) of the Act for regulation to be made to apply the Act to 'telecommunication system or other information technology', but no such regulations have been made at the date of publication of this guide.
302	Such systems include the Bolero International Limited and ESS Databridge systems. See paragraph 314 for websites.
305	For example, the Rules for Electronic Bills of Lading produced by the Comite Maritime International (CMI) – see www.comitemaritime.org.

Appendix I
GLOSSARY OF TERMS

Term	*Explanation*
Ad valorem bills of lading	An *ad valorem* bill of lading is a bill of lading which shows, on its face, the nature and value of the goods. By stating the value, the shipper is no longer bound by the per package limitation of liability set out in the Hague or Hague-Visby Rules in Article 4, rule 5. In return for the loss of the right to limit, the shipowner is entitled to claim *ad valorem* freight – that is a freight which reflects the high value and high risk of carrying the goods.
'Clean on board' bills of lading	See paragraph 174 and **'shipped' bills of lading.**
Demise clause	There are many versions of demise clause or identity of carrier clause. Its purpose is to identify the party who is the contractual carrier under the bill of lading. Usually the clause will direct the claims to the shipowner rather than to a time charterer or operator or freight forwarder who may have been actively involved in arranging the carriage. As the shipowner, through his master and crew, has physical care of the cargo, and as the shipowner is best placed to benefit from limitation of liability regimes in most jurisdictions (although others can benefit), this arrangement is widespread, particularly in the liner trade where liner operators may give all outward appearances of being the carrier. (Note: Where the vessel is operating under a bare boat charterparty then a demise or identity of carrier clause would usually be worded to make the bare boat charterer the carrier in place of the shipowner.)
FIO, FIOS, FIOST.	All of these are variations of free in and out (the variations being free in and out stowed or free in and out stowed and trimmed) and they relate to the cost of loading and discharging. The 'free' means 'free of expense to the ship' and it means that all expenses relating to the loading and discharging of the goods are to be borne by the shippers and / or receivers. Additional words such as stowed, trimmed, or spout trimmed, all emphasise that those expenses are 'free' so far as the ship is concerned.
Freight forwarder	Often a number of shippers will be brought together by an intermediary in order to put together a substantial quantity of cargo to be shipped. The intermediary is know as a freight forwarder. Frequently the freight forwarder will gather all of the cargoes together and take from the shipowner a bill of lading covering all of them. The bill of lading is often called a **groupage** bill or **service** bill. It will name the freight forwarder as the shipper and will usually also name the freight forwarder or his agent as the consignee. The bill of lading will thus typically be a

straight or **non-negotiable** bill of lading. The individual shippers will receive from the freight forwarder a form of receipt usually in the form of a house bill of lading (that is a bill of lading issued in the freight forwarder's own form),or by obtaining from the ship a **ship's delivery order** by which the shipowner or master undertakes to release specific goods to a specific consignee or other holder of the **delivery order**. Each of these documents will then be presented either to the forwarder or his agent at the discharge port who in turn will collect the goods from the ship, or, in the case of a ships delivery order, direct from the ship's agent at the discharge port. None of these documents is unusual. The master in these situations would be principally concerned with delivering the cargo upon presentation of the bill of lading which he issued to the freight forwarder

Freight pre-paid bills of lading	These are bills of lading which record that freight has been paid against the delivery or handing over of the original bills of lading. The effect of marking the bill of lading 'freight pre-paid' is to prevent the shipowner from claiming freight from a subsequent holder of the bill of lading.
'Groupage' bills of lading	See **freight forwarder**.
'House' bills of lading	See **freight forwarder**.
Identity of carrier clause	See **demise clause**.
Liner terms	These show that the freight includes the cost of handling the cargo at the loading and discharging ports. The precise meaning may vary from port to port by reason of custom, but essentially a 'liner terms' bill is one where the shipowner is going to face some cost of handling.
Loading broker	Loading brokers are agents appointed by owners of vessels trading in a regular line to obtain cargoes for the vessels and to receive payment of freight. They usually have authority to sign and issue bills of lading but the extent of their authority is the same as that of the master in signing and issuing bills of lading.
Negotiable and non-negotiable bills of lading	A bill of lading is negotiable if it can be transferred. The bill of lading will show on its face whether this can be done. If the bill of lading uses the words 'to order' or 'bearer' or 'holder' or is left blank in terms of who is the consignee, then the bill of lading can be transferred by delivery or endorsement. This is dealt with in detail in paragraphs 215 – 225. If the bill of lading is to a named consignee and not 'to order' then the bill of lading is non-negotiable. (This is sometimes also called a 'straight' bill of lading.) The importance of a bill of lading being negotiable is that it enables its original holder to transfer, without the use of any other document, the right to receive and control possession of the goods. A non-negotiable bill of lading may be treated as a sea waybill in certain circumstances. See paragraph 241 and 242.

Notify address / notify party	This is the address of the person or party to whom the shipper requires the shipowners to give notice when the goods arrive at their destination. Often the notify address or party will be the consignee, or a consignee's agent who has been appointed to collect the goods at the discharge port, or a bank who has paid out on the goods on behalf of the buyer. See paragraph 38 for an example of its use.
'Received for shipment' bills of lading	See **'shipped' bills of lading**.
Retla clause	This clause is named after a case in which it appeared. It is a clause often used in the steel trade and it will appear on the bill of lading alongside the words 'in apparent good order and condition'. The precise wording of the clause appears at the legal note to paragraph 185.
'Service' bills of lading	See **freight forwarder**.
'Shipped' and 'received for shipment' bills of lading	Under the Hague and Hague-Visby Rules the shipper can demand a bill of lading immediately that the goods are received into the charge of the carrier ⚖. This is a received for shipment bill of lading. It may be more usual for no bill of lading to be issued until the goods have actually been shipped. That would then be a 'shipped' bill of lading and it should be issued on the date when all of the cargo covered by the bill of lading has been loaded ⚖. Where a 'received for shipment' bill of lading (or a mate's receipt) was issued at the time that the goods came into the shipowner's possession but before loading, then as and when a shipped bill of lading is issued that previous document should be surrendered. Alternatively, a 'received for shipment' bill of lading can be amended by showing the name of the ship and the date of shipment so that it becomes a **'shipped' bill of lading** ⚖.

Appendix II

RECOMMENDED STANDARD LETTER OF AUTHORITY TO ISSUE BILLS OF LADING

To:
_____

[*ship's agent or, if vessel is operating under a time charter party, time charter's agent*]

M.V.: _____

Loading at: _____

Dear Sirs

By this letter I authorise you to sign bills of lading in accordance with the following instructions:

1. You will sign legibly showing the name of your company and of the individual person who is signing, and affix any company seal alongside any such signature.

2. You will state that you are signing 'as agent for the master'.

3. You will sign bills of lading which

   (a) are strictly in accordance with mate's receipt(s), and

   (b) clearly and accurately state the cargo quantity and condition as shown on the mate's receipt(s) or on any documents referred to in those receipt(s).

4. You will ensure that for each parcel of cargo for which a separate bill of lading is required by the shipper, the correct date of completion of loading of that parcel is shown on the bill of lading.

5. You will provide, immediately upon signing, a copy of the signed bill of lading to the ship and to the owners' managers by fax at ……………..

[*If the vessel is operating under a time charter party, add the following clause:*

6. *Any reference in the bill(s) of lading to a charter party shall, in the absence of contrary instructions, show the date of the head charter party between the owners of the vessel and their time charterers, namely …………….. If contrary instructions are given then you are to seek guidance from me or from owners before inserting a different date in the bill of lading.*]

Your authority to sign this bill of lading is conditional upon your complying with all of the above instructions.

This authority to sign cannot be sub-delegated to any other party without my or owners' consent.

Yours faithfully

_____
Master

Appendix III

P&I CLUB CIRCULARS ON STANDARD LETTERS OF INDEMNITY

CIRCULAR OF FEBRUARY 2001

Bills of lading - delivery of cargo
Standard forms of letters of indemnity to be given in return for:
(a) *delivery of cargo without production of the original bill of lading*
(b) *delivery of cargo at a port other than that stated in the bill of lading*
(c) *delivery of cargo at a port other than that stated in the bill of lading and without production of the original bill of lading*

In December 1998, the International Group of P&I Clubs issued a Circular to Members recommending revised wordings of the standard form Letters of Indemnity for use by Members in circumstances where they are requested to deliver cargo without production of the original bill of lading and/or to deliver cargo at a port other than that stated in the bill of lading.

As a result of comment from shipowners and shipowners' organisations, a further review of the wordings has been undertaken and further modifications to the standard wordings have now been made. Moreover, discussions have taken place between the International Group and the British Bankers Association (BBA) and a separate standard wording has been agreed on the basis of which banks members of the BBA will now be prepared in principle to join in the Letters of Indemnity while, through the auspices of the International Chamber of Commerce, the BBA will endeavour to promote this agreed standard wording within the international business community. The BBA has also given its general approval to this Circular.

In consequence of the agreement reached with the BBA, the three recommended standard form Letters of Indemnity are now issued in two versions: INT GROUP A (for delivery of cargo without production of the original bill of lading), INT GROUP B (for delivery of cargo at a port other than that stated in the bill of lading against production of at least one original bill of lading), and INT GROUP C (for delivery of cargo at a port other than that stated in the bill of lading and without production of the original bill of lading) for use when the commercial party requesting delivery (the "Requestor") will alone be signing the Letter of Indemnity, and INT GROUP AA, INT GROUP BB and INT GROUP CC for use when a bank will be joining in the Letter of Indemnity and which forms incorporate, in addition to the same indemnities given by the Requestor under INT GROUP A, B and C, the separate standard wording agreed with the banks.

The principal features of the new wordings are explained below.

Financial Limit
The liability of the Requestor should generally not be limited. However, where a bank is to join in the Letter of Indemnity it will generally insist upon a fixed monetary limit. The amount of the limit must be a matter for negotiation in order that it properly reflects the potential exposure in the particular circumstances, taking into account, inter alia, the sound market value of the cargo at the time of delivery, but it is recommended that the limit should be a minimum of 200% of the sound market value of the cargo at the time of delivery.

Duration of security
Under INT GROUP A and AA, the liability of the Requestor (and, hence, the bank under AA) terminates upon the delivery of all original bills of lading to the shipowner. If the original bills of lading are not delivered to the shipowner, the Requestor's liability under the Letter of Indemnity continues.

Subject to delivery of all original bills of lading as stated, and to the two exceptions described below, the bank's liability under INT GROUP AA is for an initial period of six years, but which is automatically renewable from time to time for further periods of two years at the request of the shipowner. The exceptions are (1) that, rather than agree to an extension of its liability, the bank has the option of discharging its liability by paying the maximum amount payable under its indemnity and (2) that, in the event of a demand being made by the shipowner to the bank for payment under the indemnity before the termination date, or in the event of the bank being notified by the shipowner of the commencement of legal proceedings against the shipowner before the termination date, the liability of the bank will continue until the demand has been paid or the legal proceedings have been concluded, the bank, if called upon so to do, paying the amount of any judgment or settlement payable by the shipowner if the Requestor has failed to do so.

Under INT GROUP B, C, BB and CC, since it is possible for a claim to be pursued against a shipowner for delivering cargo at a port other than that stated in the bill of lading despite cargo being delivered against production of the original bill of lading, or all original bills of lading being subsequently delivered to the shipowner (in particular, in circumstances where a charterer may require a cargo owner to receive his cargo at such other port against his wishes and request the shipowner to accommodate his request), the liability of the Requestor will continue until it can be established to the satisfaction of the shipowner that no such claim will be made.

Accordingly, unless the shipowner is satisfied that no claim of this nature will be made, the liability of the bank under INT GROUP BB and CC will be as described under INT GROUP AA above.

Scope of security

The Requestor is obliged to provide bail or other security not only to prevent or lift the arrest of the ship the subject matter of the indemnity, but also any other ship in the same or associated ownership, management or control. In addition, the Requestor is obliged to provide bail or other security to prevent interference in the use or trading of the ship, such as a caveat being entered on the ship's registry to prevent the sale of the ship the subject matter of the indemnity.

Where a bank joins in the Letter of Indemnity it will generally not agree to provide bail or other security. However, the bank will pay any amount up to the limit of its liability under the Letter of Indemnity in order to enable the shipowner to arrange the provision of security if the Requestor fails to provide bail or other security.

Tankers

A provision designed to give greater security to tankers has been incorporated, whereby requested delivery of a bulk liquid or gas cargo to a terminal or facility, or to another ship, lighter or barge is to be deemed to be delivery to the party to whom delivery has been requested.

Members are again reminded that, unless the Association's Committee otherwise determines, there is no cover in respect of liabilities arising out of the delivery of cargo without production of the original bill of lading and/or delivery at a port other than that stated in the bill of lading and that, in such circumstances, Members are strongly advised to ensure that they are fully satisfied with the financial standing and authority of those who are to issue and sign these indemnities.

The standard form Letters of Indemnity are designed to cover a broad range of trades and operations, and Members may wish to modify the standard forms to suit particular requirements. However, in this event, it must be appreciated that if a bank is to join in the Letter of Indemnity there may be limited scope for amendment, and that the Requestor's bank will have to be consulted if any material change is contemplated. The Managers will be pleased to advise Members regarding any proposed modification.

Finally, it is not uncommon for Members to be requested by charterers to agree clauses in charter parties which expressly provide for the delivery of cargo without production of bills of lading and/or at ports other than those stated in the bills of lading against Letters of Indemnity. Members are strongly advised not to accept such clauses and it is recommended that Members seek advice from the Managers before responding to such requests.

CIRCULAR OF OCTOBER 2010

Delivery of cargo without production of bills of lading

Following the decision in the English Commercial Court in the case of Farenco Shipping Co Ltd -v- Daebo Shipping Co Ltd (LLR (2009) Vol 1 81) (the *Bremen Max*) the International Group of P&I Clubs recommends that Members take two further precautions if they choose to accept a Letter of Indemnity for delivery of cargo without production of the original bill of lading. The precautions relate to:

1. The identity of the party to whom delivery is to be given

The opening paragraph of the Letter of Indemnity includes a number of insertion instructions in brackets which are to be completed when the Letter of Indemnity is issued. This Circular deals with the identity of the party to whom delivery is to be made which appears as:

[insert name of party to whom delivery is to be made]

Recommendation: As well as inserting the name of the specific party (person or company) to whom delivery is to be made, Members should request that the blank section be completed as follows:

"X [name of the specific party] or to such party as you believe to be or to represent X or to be acting on behalf of X".

Reason: If a specific party only is named in the Letter of Indemnity, the Member may be assuming the burden of properly identifying that party. If the Member then mis-identifies the party, and delivers to some other party, there is then the risk that the Member is not entitled to indemnity, because he has not satisfied the pre-conditions in the Letter of Indemnity for delivery to the named party. The wording suggested above is designed to ensure so far as possible, that if the Member believes that the party to whom physical delivery of the cargo is given is X or is acting on behalf of X, he can rely on the Letter of Indemnity.

2. Timing of demands under the Letter of Indemnity

In the event that a Member delivers cargo without production of the bill of lading in return for a Letter of Indemnity and an allegation is subsequently made against the Member that it has mis-delivered the cargo, accompanied by a security demand from the claimant, then the Member should immediately give notice to the issuer of the Letter of Indemnity that:

(a) a claim has been notified
(b) security has been demanded from the Member
(c) the Member now requires to be secured by the issuer in accordance with paragraph 3 of the Letter of Indemnity.

It is essential that this is done before the Member provides any security itself to the original claimant.

Reason: The Member may prejudice his right to demand and receive security under the Letter of Indemnity if he provides security to the claimant before making his own demand for security under Clause 3 of the Letter of Indemnity.

Appendix IV
STANDARD LETTERS OF INDEMNITY

These letters of indemnity should be used in accordance with the guidance provided by the International Group of P&I Clubs in Appendix III and attention is particularly drawn to the circular dated October 2010.

INT GROUP A: INTERNATIONAL GROUP LETTER OF INDEMNITY TO BE GIVEN IN RETURN FOR DELIVERING CARGO WITHOUT PRODUCTION OF THE ORIGINAL BILL OF LADING

To: [insert name of Owners] [insert date]

The Owners of the [insert name of ship]
[insert address]

Dear Sirs

Ship: [insert name of ship]

Voyage: [insert load and discharge ports as stated in the bill of lading]

Cargo: [insert description of cargo]

Bill of lading: [insert identification numbers, date and place of issue]

The above cargo was shipped on the above ship by [insert name of shipper] and consigned to [insert name of consignee or party to whose order the bill of lading is made out, as appropriate] for delivery at the port of [insert name of discharge port stated in the bill of lading] but the bill of lading has not arrived and we, [insert name of party requesting delivery], hereby request you to deliver the said cargo to [insert name of party to whom delivery is to be made] at [insert place where delivery is to be made] without production of the original bill of lading.

In consideration of your complying with our above request, we hereby agree as follows:-

1. To indemnify you, your servants and agents and to hold all of you harmless in respect of any liability, loss, damage or expense of whatsoever nature which you may sustain by reason of delivering the cargo in accordance with our request.

2. In the event of any proceedings being commenced against you or any of your servants or agents in connection with the delivery of the cargo as aforesaid, to provide you or them on demand with sufficient funds to defend the same.

3. If, in connection with the delivery of the cargo as aforesaid, the ship, or any other ship or property in the same or associated ownership, management or control, should be arrested or detained or should the arrest or detention thereof be threatened, or should there be any interference in the use or trading of the vessel (whether by virtue of a caveat being entered on the ship's registry or otherwise howsoever), to provide on demand such bail or other security as may be required to prevent such arrest or detention or to secure the release of such ship or property or to remove such interference and to indemnify you in respect of any liability, loss, damage or expense caused by such arrest or detention or threatened arrest or detention or such interference, whether or not such arrest or detention or threatened arrest or detention or such interference may be justified.

4. If the place at which we have asked you to make delivery is a bulk liquid or gas terminal or facility, or another ship, lighter or barge, then delivery to such terminal, facility, ship, lighter or barge shall be deemed to be delivery to the party to whom we have requested you to make such delivery.

5. As soon as all original bills of lading for the above cargo shall have come into our possession, to deliver the same to you, or otherwise to cause all original bills of lading to be delivered to you, whereupon our liability hereunder shall cease.

6. The liability of each and every person under this indemnity shall be joint and several and shall not be conditional upon your proceeding first against any person, whether or not such person is party to or liable under this indemnity.

7. This indemnity shall be governed by and construed in accordance with English law and each and every person liable under this indemnity shall at your request submit to the jurisdiction of the High Court of Justice of England.

Yours faithfully
For and on behalf of

[insert name of Requestor]
The Requestor

INT GROUP B: INTERNATIONAL GROUP LETTER OF INDEMNITY TO BE GIVEN IN RETURN FOR DELIVERING CARGO AT A PORT OTHER THAN THAT STATED IN THE BILL OF LADING

To: [insert name of Owners] [insert date]
The Owners of the [insert name of ship]
[insert address]

Dear Sirs

Ship: [insert name of ship]

Voyage: [insert load and discharge ports as stated in the bill of lading]

Cargo: [insert description of cargo]

Bill of lading: [insert identification number, date and place of issue]

The above cargo was shipped on the above ship by [insert name of shipper] and consigned to [insert name of consignee or party to whose order the bill of lading is made out, as appropriate] for delivery at the port of [insert name of discharge port stated in the bill of lading] but we, [insert name of party requesting substituted delivery], hereby request you to order the ship to proceed to and deliver the said cargo at [insert name of substitute port or place of delivery] against production of at least one original bill of lading.

In consideration of your complying with our above request, we hereby agree as follows:-

1. To indemnify you, your servants and agents and to hold all of you harmless in respect of any liability, loss, damage or expense of whatsoever nature which you may sustain by reason of the ship proceeding and giving delivery of the cargo against production of at least one original bill of lading in accordance with our request.

2. In the event of any proceedings being commenced against you or any of your servants or agents in connection with the ship proceeding and giving delivery of the cargo as aforesaid, to provide you or them on demand with sufficient funds to defend the same.

3. If, in connection with the delivery of the cargo as aforesaid, the ship, or any other ship or property in the same or associated ownership, management or control, should be arrested or detained or should the arrest or detention thereof be threatened, or should there be any interference in the use or trading of the vessel (whether by virtue of a caveat being entered on the ship's registry or otherwise howsoever), to provide on demand such bail or other security as may be required to prevent such arrest or detention or to secure the release of such ship or property or to remove such interference and to indemnify you in respect of any liability, loss, damage or expense caused by such arrest or detention or threatened arrest or detention or such interference, whether or not such arrest or detention or threatened arrest or detention or such interference may be justified.

4. The liability of each and every person under this indemnity shall be joint and several and shall not be conditional upon your proceeding first against any person, whether or not such person is party to or liable under this indemnity.

5. This indemnity shall be governed by and construed in accordance with English law and each and every person liable under this indemnity shall at your request submit to the jurisdiction of the High Court of Justice of England.

Yours faithfully
For and on behalf of
[insert name of Requestor]
The Requestor

INT GROUP C: INTERNATIONAL GROUP LETTER OF INDEMNITY TO BE GIVEN IN RETURN FOR DELIVERING CARGO AT A PORT OTHER THAN THAT STATED IN THE BILL OF LADING AND WITHOUT PRODUCTION OF THE ORIGINAL BILL OF LADING

To: [insert name of Owners] [insert date]
The Owners of the [insert name of ship]
[insert address]

Dear Sirs

Ship: [insert name of ship]

Voyage: [insert load and discharge ports as stated in the bill of lading]

Cargo: [insert description of cargo]

Bill of lading: [insert identification number, date and place of issue]

The above cargo was shipped on the above vessel by [insert name of shipper] and consigned to [insert name of consignee or party to whose order the bills of lading are made out, as appropriate] for delivery at the port of [insert name of discharge port stated in the bills of lading] but we, [insert name of party requesting substituted delivery], hereby request you to order the vessel to proceed to and deliver the said cargo at [insert name of substitute port or place of delivery] to [insert name of party to whom delivery is to be made] without production of the original bill of lading.

In consideration of your complying with our above request, we hereby agree as follows:-

1. To indemnify you, your servants and agents and to hold all of you harmless in respect of any liability, loss, damage or expense of whatsoever nature which you may sustain by reason of the ship proceeding and giving delivery of the cargo in accordance with our request.

2. In the event of any proceedings being commenced against you or any of your servants or agents in connection with the ship proceeding and giving delivery of the cargo as aforesaid, to provide you or them on demand with sufficient funds to defend the same.

3. If, in connection with the delivery of the cargo as aforesaid, the ship, or any other ship or property in the same or associated ownership, management or control, should be arrested or detained or should the arrest or detention thereof be threatened, or should there be any interference in the use or trading of the vessel (whether by virtue of a caveat being entered on the ship's registry or otherwise howsoever), to provide on demand such bail or other security as may be required to prevent such arrest or detention or to secure the release of such ship or property or to remove such interference and to indemnify you in respect of any liability, loss, damage or expense caused by such arrest or detention or threatened arrest or detention or such interference, whether or not such arrest or detention or threatened arrest or detention or such interference may be justified.

4. If the place at which we have asked you to make delivery is a bulk liquid or gas terminal or facility, or another ship, lighter or barge, then delivery to such terminal, facility, ship, lighter or barge shall be deemed to be delivery to the party to whom we have requested you to make such delivery.

5. As soon as all original bills of lading for the above cargo shall have come into our possession, to deliver the same to you, or otherwise to cause all original bills of lading to be delivered to you.

6. The liability of each and every person under this indemnity shall be joint and several and shall not be conditional upon your proceeding first against any person, whether or not such person is party to or liable under this indemnity.

7. This indemnity shall be governed by and construed in accordance with English law and each and every person liable under this indemnity shall at your request submit to the jurisdiction of the High Court of Justice of England.

Yours faithfully
For and on behalf of
[insert name of Requestor]
The Requestor

STANDARD LETTER FOR BANKS TO JOIN IN INTERNATIONAL GROUP LETTERS OF INDEMNITY: APPENDING THIS LETTER TO INT GROUP A, B AND C LETTERS CONVERTS THEM TO INT GROUP AA, BB AND CC RESPECTIVELY

We, [insert name of the Bank], hereby agree to join in this Indemnity providing always that the Bank's liability:-

1. shall be restricted to payment of specified sums of money demanded in relation to the Indemnity (and shall not extend to the provision of bail or other security)

2. shall be to make payment to you forthwith on your written demand in the form of a signed letter certifying that the amount demanded is a sum due to be paid to you under the terms of the Indemnity and has not been paid to you by the Requestor or is a sum which represents monetary compensation due to you in respect of the failure by the Requestor to fulfil its obligations to you under the Indemnity. For the avoidance of doubt the Bank hereby confirms that:-

    (a) such compensation shall include, but not be limited to, payment of any amount up to the amount stated in proviso 3 below in order to enable you to arrange the provision of security to release the ship (or any other ship in the same or associated ownership, management or control) from arrest or to prevent any such arrest or to prevent any interference in the use or trading of the ship, or other ship as aforesaid, and

    (b) in the event that the amount of compensation so paid is less than the amount stated in proviso 3 below, the liability of the Bank hereunder shall continue but shall be reduced by the amount of compensation paid.

3. shall be limited to a sum or sums not exceeding in aggregate [insert currency and amount in figures and words]

4. subject to proviso 5 below, shall terminate on [date six years from the date of the Indemnity] (the 'Termination Date'), except in respect of any demands for payment received by the Bank hereunder at the address indicated below on or before that date.

5. shall be extended at your request from time to time for a period of two calendar years at a time provided that:-

    a) the Bank shall receive a written notice signed by you and stating that the Indemnity is required by you to remain in force for a further period of two years, and

    b) such notice is received by the Bank at the address indicated below on or before the then current Termination Date.

    Any such extension shall be for a period of two years from the then current Termination Date and, should the Bank for any reason be unwilling to extend the Termination Date, the Bank shall discharge its liability by the payment to you of the maximum sum payable hereunder (or such lesser sum as you may require).

    However, in the event of the Bank receiving a written notice signed by you, on or before the then current Termination Date, stating that legal proceedings have been commenced against you as a result of your having delivered the said cargo as specified in the Indemnity, the Bank agrees that its liability hereunder will not terminate until receipt by the Bank of your signed written notice stating that all legal proceedings have been concluded and that any sum or sums payable to you by the Requestor and/or the Bank in connection therewith have been paid and received in full and final settlement of all liabilities arising under the Indemnity.

6. shall be governed by and construed in accordance with the law governing the Indemnity and the Bank agrees to submit to the jurisdiction of the court stated within the Indemnity.

It should be understood that, where appropriate, the Bank will only produce and deliver to you all original bills of lading should the same come into the Bank's possession, but the Bank agrees that, in that event, it shall do so.

The Bank agrees to promptly notify you in the event of any change in the full details of the office to which any demand or notice is to be addressed and which is stated below and it is agreed that you shall also promptly notify the Bank in the event of any change in your address as stated above.

Please quote the Bank's Indemnity Ref _____ in all correspondence with the Bank and any demands for payment and notices hereunder.

Yours faithfully
For and on behalf of
[insert name of bank]
[insert full details of the office to which any demand or notice is to be addressed]

Appendix V
HAGUE RULES

International Convention for the Unification of certain Rules of Law relating to Bills of Lading, signed at Brussels on August 25, 1924

Article 1.

In this convention the following words are employed, with the meanings set out below:-

(a) "Carrier" includes the owner or the charterer who enters into a contract of carriage with a shipper.

(b) "Contract of carriage" applies only to contracts of carriage covered by a bill of lading or any similar document of title, in so far as such document relates to the carriage of goods by sea, including any bill of lading or any similar document as aforesaid issued under or pursuant to a charter party from the moment at which such bill of lading or similar document of title regulates the relations between a carrier and a holder of the same.

(c) "Goods" includes goods, wares, merchandise, and articles of every kind whatsoever except live animals and cargo which by the contract of carriage is stated as being carried on deck and is so carried.

(d) "Ship" means any vessel used for the carriage of goods by sea.

(e) "Carriage of goods" covers the period from the time when the goods are loaded on to the time they are discharged from the ship.

Article 2.

Subject to the provisions of Article 6, under every contract of carriage of goods by sea the carrier, in relation to the, loading, handling, stowage, carriage, custody, care and discharge of such goods, shall be subject to the responsibilities and liabilities, and entitled to the rights and immunities hereinafter set forth.

Article 3.

1. The carrier shall be bound before and at the beginning of the voyage to exercise due diligence to-

    (a) Make the ship, seaworthy.

    (b) Properly man, equip and supply the ship.

    (c) Make the holds, refrigerating and cool chambers, and all other parts of the ship in which goods are carried, fit and safe for their reception, carriage and preservation.

2. Subject to the provisions of Article 4, the carrier shall properly and carefully load, handle, stow, carry, keep, care for, and discharge the goods carried.

3. After receiving the goods into his charge the carrier or the master or agent of the carrier shall, on demand of the shipper, issue to the shipper a bill of lading showing among other things-

    (a) The leading marks necessary for identification of the goods as the same are furnished in writing by the shipper before the loading of such goods starts, provided such marks are stamped or otherwise shown clearly upon the goods if uncovered, or on the cases or coverings in which such goods are contained, in such a manner as should ordinarily remain legible until the end of the voyage.

    (b) Either the number of packages or pieces, or the quantity, or weight, as the case may be, as furnished in writing by the shipper.

    (c) The apparent order and condition of the goods.

HAGUE RULES

Provided that no carrier, master or agent of the carrier shall be bound to state or show in the bill of lading any marks, number, quantity, or weight which he has reasonable ground for suspecting not accurately to represent the goods actually received, or which he has had no reasonable means of checking.

4. Such a bill of lading shall be *primâ facie* evidence of the receipt by the carrier of the goods as therein described in accordance with paragraph 3 (a), (b) and (c).

5. The shipper shall be deemed to have guaranteed to the carrier the accuracy at the time of shipment of the marks, number, quantity and weight, as furnished by him, and the shipper shall indemnify the carrier against all loss, damages and expenses arising or resulting from inaccuracies in such particulars. The right of the carrier to such indemnity shall in no way limit his responsibility and liability under the contract of carriage to any person other than the shipper.

6. Unless notice of loss or damage and the general nature of such loss or damage be given in writing to the carrier or his agent at the port of discharge before or at the time of the removal of the goods into the custody of the person entitled to delivery thereof under the contract of carriage, or, if the loss or damage be not apparent, within three days, such removal shall be *primâ facie* evidence of the delivery by the carrier of the goods as described in the bill of lading.

   The notice in writing need not be given if the state of the goods has, at the time of their receipt, been the subject of joint survey or inspection.

   In any event the carrier and the ship shall be discharged from all liability in respect of loss or damage unless suit is brought within one year after delivery of the goods or the date when the goods should have been delivered.

   In the case of any actual or apprehended loss or damage the carrier and the receiver shall give all reasonable facilities to each other for inspecting and tallying the goods.

7. After the goods are loaded the bill of lading to be issued by the carrier, master, or agent of the carrier, to the shipper shall, if the shipper so demands, be a "shipped" bill of lading, provided that if the shipper shall have previously taken up any document of title to such goods, he shall surrender the same as against the issue of the "shipped" bill of lading, but at the option of the carrier such document of title may be noted at the port of shipment by the carrier, master, or agent with the name or names of the ship or ships upon which the goods have been shipped and the date or dates of shipment, and when so noted, if it shows the particulars mentioned in paragraph 3 of Article 3, shall for the purpose of this article be deemed to constitute a "shipped" bill of lading.

8. Any clause, covenant, or agreement in a contract of carriage relieving the carrier or the ship from liability for loss or damage to, or in connexion with, goods arising from negligence, fault, or failure in the duties and obligations provided in this article or lessening such liability otherwise than as provided in this convention, shall be null and void and of no effect. A benefit of insurance in favour of the carrier or similar clause shall be deemed to be a clause relieving the carrier from liability.

Article 4.

1. Neither the carrier nor the ship shall be liable for loss or damage arising or resulting from unseaworthiness unless caused by want of due diligence on the part of the carrier to make the ship seaworthy, and to secure that the ship is properly manned, equipped and supplied, and to make the holds, refrigerating and cool chambers and all other parts of the ship in which goods are carried fit and safe for their reception, carriage and preservation in accordance with the provisions of paragraph 1 of Article 3. Whenever loss or damage has resulted from unseaworthiness the burden of proving the exercise of due diligence shall be on the carrier or other person claiming exemption under this article.

2. Neither the carrier nor the ship shall be responsible for loss or damage arising or resulting from-

   (a) Act, neglect, or default of the master, mariner, pilot, or the servants of the carrier in the navigation or in the management of the ship.

   (b) Fire, unless caused by the actual fault or privity of the carrier.

HAGUE RULES

- (c) Perils, dangers and accidents of the sea or other navigable waters.
- (d) Act of God.
- (e) Act of war.
- (f) Act of public enemies.
- (g) Arrest or restraint of princes, rulers or people, or seizure under legal process.
- (h) Quarantine restrictions.
- (i) Act or omission of the shipper or owner of the goods, his agent or representative.
- (j) Strikes or lockouts or stoppage or restraint of labour from whatever cause, whether partial or general.
- (k) Riots and civil commotions.
- (l) Saving or attempting to save life or property at sea.
- (m) Wastage in bulk or weight or any other loss or damage arising from inherent defect, quality or vice of the goods.
- (n) Insufficiency of packing.
- (o) Insufficiency or inadequacy of marks.
- (p) Latent defects not discoverable by due diligence.
- (q) Any other cause arising without the actual fault or privity of the carrier, or without the fault or neglect of the agents or servants of the carrier, but the burden of proof shall be on the person claiming the benefit of this exception to show that neither the actual fault or privity of the carrier nor the fault or neglect of the agents or servants of the carrier contributed to the loss or damage.

3. The shipper shall not be responsible for loss or damage sustained by the carrier or the ship arising or resulting from any cause without the act, fault or neglect of the shipper, his agents or his servants.

4. Any deviation in saving or attempting to save life or property at sea or any reasonable deviation shall not be deemed to be an infringement or breach of this convention or of the contract of carriage, and the carrier shall not be liable for any loss or damage resulting therefrom.

5. Neither the carrier nor the ship shall in any event be or become liable for any loss or damage to or in connexion with goods in an amount exceeding £100 per package or unit, or the equivalent of that sum in other currency unless the nature and value of such goods have been declared by the shipper before shipment and inserted, in the bill of lading.

    This declaration if embodied in the bill of lading shall be *primâ facie* evidence, but shall not be binding or conclusive on the carrier.

    By agreement between the carrier, master or agent of the carrier and the shipper another maximum amount than that mentioned in this paragraph may be fixed, provided that such maximum shall not be less than the figure above named.

    Neither the carrier nor the ship shall be responsible in any event for loss or damage to, or in connexion with, goods if the nature or value thereof has been knowingly misstated by the shipper in the bill of lading.

6. Goods of an inflammable, explosive or dangerous nature to the shipment whereof the carrier, master or agent of the carrier has not consented with knowledge of their nature and character, may at any time before discharge be landed at any place, or destroyed or rendered innocuous by the carrier without compensation and the shipper of such goods shall be liable, for all damages and expenses directly or indirectly arising out of or resulting from such shipment. If any such goods shipped with such knowledge and consent shall become a danger to the ship or cargo, they may in like manner be landed at any place, or destroyed or rendered innocuous by the, carrier without liability on the part of the carrier except to general average, if any.

HAGUE RULES

Article 5.

A carrier shall be at liberty to surrender in whole or in part all or any of his rights and immunities or to increase any of his responsibilities and obligations under this convention, provided such surrender or increase shall be embodied in the bill of lading issued to the shipper. The provisions of this convention shall not be applicable to charter parties, but if bills of lading are issued in the case of a ship under a charter party they shall comply with the terms of this convention. Nothing in these rules shall be held to prevent the insertion in a bill of lading of any lawful provision regarding general average.

Article 6.

Notwithstanding the provisions of the preceding articles, a carrier, master or agent of the carrier and a shipper shall in regard to any particular goods be at liberty to enter into any agreement in any terms as to the responsibility and liability of the carrier for such goods, and as to the rights and immunities of the carrier in respect of such goods, or his obligation as to seaworthiness, so far as this stipulation is not contrary to public policy, or the care or diligence of his servants or agents in regard to the loading, handling, stowage, carriage, custody, care and discharge of the goods carried by sea, provided that in this case no bill of lading has been or shall be issued and that the terms agreed shall be embodied in a receipt which shall be a non-negotiable document and shall be marked as such.

Any agreement so entered into shall have full legal effect.

Provided that this article shall not apply to ordinary commercial shipments made in the ordinary course of trade, but only to other shipments where the character or condition of the property to be carried or the circumstances, terms and conditions under which the carriage is to be performed are such as reasonably to justify a special agreement.

Article 7.

Nothing herein contained shall prevent a carrier or a shipper from entering into any agreement, stipulation, condition, reservation or exemption as to the responsibility and liability of the carrier or the ship for the loss or damage to, or in connexion with, the custody and care and handling of goods prior to the loading on, and subsequent to, the discharge from the ship on which the goods are carried by sea.

Article 8.

The provisions of this convention shall not affect the rights and obligations of the carrier under any statute for the time being in force relating to the limitation of the liability of owners of sea-going vessels.

Article 9.

The monetary limits mentioned in this convention are to be taken to be gold value

Those contracting States in which the pound sterling is not a monetary unit reserve to themselves the right of translating the sums indicated in this convention in terms of pound sterling into terms of their own monetary system in round figures.

The national laws may reserve to the debtor the right of discharging his debt in national currency according to the rate of exchange prevailing on the day of the arrival of the ship at the port of discharge of the goods concerned.

Article 10.

The provisions of this convention shall apply to all bills of lading issued in any of the contracting States.

Article 11.

After an interval of not more than two years from the day on which the convention is signed the Belgian Government shall place itself in communication with the Governments of the high contracting parties which have declared themselves prepared to ratify the convention, with a view to deciding whether it shall be put into force. The ratifications shall be deposited at Brussels at a date to be fixed by agreement among the said Governments. The first deposit of ratifications shall be recorded in a *procès-verbal* signed by the representatives of the Powers which take part therein and by the Belgian Minister for Foreign Affairs.

The subsequent deposit of ratifications shall be made by means of a written notification, addressed to the Belgian Government and accompanied by the instrument of ratification.

A duly certified copy of the *procès-verbal* relating to the first deposit of ratifications, of the notifications referred to in the previous paragraph, and also of the instruments of ratification accompanying them, shall be immediately sent by the Belgian Government through the diplomatic channel to the Powers who have signed this convention or who have acceded to it. In the cases contemplated in the preceding paragraph, the said Government shall inform them at the same time of the date on which it received the notification.

Article 12.

Non-signatory States may accede to the present convention whether or not they have been represented at the International Conference at Brussels.

A State which desires to accede shall notify its intention in writing to the Belgian Government, forwarding to it the document of accession, which shall be deposited in the archives of the said Government.

The Belgian Government shall immediately forward to all the States which have signed or acceded to the convention a duly certified copy of the notification and of the act of accession, mentioning the date on which it received the notification.

Article 13.

The high contracting parties may at the time of signature, ratification or accession declare that their acceptance of the present convention does not include any or all of the self-governing dominions, or of the colonies, overseas possessions, protectorates or territories under their sovereignty or authority, and they may subsequently accede separately on behalf of any self-governing dominion, colony, overseas possession, protectorate or territory excluded in their declaration. They may also denounce the convention separately in accordance with its provisions in respect of any self-governing dominion, or any colony, overseas possession, protectorate or territory under their sovereignty or authority.

Article 14.

The present convention shall take effect, in the case of the States which have taken part in the first deposit of ratifications, one year after the date of the protocol recording such deposit. As respects the States which ratify subsequently or which accede, and also in cases in which the convention is subsequently put into effect in accordance with Article 13, it shall take effect six months after the notifications specified in paragraph 2 of Article 11 and paragraph 2 of Article 12 have been received by the Belgian Government.

Article 15.

In the event of one of the contracting States wishing to denounce the present convention, the denunciation shall be notified in writing to the Belgian Government, which shall immediately communicate a duly certified copy of the notification to all the other States, informing them of the date on which it was received.

The denunciation shall only operate in respect of the State which made the notification, and on the expiry of one year after the notification has reached the Belgian Government.

Article 16.

Any one of the contracting States shall have the right to call for a fresh conference with a view to considering possible amendments.

A State which would exercise this right should notify its intention to the other States through the Belgian Government, which would make arrangements for convening the Conference.

Done at Brussels, in a single copy, the 25th August, 1924.

Appendix VI
HAGUE-VISBY RULES

Hague Rules as amended by the Brussels Protocol of 23 February 1968 and by the protocol signed at Brussels on 21 December 1979*

Article 1.
In these Rules the following words are employed, with the meanings set out below:
(a) "Carrier" includes the owner or the charterer who enters into a contract of carriage with a shipper.
(b) "Contract of carriage" applies only to contracts of carriage covered by a bill of lading or any similar document of title, in so far as such document relates to the carriage of goods by sea, including any bill of lading or any similar document as aforesaid issued under or pursuant to a charter party from the moment at which such bill of lading or similar document of title regulates the relations between a carrier and a holder of the same.
(c) "Goods" includes goods, wares, merchandise, and articles of every kind whatsoever except live animals and cargo which by the contract of carriage is stated as being carried on deck and is so carried.
(d) "Ship" means any vessel used for the carriage of goods by sea.
(e) "Carriage of goods" covers the period from the time when the goods are loaded on to the time they are discharged from the ship.

Article 2.
Subject to the provisions of Article 6, under every contract of carriage of goods by sea the carrier, in relation to the loading, handling, stowage, carriage, custody, care and discharge of such goods, shall be subject to the responsibilities and liabilities and entitled to the rights and immunities hereinafter set forth.

Article 3.
1. The carrier shall be bound before and at the beginning of the voyage to exercise due diligence to:
   (a) Make the ship seaworthy;
   (b) Properly man, equip and supply the ship;
   (c) Make the holds, refrigerating and cool chambers, and all other parts of the ship in which goods are carried, fit and safe for their reception, carriage and preservation.
2. Subject to the provisions of Article 4, the carrier shall properly and carefully load, handle, stow, carry, keep, care for, and discharge the goods carried.
3. After receiving the goods into his charge the carrier or the master or agent of the carrier shall, on demand of the shipper, issue to the shipper a bill of lading showing among other things:
   (a) The leading marks necessary for identification of the goods as the same are furnished in writing by the shipper before the loading of such goods starts, provided such marks are stamped or otherwise shown clearly upon the goods if uncovered, or on the cases or coverings in which such goods are contained, in such a manner as should ordinarily remain legible until the end of the voyage.

---

* By a protocol in 1979 (the SDR Protocol) the Hague-Visby Rules were amended so that the calculation of limitation of liability was based on the special drawing right as defined by the International Monetary Fund rather than a fixed number of Poincare Francs as contained in the original 1968 Protocol. The Merchant Shipping Act 1981 section 2 enacts the provisions of the SDR Protocol under English law. Not all countries which have acceded to, ratified or enacted the Hague-Visby Rules have enacted the SDR Protocol - see appendix VIII.

HAGUE-VISBY RULES

(b) Either the number of packages or pieces, or the quantity, or weight, as the case may be, as furnished in writing by the shipper.

(c) The apparent order and condition of the goods.

Provided that no carrier, master or agent of the carrier shall be bound to state or show in the bill of lading any marks, number, quantity or weight which he has reasonable ground for suspecting not accurately to represent the goods actually received, or which he has had no reasonable means of checking.

4. Such a bill of lading shall be prima facie evidence of the receipt by the carrier of the goods as therein described in accordance with paragraph 3 (a), (b) and (c). However, proof to the contrary shall not be admissible when the bill of lading has been transferred to a third party acting in good faith.

5. The shipper shall be deemed to have guaranteed to the carrier the accuracy at the time of shipment of the marks, number, quantity and weight, as furnished by him, and the shipper shall indemnify the carrier against all loss, damages and expenses arising or resulting from inaccuracies in such particulars. The right of the carrier to such indemnity shall in no way limit his responsibility and liability under the contract of carriage to any person other than the shipper.

6. Unless notice of loss or damage and the general nature of such loss or damage be given in writing to the carrier or his agent at the port of discharge before or at the time of the removal of the goods into the custody of the person entitled to delivery thereof under the contract of carriage, or, if the loss or damage be not apparent, within three days, such removal shall be prima facie evidence of the delivery by the carrier of the goods as described in the bill of lading.

The notice in writing need not be given if the state of the goods has, at the time of their receipt, been the subject of joint survey or inspection.

Subject to paragraph 6*bis* the carrier and the ship shall in any event be discharged from all liability whatsoever in respect of the goods, unless suit is brought within one year of their delivery or of the date when they should have been delivered. This period, may however, be extended if the parties so agree after the cause of action has arisen.

In the case of any actual or apprehended loss or damage the carrier and the receiver shall give all reasonable facilities to each other for inspecting and tallying the goods.

6*bis*. An action for indemnity against a third person may be brought even after the expiration of the year provided for in the preceding paragraph if brought within the time allowed by the law of the Court seized of the case. However, the time allowed shall be not less than three months, commencing from the day when the person bringing such action for indemnity has settled the claim or has been served with process in the action against himself.

7. After the goods are loaded the bill of lading to be issued by the carrier, master, or agent of the carrier, to the shipper shall, if the shipper so demands be a 'shipped' bill of lading, provided that if the shipper shall have previously taken up any document of title to such goods, he shall surrender the same as against the issue of the 'shipped' bill of lading, but at the option of the carrier such document of title may be noted at the port of shipment by the carrier, master, or agent with the name or names of the ship or ships upon which the goods have been shipped and the date or dates of shipment, and when so noted, if it shows the particulars mentioned in paragraph 3 of Article III, shall for the purpose of this article be deemed to constitute a 'shipped' bill of lading.

8. Any clause, covenant, or agreement in a contract of carriage relieving the carrier or the ship from liability for loss or damage to, or in connection with, goods arising from negligence, fault, or failure in the duties and obligations provided in this article or lessening such liability otherwise than as provided in these Rules, shall be null and void and of no effect. A benefit of insurance in favour of the carrier or similar clause shall be deemed to be a clause relieving the carrier from liability.

Article 4.

1. Neither the carrier nor the ship shall be liable for loss or damage arising or resulting from unseaworthiness unless caused by want of due diligence on the part of the carrier to make the ship

seaworthy, and to secure that the ship is properly manned, equipped and supplied, and to make the holds, refrigerating and cool chambers and all other parts of the ship in which goods are carried fit and safe for their reception, carriage and preservation in accordance with the provisions of paragraph 1 of Article 3. Whenever loss or damage has resulted from unseaworthiness the burden of proving the exercise of due diligence shall be on the carrier or other person claiming exemption under this article.

2. Neither the carrier nor the ship shall be responsible for loss or damage arising or resulting from:
   (a) Act, neglect, or default of the master, mariner, pilot, or the servants of the carrier in the navigation or in the management of the ship.
   (b) Fire, unless caused by the actual fault or privity of the carrier.
   (c) Perils, dangers and accidents of the sea or other navigable waters.
   (d) Act of God.
   (e) Act of war.
   (f) Act of public enemies.
   (g) Arrest or restraint of princes, rulers or people, or seizure under legal process.
   (h) Quarantine restrictions.
   (i) Act or omission of the shipper or owner of the goods, his agent or representative.
   (j) Strikes or lockouts or stoppage or restraint of labour from whatever cause, whether partial or general.
   (k) Riots and civil commotions.
   (l) Saving or attempting to save life or property at sea.
   (m) Wastage in bulk of weight or any other loss or damage arising from inherent defect, quality or vice of the goods.
   (n) Insufficiency of packing.
   (o) Insufficiency or inadequacy of marks.
   (p) Latent defects not discoverable by due diligence.
   (q) Any other cause arising without the actual fault or privity of the carrier, or without the fault or neglect of the agents or servants of the carrier, but the burden of proof shall be on the person claiming the benefit of this exception to show that neither the actual fault or privity of the carrier nor the fault or neglect of the agents or servants of the carrier contributed to the loss or damage.

3. The shipper shall not be responsible for loss or damage sustained by the carrier or the ship arising or resulting from any cause without the act, fault or neglect of the shipper, his agents or his servants.

4. Any deviation in saving or attempting to save life or property at sea or any reasonable deviation shall not be deemed to be an infringement or breach of these Rules or of the contract of carriage, and the carrier shall not be liable for any loss or damage resulting therefrom.

5. (a) Unless the nature and value of such goods have been declared by the shipper before shipment and inserted in the bill of lading, neither the carrier nor the ship shall in any event be or become liable for any loss or damage to or in connection with the goods in an amount exceeding 666.67 units of account per package or unit or 2 units of account per kilogramme of gross weight of the goods lost or damaged, whichever is the higher.
   (b) The total amount recoverable shall be calculated by reference to the value of such goods at the place and time at which the goods are discharged from the ship in accordance with the contract or should have been so discharged.

   The value of the goods shall be fixed according to the commodity exchange price, or, if there be no such price, according to the current market price, or, if there be no commodity exchange price or current market price, by reference to the normal value of goods of the same kind and quality.

(c) Where a container, pallet or similar article of transport is used to consolidate goods, the number of packages or units enumerated in the bill of lading as packed in such article of transport shall be deemed the number of packages or units for the purpose of this paragraph as far as these packages or units are concerned. Except as aforesaid such article of transport shall be considered the package or unit.

(d) The unit of account mentioned in this article is the special drawing right as defined by the International Monetary Fund. The amounts mentioned in sub-paragraph (a) of this paragraph shall be converted into national currency on the basis of the value of that currency on a date to be determined by the law of the Court seized of the case.

(e) Neither the carrier nor the ship shall be entitled to the benefit of the limitation of liability provided for in this paragraph if it is proved that the damage resulted from an act or omission of the carrier done with intent to cause damage, or recklessly and with knowledge that damage would probably result.

(f) The declaration mentioned in sub-paragraph (a) of this paragraph, if embodied in the bill of lading, shall be *prima facie* evidence, but shall not be binding or conclusive on the carrier.

(g) By agreement between the carrier, master or agent of the carrier and the shipper other maximum amounts than those mentioned in sub-paragraph (a) of this paragraph may be fixed, provided that no maximum amount so fixed shall be less than the appropriate maximum mentioned in that sub-paragraph.

(h) Neither the carrier nor the ship shall be responsible in any event for loss or damage to, or in connection with, goods if the nature or value thereof has been knowingly mis-stated by the shipper in the bill of lading.

6. Goods of an inflammable, explosive or dangerous nature to the shipment whereof the carrier, master or agent of the carrier has not consented with knowledge of their nature and character, may at any time before discharge be landed at any place, or destroyed or rendered innocuous by the carrier without compensation and the shipper of such goods shall be liable for all damages and expenses directly or indirectly arising out of or resulting from such shipment. If any such goods shipped with such knowledge and consent shall become a danger to the ship or cargo, they may in like manner be landed at any place, or destroyed or rendered innocuous by the carrier without liability on the part of the carrier except to general average, if any.

Article 4*bis*.

1. The defences and limits of liability provided for in these Rules shall apply in any action against the carrier in respect of loss or damage to goods covered by a contract of carriage whether the action be founded in contract or in tort.

2. If such an action is brought against a servant or agent of the carrier (such servant or agent not being an independent contractor), such servant or agent shall be entitled to avail himself of the defences and limits of liability which the carrier is entitled to invoke under these Rules.

3. The aggregate of the amounts recoverable from the carrier, and such servants and agents, shall in no case exceed the limit provided for in these Rules.

4. Nevertheless, a servant or agent of the carrier shall not be entitled to avail himself of the provisions of this article, if it is proved that the damage resulted from an act or omission of the servant or agent done with intent to cause damage or recklessly and with knowledge that damage would probably result.

Article 5.

A carrier shall be at liberty to surrender in whole or in part all or any of his rights and immunities or to increase any of his responsibilities and obligations under these Rules, provided such surrender or increase shall be embodied in the bill of lading issued to the shipper. The provisions of these Rules shall not be applicable to charter parties, but if bills of lading are issued in the case of a ship under a

HAGUE-VISBY RULES

charter party they shall comply with the terms of these Rules. Nothing in these Rules shall be held to prevent the insertion in a bill of lading of any lawful provision regarding general average.

Article 6.

Notwithstanding the provisions of the preceding articles, a carrier, master or agent of the carrier and a shipper shall in regard to any particular goods be at liberty to enter into any agreement in any terms as to the responsibility and liability of the carrier for such goods, and as to the rights and immunities of the carrier in respect of such goods, or his obligation as to seaworthiness, so far as this stipulation is not contrary to public policy, or the care or diligence of his servants or agents in regard to the loading, handling, stowage, carriage, custody, care and discharge of the goods carried by sea, provided that in this case no bill of lading has been or shall be issued and that the terms agreed shall be embodied in a receipt which shall be a non-negotiable document and shall be marked as such.

An agreement so entered into shall have full legal effect.

Provided that this article shall not apply to ordinary commercial shipments made in the ordinary course of trade, but only to other shipments where the character or condition of the property to be carried or the circumstances, terms and conditions under which the carriage is to be performed are such as reasonably to justify a special agreement.

Article 7.

Nothing herein contained shall prevent a carrier or a shipper from entering into any agreement, stipulation, condition, reservation or exemption as to the responsibility and liability of the carrier or the ship for the loss or damage to, or in connection with, the custody and care and handling of goods prior to the loading on, and subsequent to the discharge from, the ship on which the goods are carried by sea.

Article 8.

The provisions of these Rules shall not affect the rights and obligations of the carrier under any statute for the time being in force relating to the limitation of the liability of owners of sea-going vessels.

Article 9.

These Rules shall not affect the provisions of any international Convention or national law governing liability for nuclear damage.

Article 10.

The provisions of these Rules shall apply to every bill of lading relating to the carriage of goods between ports in two different States if

(a) the Bill of Lading is issued in a contracting State, or

(b) the carriage is from a port in a contracting State, or

(c) the contract contained in or evidenced by the Bill of Lading provides that these Rules or legislation of any State giving effect to them are to govern the contract;

whatever may be the nationality of the ship, the carrier, the shipper, the consignee, or any other interested person.

(The last two paragraphs of this article are not reproduced. They require contracting States to apply the Rules to bills of lading mentioned in the article and authorise them to apply the Rules to other bills of lading).

(Articles 11 to 16 of the International Convention for the Unification of certain Rules of Law relating to Bills of Lading signed at Brussels on 25 August 1924 (the Hague Rules) are not reproduced here. They deal with the coming into force of the Convention, procedure for ratification, accession and denunciation and the right to call for a fresh conference to consider amendments to the Rules contained in the Convention. See appendix V).

Appendix VII
HAMBURG RULES

United Nations Convention on the Carriage of Goods by Sea, 1978

PREAMBLE

THE STATES PARTIES TO THIS CONVENTION,

HAVING RECOGNIZED the desirability of determining by agreement certain rules relating to the carriage of goods by sea,

HAVING DECIDED to conclude a convention for this purpose and have thereto agreed as follows:

PART I. GENERAL PROVISIONS

Article 1. Definitions

In this Convention:

1. "Carrier" means any person by whom or in whose name a contract of carriage of goods by sea has been concluded with a shipper.
2. "Actual carrier" means any person to whom the performance of the carriage of the goods, or of part of the carriage, has been entrusted by the carrier, and includes any other person to whom such performance has been entrusted.
3. "Shipper" means any person by whom or in whose name or on whose behalf a contract of carriage of goods by sea has been concluded with a carrier, or any person by whom or in whose name or on whose behalf the goods are actually delivered to the carrier in relation to the contract of carriage by sea.
4. "Consignee" means the person entitled to take delivery of the goods.
5. "Goods" includes live animals; where the goods are consolidated in a container, pallet or similar article of transport or where they are packed, goods includes such article of transport or packaging if supplied by the shipper.
6. "Contract of carriage by sea" means any contract whereby the carrier undertakes against payment of freight to carry goods by sea from one port to another; however, a contract which involves carriage by sea and also carriage by some other means is deemed to be a contract of carriage by sea for the purposes of this Convention only in so far as it relates to the carriage by sea.
7. "Bill of lading" means a document which evidences a contract of carriage by sea and the taking over or loading of the goods by the carrier, and by which the carrier undertakes to deliver the goods against surrender of the document. A provision in the document that the goods are to be delivered to the order of a named person, or to order, or to bearer, constitutes such an undertaking.
8. "Writing" includes, inter alia, telegram and telex.

Article 2. Scope of application

1. The provisions of this Convention are applicable to all contracts of carriage by sea between two different States, if:
(a) the port of loading as provided for in the contract of carriage by sea is located in a Contracting State, or
(b) the port of discharge as provided for in the contract of carriage by sea is located in a Contracting State, or
(c) one of the optional ports of discharge provided for in the contract of carriage by sea is the actual port of discharge and such port is located in a Contracting State, or
(d) the bill of lading or other document evidencing the contract of carriage by sea is issued in a Contracting State, or
(e) the bill of lading or other document evidencing the contract of carriage by sea provides that the provisions of this Convention or the legislation of any State giving effect to them are to govern the contract.
2. The provisions of this Convention are applicable without regard to the nationality of the ship, the carrier, the actual carrier, the shipper, the consignee or any other interested person.
3. The provisions of this Convention are not applicable to charter-parties. However, where a bill of lading is issued

HAMBURG RULES

pursuant to a charter-party, the provisions of the Convention apply to such a bill of lading if it governs the relation between the carrier and the holder of the bill of lading, not being the charterer.

4. If a contract provides for future carriage of goods in a series of shipments during an agreed period, the provisions of this Convention apply to each shipment. However, where a shipment is made under a charter-party, the provisions of paragraph 3 of this article apply.

Article 3. Interpretation of the Convention

In the interpretation and application of the provisions of this Convention regard shall be had to its international character and to the need to promote uniformity.

PART II. LIABILITY OF THE CARRIER

Article 4. Period of responsibility

1. The responsibility of the carrier for the goods under this Convention covers the period during which the carrier is in charge of the goods at the port of loading, during the carriage and at the port of discharge.
2. For the purpose of paragraph 1 of this article, the carrier is deemed to be in charge of the goods
(a) from the time he has taken over the goods from:
(i) the shipper, or a person acting on his behalf; or
(ii) an authority or other third party to whom, pursuant to law or regulations applicable at the port of loading, the goods must be handed over for shipment;
(b) until the time he has delivered the goods:
(i) by handing over the goods to the consignee; or
(ii) in cases where the consignee does not receive the goods from the carrier, by placing them at the disposal of the consignee in accordance with the contract or with the law or with the usage of the particular trade, applicable at the port of discharge; or
(iii) by handing over the goods to an authority or other third party to whom, pursuant to law or regulations applicable at the port of discharge, the goods must be handed over.
3. In paragraphs 1 and 2 of this article, reference to the carrier or to the consignee means, in addition to the carrier or the consignee, the servants or agents, respectively of the carrier or the consignee.

Article 5. Basis of liability

1. The carrier is liable for loss resulting from loss of or damage to the goods, as well as from delay in delivery, if the occurrence which caused the loss, damage or delay took place while the goods were in his charge as defined in article 4, unless the carrier proves that he, his servants or agents took all measures that could reasonably be required to avoid the occurrence and its consequences.
2. Delay in delivery occurs when the goods have not been delivered at the port of discharge provided for in the contract of carriage by sea within the time expressly agreed upon or, in the absence of such agreement, within the time which it would be reasonable to require of a diligent carrier, having regard to the circumstances of the case.
3. The person entitled to make a claim for the loss of goods may treat the goods as lost if they have not been delivered as required by article 4 within 60 consecutive days following the expiry of the time for delivery according to paragraph 2 of this article.
4. (a) The carrier is liable
(i) for loss of or damage to the goods or delay in delivery caused by fire, if the claimant proves that the fire arose from fault or neglect on the part of the carrier, his servants or agents;
(ii) for such loss, damage or delay in delivery which is proved by the claimant to have resulted from the fault or neglect of the carrier, his servants or agents in taking all measures that could reasonably be required to put out the fire and avoid or mitigate its consequences.
(b) In case of fire on board the ship affecting the goods, if the claimant or the carrier so desires, a survey in accordance with shipping practices must be held into the cause and circumstances of the fire, and a copy of the surveyors report shall be made available on demand to the carrier and the claimant.
5. With respect to live animals, the carrier is not liable for loss, damage or delay in delivery resulting from any

special risks inherent in that kind of carriage. If the carrier proves that he has complied with any special instructions given to him by the shipper respecting the animals and that, in the circumstances of the case, the loss, damage or delay in delivery could be attributed to such risks, it is presumed that the loss, damage or delay in delivery was so caused, unless there is proof that all or a part of the loss, damage or delay in delivery resulted from fault or neglect on the part of the carrier, his servants or agents.

6. The carrier is not liable, except in general average, where loss, damage or delay in delivery resulted from measures to save life or from reasonable measures to save property at sea.

7. Where fault or neglect on the part of the carrier, his servants or agents combines with another cause to produce loss, damage or delay in delivery, the carrier is liable only to the extent that the loss, damage or delay in delivery is attributable to such fault or neglect, provided that the carrier proves the amount of the loss, damage or delay in delivery not attributable thereto.

Article 6. Limits of liability

1. (a) The liability of the carrier for loss resulting from loss of or damage to goods according to the provisions of article 5 is limited to an amount equivalent to 835 units of account per package or other shipping unit or 2.5 units of account per kilogram of gross weight of the goods lost or damaged, whichever is the higher.

(b) The liability of the carrier for delay in delivery according to the provisions of article 5 is limited to an amount equivalent to two and a half times the freight payable for the goods delayed, but not exceeding the total freight payable under the contract of carriage of goods by sea.

(c) In no case shall the aggregate liability of the carrier, under both subparagraphs (a) and (b) of this paragraph, exceed the limitation which would be established under subparagraph (a) of this paragraph for total loss of the goods with respect to which such liability was incurred.

2. For the purpose of calculating which amount is the higher in accordance with paragraph 1 (a) of this article, the following rules apply:

(a) Where a container, pallet or similar article of transport is used to consolidate goods, the package or other shipping units enumerated in the bill of lading, if issued, or otherwise in any other document evidencing the contract of carriage by sea, as packed in such article of transport are deemed packages or shipping units. Except as aforesaid the goods in such article of transport are deemed one shipping unit.

(b) In cases where the article of transport itself has been lost or damaged, that article of transport, if not owned or otherwise supplied by the carrier, is considered one separate shipping unit.

3. Unit of account means the unit of account mentioned in article 26.

4. By agreement between the carrier and the shipper, limits of liability exceeding those provided for in paragraph 1 may be fixed.

Article 7. Application to non-contractual claims

1. The defences and limits of liability provided for in this Convention apply in any action against the carrier in respect of loss of or damage to the goods covered by the contract of carriage by sea, as well as of delay in delivery whether the action is founded in contract, in tort or otherwise.

2. If such an action is brought against a servant or agent of the carrier, such servant or agent, if he proves that he acted within the scope of his employment, is entitled to avail himself of the defences and limits of liability which the carrier is entitled to invoke under this Convention.

3. Except as provided in article 8, the aggregate of the amounts recoverable from the carrier and from any persons referred to in paragraph 2 of this article shall not exceed the limits of liability provided for in this Convention.

Article 8. Loss of right to limit responsibility

1. The carrier is not entitled to the benefit of the limitation of liability provided for in article 6 if it is proved that the loss, damage or delay in delivery resulted from an act or omission of the carrier done with the intent to cause such loss, damage or delay, or recklessly and with knowledge that such loss, damage or delay would probably result.

2. Notwithstanding the provisions of paragraph 2 of article 7, a servant or agent of the carrier is not entitled to the benefit of the limitation of liability provided for in article 6 if it is proved that the loss, damage or delay in delivery resulted from an act or omission of such servant or agent, done with the intent to cause such loss, damage or delay, or recklessly and with knowledge that such loss, damage or delay would probably result.

Article 9. Deck cargo

1. The carrier is entitled to carry the goods on deck only if such carriage is in accordance with an agreement with the shipper or with the usage of the particular trade or is required by statutory rules or regulations.
2. If the carrier and the shipper have agreed that the goods shall or may be carried on deck, the carrier must insert in the bill of lading or other document evidencing the contract of carriage by sea a statement to that effect. In the absence of such a statement the carrier has the burden of proving that an agreement for carriage on deck has been entered into; however, the carrier is not entitled to invoke such an agreement against a third party, including a consignee, who has acquired the bill of lading in good faith.
3. Where the goods have been carried on deck contrary to the provisions of paragraph 1 of this article or where the carrier may not under paragraph 2 of this article invoke an agreement for carriage on deck, the carrier, notwithstanding the provisions of paragraph 1 of article 5, is liable for loss of or damage to the goods, as well as for delay in delivery, resulting solely from the carriage on deck, and the extent of his liability is to be determined in accordance with the provisions of article 6 or article 8 of this Convention, as the case may be.
4. Carriage of goods on deck contrary to express agreement for carriage under deck is deemed to be an act or omission of the carrier within the meaning of article 8.

Article 10. Liability of the carrier and actual carrier

1. Where the performance of the carriage or part thereof has been entrusted to an actual carrier, whether or not in pursuance of a liberty under the contract of carriage by sea to do so, the carrier nevertheless remains responsible for the entire carriage according to the provisions of this Convention. The carrier is responsible, in relation to the carriage performed by the actual carrier, for the acts and omissions of the actual carrier and of his servants and agents acting within the scope of their employment.
2. All the provisions of this Convention governing the responsibility of the carrier also apply to the responsibility of the actual carrier for the carriage performed by him. The provisions of paragraphs 2 and 3 of article 7 and of paragraph 2 of article 8 apply if an action is brought against a servant or agent of the actual carrier.
3. Any special agreement under which the carrier assumes obligations not imposed by this Convention or waives rights conferred by this Convention affects the actual carrier only if agreed to by him expressly and in writing. Whether or not the actual carrier has so agreed, the carrier nevertheless remains bound by the obligations or waivers resulting from such special agreement.
4. Where and to the extent that both the carrier and the actual carrier are liable, their liability is joint and several.
5. The aggregate of the amounts recoverable from the carrier, the actual carrier and their servants and agents shall not exceed the limits of liability provided for in this Convention.
6. Nothing in this article shall prejudice any right of recourse as between the carrier and the actual carrier.

Article 11. Through carriage

1. Notwithstanding the provisions of paragraph 1 of article 10, where a contract of carriage by sea provides explicitly that a specified part of the carriage covered by the said contract is to be performed by a named person other than the carrier, the contract may also provide that the carrier is not liable for loss, damage or delay in delivery caused by an occurrence which takes place while the goods are in the charge of the actual carrier during such part of the carriage. Nevertheless, any stipulation limiting or excluding such liability is without effect if no judicial proceedings can be instituted against the actual carrier in a court competent under paragraph 1 or 2 of article 21. The burden of proving that any loss, damage or delay in delivery has been caused by such an occurrence rests upon the carrier.
2. The actual carrier is responsible in accordance with the provisions of paragraph 2 of article 10 for loss, damage or delay in delivery caused by an occurrence which takes place while the goods are in his charge.

PART III. LIABILITY OF THE SHIPPERS

Article 12. General rule

The shipper is not liable for loss sustained by the carrier or the actual carrier, or for damage sustained by the ship, unless such loss or damage was caused by the fault or neglect of the shipper, his servants or agents. Nor is any servant or agent of the shipper liable for such loss or damage unless the loss or damage was caused by fault or neglect on his part.

HAMBURG RULES

Article 13. Special rules on dangerous goods

1. The shipper must mark or label in a suitable manner dangerous goods as dangerous.
2. Where the shipper hands over dangerous goods to the carrier or an actual carrier, as the case may be, the shipper must inform him of the dangerous character of the goods and, if necessary, of the precautions to be taken. If the shipper fails to do so and such carrier or actual carrier does not otherwise have knowledge of their dangerous character:
   (a) the shipper is liable to the carrier and any actual carrier for the loss resulting from the shipment of such goods, and
   (b) the goods may at any time be unloaded, destroyed or rendered innocuous, as the circumstances may require, without payment of compensation.
3. The provisions of paragraph 2 of this article may not be invoked by any person if during the carriage he has taken the goods in his charge with knowledge of their dangerous character.
4. If, in cases where the provisions of paragraph 2, subparagraph (b), of this article do not apply or may not be invoked, dangerous goods become an actual danger to life or property, they may be unloaded, destroyed or rendered innocuous, as the circumstances may require, without payment of compensation except where there is an obligation to contribute in general average or where the carrier is liable in accordance with the provisions of article 5.

PART IV. TRANSPORT DOCUMENTS

Article 14. Issue of bill of lading

1. When the carrier or the actual carrier takes the goods in his charge, the carrier must, on demand of the shipper, issue to the shipper a bill of lading.
2. The bill of lading may be signed by a person having authority from the carrier. A bill of lading signed by the master of the ship carrying the goods is deemed to have been signed on behalf of the carrier.
3. The signature on the bill of lading may be in handwriting, printed in facsimile, perforated, stamped, in symbols, or made by any other mechanical or electronic means, if not inconsistent with the law of the country where the bill of lading is issued.

Article 15. Contents of bill of lading

1. The bill of lading must include, inter alia, the following particulars:
   (a) the general nature of the goods, the leading marks necessary for identification of the goods, an express statement, if applicable, as to the dangerous character of the goods, the number of packages or pieces, and the weight of the goods or their quantity otherwise expressed, all such particulars as furnished by the shipper;
   (b) the apparent condition of the goods;
   (c) the name and principal place of business of the carrier;
   (d) the name of the shipper;
   (e) the consignee if named by the shipper;
   (f) the port of loading under the contract of carriage by sea and the date on which the goods were taken over by the carrier at the port of loading;
   (g) the port of discharge under the contract of carriage by sea;
   (h) the number of originals of the bill of lading, if more than one;
   (i) the place of issuance of the bill of lading;
   (j) the signature of the carrier or a person acting on his behalf;
   (k) the freight to the extent payable by the consignee or other indication that freight is payable by him;
   (l) the statement referred to in paragraph 3 of article 23;
   (m) the statement, if applicable, that the goods shall or may be carried on deck;
   (n) the date or the period of delivery of the goods at the port of discharge if expressly agreed upon between the parties; and
   (o) any increased limit or limits of liability where agreed in accordance with paragraph 4 of article 6.

2. After the goods have been loaded on board, if the shipper so demands, the carrier must issue to the shipper a "shipped" bill of lading which, in addition to the particulars required under paragraph 1 of this article, must state that the goods are on board a named ship or ships, and the date or dates of loading. If the carrier has previously issued to the shipper a bill of lading or other document of title with respect to any of such goods, on request of the carrier the shipper must surrender such document in exchange for a "shipped" bill of lading. The carrier may amend any previously issued document in order to meet the shippers demand for a "shipped" bill of lading if, as amended, such document includes all the information required to be contained in a "shipped" bill of lading.
3. The absence in the bill of lading of one or more particulars referred to in this article does not affect the legal character of the document as a bill of lading provided that it nevertheless meets the requirements set out in paragraph 7 of article 1.

Article 16. Bills of lading: reservations and evidentiary effect

1. If the bill of lading contains particulars concerning the general nature, leading marks, number of packages of pieces, weight or quantity of the goods which the carrier or other person issuing the bill of lading on his behalf knows or has reasonable grounds to suspect do not accurately represent the goods actually taken over or, where a "shipped" bill of lading is issued, loaded, or if he had no reasonable means of checking such particulars, the carrier or such other person must insert in the bill of lading a reservation specifying these inaccuracies, grounds of suspicion or the absence of reasonable means of checking.
2. If the carrier or other person issuing the bill of lading on his behalf fails to note on the bill of lading the apparent condition of the goods, he is deemed to have noted on the bill of lading that the goods were in apparent good condition.
3. Except for particulars in respect of which and to the extent to which a reservation permitted under paragraph 1 of this article has been entered:
(a) the bill of lading is prima facie evidence of the taking over or, where a "shipped" bill of lading is issued, loading, by the carrier of the goods as described in the bill of lading; and
(b) proof to the contrary by the carrier is not admissible if the bill of lading has been transferred to a third party, including a consignee, who in good faith has acted in reliance on the description of the goods therein.
4. A bill of lading which does not, as provided in paragraph 1, subparagraph (k), of article 15, set forth the freight or otherwise indicate that freight is payable by the consignee or does not set forth demurrage incurred at the port of loading payable by the consignee, is prima facie evidence that no freight or such demurrage is payable by him. However, proof to the contrary by the carrier is not admissible when the bill of lading has been transferred to a third party, including a consignee, who in good faith has acted in reliance on the absence in the bill of lading of any such indication.

Article 17. Guarantees by the shipper

1. The shipper is deemed to have guaranteed to the carrier the accuracy of particulars relating to the general nature of the goods, their marks, number, weight and quantity as furnished by him for insertion in the bill of lading. The shipper must indemnify the carrier against the loss resulting from inaccuracies in such particulars. The shipper remains liable even if the bill of lading has been transferred by him. The right of the carrier to such indemnity in no way limits his liability under the contract of carriage by sea to any person other than the shipper.
2. Any letter of guarantee or agreement by which the shipper undertakes to indemnify the carrier against loss resulting from the issuance of the bill of lading by the carrier, or by a person acting on his behalf, without entering a reservation relating to particulars furnished by the shipper for insertion in the bill of lading, or to the apparent condition of the goods, is void and of no effect as against any third party, including a consignee, to whom the bill of lading has been transferred.
3. Such a letter of guarantee or agreement is valid as against the shipper unless the carrier or the person acting on his behalf, by omitting the reservation referred to in paragraph 2 of this article, intends to defraud a third party, including a consignee, who acts in reliance on the description of the goods in the bill of lading. In the latter case, if the reservation omitted relates to particulars furnished by the shipper for insertion in the bill of lading, the carrier has no right of indemnity from the shipper pursuant to paragraph 1 of this article.
4. In the case of intended fraud referred to in paragraph 3 of this article, the carrier is liable, without the benefit of the limitation of liability provided for in this Convention, for the loss incurred by a third party, including a consignee, because he has acted in reliance on the description of the goods in the bill of lading.

HAMBURG RULES

Article 18. Documents other than bills of lading

Where a carrier issues a document other than a bill of lading to evidence the receipt of the goods to be carried, such a document is prima facie evidence of the conclusion of the contract of carriage by sea and the taking over by the carrier of the goods as therein described.

PART V. CLAIMS AND ACTIONS

Article 19. Notice of loss, damage or delay

1. Unless notice of loss or damage, specifying the general nature of such loss or damage, is given in writing by the consignee to the carrier not later than the working day after the day when the goods were handed over to the consignee, such handing over is prima facie evidence of the delivery by the carrier of the goods as described in the document of transport or, if no such document has been issued, in good condition.

2. Where the loss or damage is not apparent, the provisions of paragraph 1 of this article apply correspondingly if notice in writing is not given within 15 consecutive days after the day when the goods were handed over to the consignee.

3. If the state of the goods at the time they were handed over to the consignee has been the subject of a joint survey or inspection by the parties, notice in writing need not be given of loss or damage ascertained during such survey or inspection.

4. In the case of any actual or apprehended loss or damage, the carrier and the consignee must give all reasonable facilities to each other for inspecting and tallying the goods.

5. No compensation shall be payable for loss resulting from delay in delivery unless a notice has been given in writing to the carrier within 60 consecutive days after the day when the goods were handed over to the consignee.

6. If the goods have been delivered by an actual carrier, any notice given under this article to him shall have the same effect as if it had been given to the carrier; and any notice given to the carrier shall have effect as if given to such actual carrier.

7. Unless notice of loss or damage, specifying the general nature of the loss or damage, is given in writing by the carrier or actual carrier to the shipper not later than 90 consecutive days after the occurrence of such loss or damage or after the delivery of the goods in accordance with paragraph 2 of article 4, whichever is later, the failure to give such notice is prima facie evidence that the carrier or the actual carrier has sustained no loss or damage due to the fault or neglect of the shipper, his servants or agents.

8. For the purpose of this article, notice given to a person acting on the carriers or the actual carriers behalf, including the master or the officer in charge of the ship, or to a person acting on the shippers behalf is deemed to have been given to the carrier, to the actual carrier or to the shipper, respectively.

Article 20. Limitation of actions

1. Any action relating to carriage of goods under this Convention is time-barred if judicial or arbitral proceedings have not been instituted within a period of two years.

2. The limitation period commences on the day on which the carrier has delivered the goods or part thereof or, in cases where no goods have been delivered, on the last day on which the goods should have been delivered.

3. The day on which the limitation period commences is not included in the period.

4. The person against whom a claim is made may at any time during the running of the limitation period extend that period by a declaration in writing to the claimant. This period may be further extended by another declaration or declarations.

5. An action for indemnity by a person held liable may be instituted even after the expiration of the limitation period provided for in the preceding paragraphs if instituted within the time allowed by the law of the State where proceedings are instituted. However, the time allowed shall not be less than 90 days commencing from the day when the person instituting such action for indemnity has settled the claim or has been served with process in the action against himself.

Article 21. Jurisdiction

1. In judicial proceedings relating to carriage of goods under this Convention the plaintiff, at his option, may institute an action in a court which according to the law of the State where the court is situated, is competent and within the jurisdiction of which is situated one of the following places:

(a) the principal place of business or, in the absence thereof, the habitual residence of the defendant; or

(b) the place where the contract was made, provided that the defendant has there a place of business, branch or agency through which the contract was made; or

(c) the port of loading or the port of discharge; or

(d) any additional place designated for that purpose in the contract of carriage by sea.

2.(a) Notwithstanding the preceding provisions of this article, an action may be instituted in the courts of any port or place in a Contracting State at which the carrying vessel or any other vessel of the same ownership may have been arrested in accordance with applicable rules of the law of that State and of international law. However, in such a case, at the petition of the defendant, the claimant must remove the action, at his choice, to one of the jurisdictions referred to in paragraph 1 of this article for the determination of the claim, but before such removal the defendant must furnish security sufficient to ensure payment of any judgement that may subsequently be awarded to the claimant in the action.

(b) All questions relating to the sufficiency or otherwise of the security shall be determined by the court of the port or place of the arrest.

3. No judicial proceedings relating to carriage of goods under this Convention may be instituted in a place not specified in paragraph 1 or 2 of this article. The provisions of this paragraph do not constitute an obstacle to the jurisdiction of the Contracting States for provisional or protective measures.

4.(a) Where an action has been instituted in a court competent under paragraphs 1 or 2 of this article or where judgement has been delivered by such a court, no new action may be started between the same parties on the same grounds unless the judgement of the court before which the first action was instituted is not enforceable in the country in which the new proceedings are instituted;

(b) For the purpose of this article, the institution of measures with a view to obtaining enforcement of a judgement is not to be considered as the starting of a new action;

(c) For the purpose of this article, the removal of an action to a different court within the same country, or to a court in another country, in accordance with paragraph 2 (a) of this article, is not to be considered as the starting of a new action.

5. Notwithstanding the provisions of the preceding paragraphs, an agreement made by the parties, after a claim under the contract of carriage by sea has arisen, which designates the place where the claimant may institute an actions, is effective.

Article 22. Arbitration

1. Subject to the provisions of this article, parties may provide by agreement evidenced in writing that any dispute that may arise relating to carriage of goods under this Convention shall be referred to arbitration.

2. Where a charter-party contains a provision that disputes arising thereunder shall be referred to arbitration and a bill of lading issued pursuant to the charter-party does not contain special annotation providing that such provision shall be binding upon the holder of the bill of lading, the carrier may not invoke such provision as against a holder having acquired the bill of lading in good faith.

3. The arbitration proceedings shall, at the option of the claimant, be instituted at one of the following places:

(a) a place in a State within whose territory is situated:

(i) the principal place of business of the defendant or, in the absence thereof, the habitual residence of the defendant; or

(ii) the place where the contract was made, provided that the defendant has there a place of business, branch or agency through which the contract was made; or

(iii) the port of loading or the port of discharge; or

(b) any place designated for that purpose in the arbitration clause or agreement.

4. The arbitrator or arbitration tribunal shall apply the rules of this Convention.

5. The provisions of paragraphs 2 and 4 of this article are deemed to be part of every arbitration clause or agreement, and any term of such clause or agreement which is inconsistent therewith is null and void.

6. Nothing in this article affects the validity of an agreement relating to arbitration made by the parties after the claim under the contract of carriage by sea has arisen.

PART VI. SUPPLEMENTARY PROVISIONS

Article 23. Contractual stipulations

1. Any stipulation in a contract of carriage by sea, in a bill of lading, or in any other document evidencing the contract of carriage by sea is null and void to the extent that it derogates, directly or indirectly, from the provisions of this Convention. The nullity of such a stipulation does not affect the validity of the other provisions of the contract or document of which it forms a part. A clause assigning benefit of insurance of goods in favour of the carrier, or any similar clause, is null and void.

2. Notwithstanding the provisions of paragraph 1 of this article, a carrier may increase his responsibilities and obligations under this Convention.

3. Where a bill of lading or any other document evidencing the contract of carriage by sea is issued, it must contain a statement that the carriage is subject to the provisions of this Convention which nullify any stipulation derogating therefrom to the detriment of the shipper or the consignee.

4. Where the claimant in respect of the goods has incurred loss as a result of a stipulation which is null and void by virtue of the present article, or as a result of the omission of the statement referred to in paragraph 3 of this article, the carrier must pay compensation to the extent required in order to give the claimant compensation in accordance with the provisions of this Convention for any loss of or damage to the goods as well as for delay in delivery. The carrier must, in addition, pay compensation for costs incurred by the claimant for the purpose of exercising his right, provided that costs incurred in the action where the foregoing provision is invoked are to be determined in accordance with the law of the State where proceedings are instituted.

Article 24. General average

1. Nothing in this Convention shall prevent the application of provisions in the contract of carriage by sea or national law regarding the adjustment of general average.

2. With the exception of article 20, the provisions of this Convention relating to the liability of the carrier for loss of or damage to the goods also determine whether the consignee may refuse contribution in general average and the liability of the carrier to indemnify the consignee in respect of any such contribution made or any salvage paid.

Article 25. Other conventions

1. This Convention does not modify the rights or duties of the carrier, the actual carrier and their servants and agents provided for in international conventions or national law relating to the limitation of liability of owners of seagoing ships.

2. The provisions of articles 21 and 22 of this Convention do not prevent the application of the mandatory provisions of any other multilateral convention already in force at the date of this Convention relating to matters dealt with in the said articles, provided that the dispute arises exclusively between parties having their principal place of business in States members of such other convention. However, this paragraph does not affect the application of paragraph 4 of article 22 of this Convention.

3. No liability shall arise under the provisions of this Convention for damage caused by a nuclear incident if the operator of a nuclear installation is liable for such damage:

(a) under either the Paris Convention of 29 July 1960 on Third Party Liability in the Field of Nuclear Energy as amended by the Additional Protocol of 28 January 1964, or the Vienna Convention of 21 May 1963 on Civil Liability for Nuclear Damage, or

(b) by virtue of national law governing the liability for such damage, provided that such law is in all respects as favourable to persons who may suffer damage as is either the Paris Convention or the Vienna Convention.

4. No liability shall arise under the provisions of this Convention for any loss of or damage to or delay in delivery of luggage for which the carrier is responsible under any international convention or national law relating to the carriage of passengers and their luggage by sea.

5. Nothing contained in this Convention prevents a Contracting State from applying any other international convention which is already in force at the date of this Convention and which applies mandatorily to contracts of carriage of goods primarily by a mode of transport other than transport by sea. This provision also applies to any subsequent revision or amendment of such international convention.

HAMBURG RULES

Article 26. Unit of account

1. The unit of account referred to in article 6 of this Convention is the special drawing right as defined by the International Monetary Fund. The amounts mentioned in article 6 are to be converted into the national currency of a State according to the value of such currency at the date of judgement or the date agreed upon by the parties. The value of a national currency, in terms of the special drawing right, of a Contracting State which is a member of the International Monetary Fund is to be calculated in accordance with the method of valuation applied by the International Monetary Fund in effect at the date in question for its operations and transactions. The value of a national currency, in terms of the special drawing right, of a Contracting State which is not a member of the International Monetary Fund is to be calculated in a manner determined by that State.
2. Nevertheless, those States which are not members of the International Monetary Fund and whose law does not permit the application of the provisions of paragraph 1 of this article may, at the time of signature, or at the time of ratification, acceptance, approval or accession or at any time thereafter, declare that the limits of liability provided for in this Convention to be applied in their territories shall be fixed as 12,500 monetary units per package or other shipping unit or 37.5 monetary units per kilogram of gross weight of the goods.
3. The monetary unit referred to in paragraph 2 of this article corresponds to sixty-five and a half milligrams of gold of millesimal fineness nine hundred. The conversion of the amounts referred to in paragraph 2 into the national currency is to be made according to the law of the State concerned.
4. The calculation mentioned in the last sentence of paragraph 1 and the conversion mentioned in paragraph 3 of this article is to be made in such a manner as to express in the national currency of the Contracting State as far as possible the same real value for the amounts in article 6 as is expressed there in units of account. Contracting States must communicate to the depositary the manner of calculation pursuant to paragraph 1 of this article, or the result of the conversion mentioned in paragraph 3 of this article, as the case may be, at the time of signature or when depositing their instruments of ratification, acceptance, approval or accession, or when availing themselves of the option provided for in paragraph 2 of this article and whenever there is a change in the manner of such calculation or in the result of such conversion.

PART VII. FINAL CLAUSES

Article 27. Depositary

The Secretary-General of the United Nations is hereby designated as the depositary of this Convention.

Article 28. Signature, Ratification, Acceptance, Approval, Accession

1. This Convention is open for signature by all States until 30 April 1979 at the Headquarters of the United Nations, New York.
2. This Convention is subject to ratification, acceptance or approval by the signatory States.
3. After 30 April 1979, this Convention will be open for accession by all States which are not signatory States.
4. Instruments of ratification, acceptance, approval and accession are to be deposited with the Secretary-General of the United Nations.

Article 29. Reservations

No reservations may be made to this Convention.

Article 30. Entry into force

1. This Convention enters into force on the first day of the month following the expiration of one year from the date of deposit of the twentieth instrument of ratification, acceptance, approval or accession.
2. For each State which becomes a Contracting State to this Convention after the date of the deposit of the twentieth instrument of ratification, acceptance, approval or accession, this Convention enters into force on the first day of the month following the expiration of one year after the deposit of the appropriate instrument on behalf of that State.
3. Each Contracting State shall apply the provisions of this Convention to contracts of carriage by sea concluded on or after the date of the entry into force of this Convention in respect of that State.

Article 31. Denunciation of other conventions

1. Upon becoming a Contracting State to this Convention, any State Party to the International Convention for the

HAMBURG RULES

Unification of certain Rules relating to Bills of Lading signed at Brussels on 25 August 1924 (1924 Convention) must notify the Government of Belgium as the depositary of the 1924 Convention of its denunciation of the said Convention with a declaration that the denunciation is to take effect as from the date when this Convention enters into force in respect of that State.

2. Upon the entry into force of this Convention under paragraph 1 of article 30, the depositary of this Convention must notify the Government of Belgium as the depositary of the 1924 Convention of the date of such entry into force, and of the names of the Contracting States in respect of which the Convention has entered into force.

3. The provisions of paragraphs 1 and 2 of this article apply correspondingly in respect of States Parties to the Protocol signed on 23 February 1968 to amend the International Convention for the Unification of certain Rules relating to Bills of Lading signed at Brussels on 25 August 1924.

4. Notwithstanding article 2 of this Convention, for the purposes of paragraph 1 of this article, a Contracting State may, if it deems it desirable, defer the denunciation of the 1924 Convention and of the 1924 Convention as modified by the 1968 Protocol for a maximum period of five years from the entry into force of this Convention. It will then notify the Government of Belgium of its intention. During this transitory period, it must apply to the Contracting States this Convention to the exclusion of any other one.

Article 32. Revision and amendment

1. At the request of not less than one third of the Contracting States to this Convention, the depositary shall convene a conference of the Contracting States for revising or amending it.

2. Any instrument of ratification, acceptance, approval or accession deposited after the entry into force of an amendment to this Convention is deemed to apply to the Convention as amended.

Article 33. Revision of the limitation amounts and unit of account or monetary unit

1. Notwithstanding the provisions of article 32, a conference only for the purpose of altering the amount specified in article 6 and paragraph 2 of article 26, or of substituting either or both of the units defined in paragraphs 1 and 3 of article 26 by other units is to be convened by the depositary in accordance with paragraph 2 of this article. An alteration of the amounts shall be made only because of a significant change in their real value.

2. A revision conference is to be convened by the depositary when not less than one fourth of the Contracting States so request.

3. Any decision by the conference must be taken by a two-thirds majority of the participating States. The amendment is communicated by the depositary to all the Contracting States for acceptance and to all the States signatories of the Convention for information.

4. Any amendment adopted enters into force on the first day of the month following one year after its acceptance by two thirds of the Contracting States. Acceptance is to be effected by the deposit of a formal instrument to that effect with the depositary.

5. After entry into force of an amendment a Contracting State which has accepted the amendment is entitled to apply the Convention as amended in its relations with Contracting States which have not within six months after the adoption of the amendment notified the depositary that they are not bound by the amendment.

6. Any instrument of ratification, acceptance, approval or accession deposited after the entry into force of an amendment to this Convention is deemed to apply to the Convention as amended.

Article 34. Denunciation

1. A Contracting State may denounce this Convention at any time by means of a notification in writing addressed to the depositary.

2. The denunciation takes effect on the first day of the month following the expiration of one year after the notification is received by the depositary. Where a longer period is specified in the notification, the denunciation takes effect upon the expiration of such longer period after the notification is received by the depositary.

Done at Hamburg, this thirty-first day of March, one thousand nine hundred and seventy-eight, in a single original, of which the Arabic, Chinese, English, French, Russian and Spanish texts are equally authentic.

In witness whereof the undersigned plenipotentiaries, being duly authorized by their respective Governments, have signed the present Convention.

Common understanding adopted by the United Nations Conference on the Carriage of Goods by Sea (A/CONF.89/13, annex 11).

It is the common understanding that the liability of the carrier under this Convention is based on the principle of presumed fault or neglect. This means that, as a rule, the burden of proof rests on the carrier but, with respect to certain cases, the provisions of the Convention modify this rule.

Resolution adopted by the United Nations Conference on the Carriage of Goods by Sea (A/CON.89/13, annex III)

The United Nations Conference on the Carriage of Goods by Sea,

Noting with appreciation the kind invitation of the Federal Republic of Germany to hold the Conference in Hamburg,

Being aware that the facilities placed at the disposal of the Conference and the generous hospitality bestowed on the participants by the Government of the Federal Republic of Germany and by the Free and Hanseatic City of Hamburg, have in no small measure contributed to the success of the Conference.

Expresses its gratitude to the Government and people of the Federal Republic of Germany, and

Having adopted the Convention on the Carriage of Goods by Sea on the basis of a draft Convention prepared by the United Nations Commission on International Trade Law at the request of the United Nations Conference on Trade and Development,

Expresses its gratitude to the United Nations Commission on International Trade Law and to the United Nations Conference on Trade and Development for their outstanding contribution to the simplification and harmonisation of the law of the carriage of goods by sea, and

Decides to designate the Convention adopted by the Conference as the: "UNITED NATIONS CONVENTION ON THE CARRIAGE OF GOODS BY SEA, 1978", and

Recommends that the rules embodied therein be known as the "HAMBURG RULES".

Further information about the Convention may be obtained from:

UNCITRAL Secretariat

Vienna International Centre

P.O. Box 500

A-1400 Vienna

Austria

Telex: 135612

Fax: +43 1 21345 5813

Tel: + 43 1 21345 4060

Appendix VIII
LIST OF COUNTRIES APPLYING THE CONVENTIONS

Country	Convention
Albania	HAMBURG
Algeria	HAGUE
Angola	HAGUE
Antigua & Barbuda	HAGUE
Argentina	HAGUE
Australia	HAGUE-VISBY[1]
Austria	HAMBURG
Bahamas	HAGUE
Bangladesh	HAGUE[2]
Barbados	HAMBURG
Belgium	HAGUE-VISBY[1]
Belize	HAGUE
Bermuda	HAGUE-VISBY[1]
Bolivia	HAGUE
Botswana	HAMBURG
British Antarctic Territory	HAGUE-VISBY[1]
British Virgin Islands	HAGUE-VISBY[1]
Bulgaria	HAGUE[2]
Burkina Faso	HAMBURG
Burundi	HAMBURG
Cameroon	HAMBURG
Canada	HAGUE-VISBY[2]
Cape Verde Islands	HAGUE
Cayman Islands	HAGUE-VISBY[1]
Chile	HAMBURG
China	HAGUE-VISBY[2]
Croatia	HAGUE-VISBY[1]
Cuba	HAGUE
Cyprus	HAGUE
Czech Republic	HAMBURG
Denmark	HAGUE-VISBY[1]
Dominican Rep.	HAMBURG
Ecuador	HAGUE-VISBY
Egypt	HAMBURG
Estonia	HAGUE[2]
Falklands Islands & Dependencies	HAGUE-VISBY[1]
Fiji	HAGUE
Finland	HAGUE-VISBY[1]
France	HAGUE-VISBY[1]
Gambia	HAMBURG
Georgia	HAMBURG
Germany	HAGUE-VISBY[2]

LIST OF COUNTRIES APPLYING THE CONVENTIONS

Ghana	HAGUE
Gibralta	HAGUE-VISBY
Goa	HAGUE
Greece	HAGUE-VISBY[1]
Grenada	HAGUE
Guinea	HAMBURG
Guinea Bissau	HAGUE
Guyana	HAGUE
Hong Kong	HAGUE-VISBY[1]
Hungary	HAMBURG
Iceland	HAGUE-VISBY[2]
India	HAGUE[2]
Indonesia	HAGUE-VISBY[2]
Iran	HAGUE
Iraq	HAMBURG[2]
Ireland	HAGUE/HAGUE-VISBY[2]
Isle of Man	HAGUE-VISBY[1]
Israel	HAGUE/HAGUE-VISBY[2]
Italy	HAGUE-VISBY[1]
Ivory Coast	HAGUE
Jamaica	HAGUE
Japan	HAGUE-VISBY[1]
Jordan	HAMBURG
Kazakhstan	HAMBURG
Kenya	HAMBURG
Kiribati	HAGUE
Kuwait	HAGUE
Latvia	HAGUE-VISBY[1]
Lebanon	HAMBURG
Lesotho	HAMBURG
Liberia	HAMBURG
Lithuania	HAGUE-VISBY[1]
Luxembourg	HAGUE-VISBY[1]
Malagasy Rep.	HAGUE
Malawi	HAMBURG
Malaysia	HAGUE
Mauritius	HAGUE
Mexico	HAGUE-VISBY[1]
Monaco	HAGUE
Montserrat	HAGUE-VISBY[1]
Morocco	HAMBURG
Mozambique	HAGUE
Nauru	HAGUE
Netherlands	HAGUE-VISBY
New Zealand	HAGUE-VISBY[1]
Nigeria	HAMBURG
Norway	HAGUE-VISBY[1]
Oman	HAGUE-VISBY[2]
Papua New Guinea	HAGUE
Paraguay	HAMBURG
Peru	HAGUE

LIST OF COUNTRIES APPLYING THE CONVENTIONS

Philippines	HAGUE[2]
Poland	HAGUE-VISBY[1]
Portugal	HAGUE/HAGUE-VISBY[2]
Romania	HAMBURG
Russian Federation	HAGUE-VISBY[1]
Sao Tome & Principe	HAGUE
Senegal	HAMBURG
Seychelles	HAGUE
Sierra Leone	HAMBURG
Singapore	HAGUE-VISBY[2]
Slovenia	HAGUE
Solomon Islands	HAGUE
Somalia	HAGUE
South Africa	HAGUE-VISBY[2]
South Korea	HAGUE-VISBY[2]
Spain	HAGUE-VISBY[1]
Sri Lanka	HAGUE-VISBY
St. Kitts-Nevis	HAGUE
St. Lucia	HAGUE
St. Vincent & Grenadines	HAMBURG
Sweden	HAGUE-VISBY[1]
Switzerland	HAGUE-VISBY[1]
Syria	HAMBURG
Taiwan	HAGUE[2]
Tanzania	HAMBURG
Thailand	HAGUE-VISBY[2]
Timores	HAGUE
Tonga	HAGUE-VISBY
Trinidad & Tobago	HAGUE
Tunisia	HAMBURG
Turkey	HAGUE
Turks & Caicos Islands	HAGUE-VISBY[1]
Tuvalu	HAGUE
Uganda	HAMBURG
United Kingdom	HAGUE-VISBY[1]
United Arab Emirates	HAGUE-VISBY[2]
USA	HAGUE
Vietnam	HAGUE-VISBY[2]
Zaire	HAGUE
Zambia	HAMBURG

1   States which are party to SDR Protocol
2   Countries which have introduced domestic legislation along the lines of the Hague, Hague-Visby or Hamburg Rules but which are not parties to the convention.

For an up-to-date list, contact: Treaty Section, British Foreign & Commonwealth Office, Tel: +44 20 7008 1500 or visit UK Treaties Online at http://treaties.fco.gov.uk/treaties/treaty.htm.

Appendix IX
UK CARRIAGE OF GOODS BY SEA ACT 1992

ELIZABETH II   c. **50**

Carriage of Goods by Sea Act 1992

1992 CHAPTER 50

An Act to replace the Bills of Lading Act 1855 with new provision with respect to bills of lading and certain other shipping documents. [16th July 1992]

BE IT ENACTED by the Queen's most Excellent Majesty, by and with the advice and consent of the Lords Spiritual and Temporal, and Commons, in this present Parliament assembled, and by the authority of the same, as follows:—

1.—(1) This Act applies to the following documents, that is to say—   *Shipping documents etc. to which Act applies.*

   (a) any bill of lading;

   (b) any sea waybill; and

   (c) any ship's delivery order.

(2) References in this Act to a bill of lading—

   (a) do not include references to a document which is incapable of transfer either by indorsement or, as a bearer bill, by delivery without indorsement; but

   (b) subject to that, do include references to a received for shipment bill of lading.

(3) References in this Act to a sea waybill are references to any document which is not a bill of lading but-

   (a) is such a receipt for goods as contains or evidences a contract for the carriage of goods by sea; and

   (b) identifies the person to whom delivery of the goods is to be made by the carrier in accordance with that contract.

(4) References in this Act to a ship's delivery order are references to any document which is neither a bill of lading nor a sea waybill but contains an undertaking which—

(a) is given under or for the purposes of a contract for the carriage by sea of the goods to which the document relates, or of goods which include those goods; and

(b) is an undertaking by the carrier to a person identified in the document to deliver the goods to which the document relates to that person.

(5) The Secretary of State may by regulations make provision for the application of this Act to cases where a telecommunication system or any other information technology is used for effecting transactions corresponding to—

(a) the issue of a document to which this Act applies;

(b) the indorsement, delivery or other transfer of such a document; or

(c) the doing of anything else in relation to such a document.

(6) Regulations under subsection (5) above may—

(a) make such modifications of the following provisions of this Act as the Secretary of State considers appropriate in connection with the application of this Act to any case mentioned in that subsection; and

(b) contain supplemental, incidental, consequential and transitional provision;

and the power to make regulations under that subsection shall be exercisable by statutory instrument subject to annulment in pursuance of a resolution of either House of Parliament.

Rights under shipping documents.

2.—(1) Subject to the following provisions of this section, a person who becomes—

(a) the lawful holder of a bill of lading;

(b) the person who (without being an original party to the contract of carriage) is the person to whom delivery of the goods to which a sea waybill relates is to be made by the carrier in accordance with that contract; or

(c) the person to whom delivery of the goods to which a ship's delivery order relates is to be made in accordance with the undertaking contained in the order,

shall (by virtue of becoming the holder of the bill or, as the case may be, the person to whom delivery is to be made) have transferred to and vested in him all rights of suit under the contract of carriage as if he had been a party to that contract.

(2) Where, when a person becomes the lawful holder of a bill of lading, possession of the bill no longer gives a right (as against the carrier) to possession of the goods to which the bill relates, that person shall not have any rights transferred to him by virtue of subsection (1) above unless he becomes the holder of the bill—

(a) by virtue of a transaction effected in pursuance of any contractual or other arrangements made before the time when such a right to possession ceased to attach to possession of the bill; or

(b) as a result of the rejection to that person by another person of goods or documents delivered to the other person in pursuance of any such arrangements.

(3) The rights vested in any person by virtue of the operation of subsection (1) above in relation to a ship's delivery order—

(a) shall be so vested subject to the terms of the order; and

(b) where the goods to which the order relates form a part only of the goods to which the contract of carriage relates, shall be confined to rights in respect of the goods to which the order relates.

(4) Where, in the case of any document to which this Act applies—

(a) a person with any interest or right in or in relation to goods to which the document relates sustains loss or damage in consequence of a breach of the contract of carriage; but

(b) subsection (1) above operates in relation to that document so that rights of suit in respect of that breach are vested in another person,

the other person shall be entitled to exercise those rights for the benefit of the person who sustained the loss or damage to the same extent as they could have been exercised if they had been vested in the person for whose benefit they are exercised.

(5) Where rights are transferred by virtue of the operation of subsection (1) above in relation to any document, the transfer for which that subsection provides shall extinguish any entitlement to those rights which derives—

(a) where that document is a bill of lading, from a person's having been an original party to the contract of carriage; or

(b) in the case of any document to which this Act applies, from the previous operation of that subsection in relation to that document;

but the operation of that subsection shall be without prejudice to any rights which derive from a person's having been an original party to the contract contained in, or evidenced by, a sea waybill and, in relation to a ship's delivery order, shall be without prejudice to any rights deriving otherwise than from the previous operation of that subsection in relation to that order.

3.—(1) Where subsection (1) of section 2 of this Act operates in relation to any document to which this Act applies and the person in whom rights are vested by virtue of that subsection— *Liabilities under shipping documents.*

(a) takes or demands delivery from the carrier of any of the goods to which the document relates;

(b) makes a claim under the contract of carriage against the carrier in respect of any of those goods; or

(c) is a person who, at a time before those rights were vested in him, took or demanded delivery from the carrier of any of those goods,

that person shall (by virtue of taking or demanding delivery or making the claim or, in a case falling within paragraph (c) above, of having the rights vested in him) become subject to the same liabilities under that contract as if he had been a party to that contract.

(2) Where the goods to which a ship's delivery order relates form a part only of the goods to which the contract of carriage relates, the liabilities to which any person is subject by virtue of the operation of this section in relation to that order shall exclude liabilities in respect of any goods to which the order does not relate.

(3) This section, so far as it imposes liabilities under any contract on any person, shall be without prejudice to the liabilities under the contract of any person as an original party to the contract.

Representations in bills of lading.

4. A bill of lading which—

(a) represents goods to have been shipped on board a vessel or to have been received for shipment on board a vessel; and

(b) has been signed by the master of the vessel or by a person who was not the master but had the express, implied or apparent authority of the carrier to sign bills of lading,

shall, in favour of a person who has become the lawful holder of the bill, be conclusive evidence against the carrier of the shipment of the goods or, as the case may be, of their receipt for shipment.

Interpretation etc.

5.—(1) In this Act—

"bill of lading", "sea waybill" and "ship's delivery order" shall be construed in accordance with section 1 above;

"the contract of carriage"—

(a) in relation to a bill of lading or sea waybill, means the contract contained in or evidenced by that bill or waybill; and

(b) in relation to a ship's delivery order, means the contract under or for the purposes of which the undertaking contained in the order is given;

"holder", in relation to a bill of lading, shall be construed in accordance with subsection (2) below;

"information technology" includes any computer or other technology by means of which information or other matter may be recorded or communicated without being reduced to documentary form; and

1984 c. 12.

"telecommunication system" has the same meaning as in the Telecommunications Act 1984.

(2) References in this Act to the holder of a bill of lading are references to any of the following persons, that is to say—

(a) a person with possession of the bill who, by virtue of being the person identified in the bill, is the consignee of the goods to which the bill relates;

(b) a person with possession of the bill as a result of the completion, by delivery of the bill, of any indorsement of the bill or, in the case of a bearer bill, of any other transfer of the bill;

(c) a person with possession of the bill as a result of any transaction by virtue of which he would have become a holder falling within paragraph (a) or (b) above had not the transaction been effected at a time when possession of the bill no longer gave a right (as against the carrier) to possession of the goods to which the bill relates;

and a person shall be regarded for the purposes of this Act as having become the lawful holder of a bill of lading wherever he has become the holder of the bill in good faith.

(3) References in this Act to a person's being identified in a document include references to his being identified by a description which allows for the identity of the person in question to be varied, in accordance with the terms of the document, after its issue; and the reference in section 1(3)(b) of this Act to a document's identifying a person shall be construed accordingly.

(4) Without prejudice to sections 2(2) and 4 above, nothing in this Act shall preclude its operation in relation to a case where the goods to which a document relates—

(a) cease to exist after the issue of the document; or

(b) cannot be identified (whether because they are mixed with other goods or for any other reason);

and references in this Act to the goods to which a document relates shall be construed accordingly.

(5) The preceding provisions of this Act shall have effect without prejudice to the application, in relation to any case, of the rules (the Hague-Visby Rules) which for the time being have the force of law by virtue of section 1 of the Carriage of Goods by Sea Act 1971. 1971 c. 19.

6.—(1) This Act may be cited as the Carriage of Goods by Sea Act 1992. Short title, repeal, commencement and extent.

(2) The Bills of Lading Act 1855 is hereby repealed.

1855 c. 111.

(3) This Act shall come into force at the end of the period of two months beginning with the day on which it is passed; but nothing in this Act shall have effect in relation to any document issued before the coming into force of this Act.

(4) This Act extends to Northern Ireland.

© Crown copyright 1992

PRINTED IN THE UNITED KINGDOM BY PAUL FREEMAN
Controller and Chief Executive of Her Majesty's Stationery Office
and Queen's Printer of Acts of Parliament

Appendix X

P&I CLUB CIRCULARS ON ELECTRONIC (PAPERLESS) TRADING SYSTEMS

CIRCULAR OF SEPTEMBER 2010

Until February 2010 the Rules of all of the Clubs comprising the International Group of P&I Clubs (the Group) specifically excluded liabilities in respect of the carriage of cargo under all electronic, that is paperless, trading systems to the extent that the liabilities under such systems would not have arisen under a 'normal' paper system, that is one using transferable paper documentation

The Group, after reviewing a number of electronic trading systems, agreed that liabilities arising in respect of the carriage of cargo under such systems would be covered from 20 February 2010 provided that the system had first been approved by the Group. Two systems approved by the Group in their versions current at the date of this circular are that administered by Electronic Shipping Solutions (the ESS system - version DSUA v. 2009.3) and that administered by Bolero International Ltd (the Bolero system - Rulebook/Operating Procedures September 1999). The websites of the two entities are www.essdocs.com and www.bolero.net.

The legal documentation associated with the use and operation of the two systems is reviewed by the Group and its legal advisers if and when amended by either of the organisations, to ensure that any modifications introduced by them meet the Group's requirements.

Traditional exclusions of cover under Club Rules relating to the carriage of cargo, will of course continue to apply in respect of ESS and Bolero in the same way as for paper systems, eg discharge at a port or place other than the port or place provided for in the contract of carriage, the issue / creation of an ante or post dated electronic document / record, delivery of cargo without the production of the negotiable electronic document / record.

Members should also be aware that participation in an electronic trading system may expose them to certain liabilities which are not of a traditional P&I nature. These may arise through shipowners or charterers who wish to participate in either the ESS or Bolero systems being required to be party to particular contractual arrangements under which they assume obligations necessary for the system to operate. Examples of such liabilities may be for breach of confidentiality undertakings or of obligations to maintain computer links. Members should be aware that, in so far as such risks are not of a traditional P&I nature, other insurance arrangements may be required.

Finally it would be helpful to the Group, in monitoring the use and development of the two systems, if Members who are using either of them would advise their Club that they are doing so and of any benefits or difficulties which they encounter, legal or practical, in the operation of either system.

CIRCULAR OF APRIL 2013

This Circular confirms approval by International Group of P&I Clubs (the Group) of an updated version of Electronics Shipping Solutions (ESS)'s electronic trading system. This version is called DSUA 2013.1 and it enables electronic trading both in respect of bills of lading and waybills. It supersedes ESS's previous electronic trading system DSUA 2009.3 which remains approved for the purposes of Club cover. DSUA 2013.1 came into effect on 18 March 2013.

Members will recall as reported in our Circular dated, 13 September 2010 (Ref: 2010/026) - Electronic (Paperless) Trading Systems - Bolero International Limited and Electronic Shipping Solutions that until February 2010 the Rules of all of the Clubs comprising the International Group of P&I Clubs (the Group) specifically excluded liabilities in respect of the carriage of cargo under all electronic, that is paperless, trading systems to the extent that the liabilities under such systems would not have arisen under a 'normal' paper system, that is one using transferable paper documentation.

The Group, after reviewing a number of electronic trading systems, agreed that liabilities arising in respect of the carriage of cargo under such systems would be covered from 20 February 2010 provided that the system had first been approved by the Group. The two systems approved by the Group in their versions current at the date of our Circular (Ref: 2010/026) - Electronic (Paperless) Trading Systems - Bolero International Limited and Electronic Shipping Solutions were that administered by Electronic Shipping Solutions (the ESS system - version DSUA 2009.3) and that administered by Bolero International Ltd (the Bolero system - Rulebook/Operating Procedures September 1999). Both those two systems continue to be approved. The websites of the two entities are www.essdocs.com and www.bolero.net.

The legal documentation associated with the use and operation of the two systems is reviewed by the Group and its legal advisers if and when amended by either of the organisations, to ensure that any modifications introduced by them meet the Group's requirements.

Traditional exclusions of cover under Club Rules relating to the carriage of cargo, will of course continue to apply in respect of ESS and Bolero in the same way as for paper systems e.g. discharge at a port or place other than the port or place provided for in the contract of carriage, the issue / creation of an ante or post-dated electronic document / record, delivery of cargo without the production of the negotiable electronic document / record.

Members should also be aware that participation in an electronic trading system may expose them to certain liabilities which are not of a traditional P&I nature. These may arise through shipowners or charterers who wish to participate in either the ESS or Bolero systems being required to be party to particular contractual arrangements under which they assume obligations necessary for the system to operate. Examples of such liabilities may be for breach of confidentiality undertakings or of obligations to maintain computer links. Members should be aware that, in so far as such risks are not of a traditional P&I nature, other insurance arrangements may be required.

Finally it would be helpful to the Group, in monitoring the use and development of the two systems, if Members who are using either of them would advise their Club that they are doing so and of any benefits or difficulties which they encounter, legal or practical, in the operation of either system.

All Clubs in the International Group of P&I Clubs have issued similar circulars.

Appendix XII

INTERNATIONAL GROUP FREQUENTLY ASKED QUESTIONS OF AUGUST 2013 ON PAPERLESS TRADING

1. What is the position of the P&I Clubs within the International Group with regard to paperless trading?

The position is set out in a 2013 circular, sent out by each Club, entitled 'Electronic (Paperless) Trading Systems – Electronic Shipping Solutions and Bolero International Ltd – updated ESSDSUA Version 2013.1'. A copy is attached to these FAQs.

The circular reflects the concern of the P&I Clubs that some systems which use electronic bills of lading may not be universally recognised as satisfactorily performing the three functions of a bill of lading which customarily underpin P&I cover, namely: as a receipt, as a document of title, and as a contract of carriage which incorporates the Hague or Hague-Visby Rules.

2. In the light of this circular, do I have P&I cover in general for liabilities arising under any electronic bills of lading?

(a) Yes, cover is available for typical P&I liabilities arising under any electronic bills of lading to the extent these liabilities would also have arisen under paper bills of lading.

(b) To the extent these liabilities would have arisen because an electronic bill of lading has been used instead of a paper bill of lading, cover is discretionary unless the electronic trading system has been approved by the International Group.

3. Have any systems been approved by the Club/International Group?

The two systems approved are those set out in the circular:

(a) Electronic Shipping Solutions DSUA 2009.3 and DSUA 2013.1 ('ESS') and

(b) Bolero International Ltd Rulebook/Operating Procedure 1999 ('Bolero').

It is always advisable to check that the system preferred bears the correct designation and is the approved version.

4. Is my position better when using one of these approved systems, than another electronic system which has not been approved?

Yes. You will have Club cover for all normal P&I liabilities arising out of the use of one of the approved systems (though not for liabilities which are of a non-traditional P&I nature – see Q6 below) and thereby avoid exposure to the risks connected with the use of non-approved systems as described in Q5 below.

However It is important to note that all exceptions and exclusions under the Club Rules continue to apply (as they would with a paper bill of lading). This includes the traditional exclusions of cover relating to the carriage of goods, such as:

- The issue or creation of an electronic document/record with a description of the cargo or its condition known to be incorrect;
- Short delivery where an electronic document/record is issued or created for an amount of cargo greater than that known to have been loaded;
- Discharge at a port or place other than the port or place provided for in the contract of carriage;
- The issue or creation of an ante or post-dated electronic document/record; and
- Delivery of the cargo without production of the negotiable electronic document/record.

5. What might the risks be if I use an unapproved electronic system?

The risk is the one set out in the answer to question 1 above i.e. that the electronic system is not recognised as performing all the functions that a paper bill of lading would have performed. One example could be that an unapproved system is found, when challenged legally, not to transfer rights in goods in the manner that the creators of the system intended. This may give rise to a dispute about ownership and mis-delivery of the cargo. Another example could be if the Hague or Hague-Visby Rules have not been effectively incorporated into the electronic bill of lading. If it is found that in each case the liability has arisen because of the use of the electronic system, then that will not be covered within normal P&I cover. It may be covered at the discretion of Club Boards.

6. The circular also says that using an electronic bill of lading may expose me to 'liabilities which are not of a traditional P&I nature'. What does this mean?

This is a reference to the kind of liabilities you face when using any electronic system or electronic interface in your office or on your ships, for example the risk of viruses, 'hacking', or the accidental release or theft of information. Simply put it is the risk of using computers. In this context, such liabilities may include, for example, those which arise under the contractual arrangements which you have to make directly with the system operator (Bolero or ESS or other, non-approved systems), such as obligations to maintain computer links, or the introduction of a virus within the operator's or a user's system. The user agreements also contain undertakings of confidentiality and could give rise to liabilities if broken.

7. Is there an insurance which can cover me for these obligations?

These are non-marine risks, and may be covered by your own business insurances. This is something which you can check with your non-marine business insurance broker. These are not in the nature of P&I risks. In insurance terms, they may be described as 'cyber-risks' or business risks.

8. What if I check with my brokers and I can find no such cover?

The answer may lie with Bolero or ESS (or other non-approved systems) who may have dealt with similar enquiries on previous occasions.

9. If I am considering using one of the approved systems and I wish to look into the Bolero Rule Book or ESS User Agreement, how can I obtain a copy?

The party inviting you to use this system should provide this for you, or put you in touch with Bolero or ESS. The Bolero Rule Book can also be accessed at: http://www.bolero.net/platform/rulebook

10. Do I need to ask you to check and approve the Rule Book or User Agreement of an approved system?

No. The International Group has approved these documents (as long as they are unamended and match the titles set out in the circular) as acceptable.

11. If I am considering using an unapproved system will the Club review the documents?

It is for you to satisfy yourself as to the manner in which the system operates. The Club cannot currently 'approve' systems other than through the IG mechanism for doing so. Unapproved system operators can of course approach the IG Secretariat for approval, and the matter would then be considered by the appropriate sub-committee comprised of Club representatives, but this is not a quick or immediate procedure.

12. Electronic systems are based on specific contractual terms rather than statutes and treaties. Is there a risk when using an approved system that the contract of carriage will not be subject to the Hague or Hague-Visby Rules and that I might therefore be deprived of my P&I cover?

No, the contractual terms for both approved systems make clear that any convention, treaty or national law that would have been applicable to carriage under a paper bill of lading will equally govern the carriage using an electronic document or record. Thus, so long as the carriage is subject to Hague or Hague Visby Rules by reference to the terms and conditions incorporated into the electronic document/record and/or by application of convention or national law as if a paper bill of lading had been issued then there will be no problem with Club cover.

If the carriage is compulsorily subject to another liability regime like the Hamburg Rules then again Club cover will remain in place as it would if the carriage were under a paper bill of lading.

BIBLIOGRAPHY

Bridge M (ed), *Benjamin's Sale of Goods*, 8th edition, Sweet & Maxwell, 2010.

Debattista C, *Bills of Lading in Export Trade*, 3rd edition, Informa, 2009.

Treitel G and Reynolds F, *Carver on Bills of Lading*, 3rd edition, Sweet & Maxwell, 2012.

Draught Surveys – Dibble J, Mitchell P and North of England P&I Association, *Draught Surveys: A Guide to Good Practice*, 2nd edition, North of England P&I Association, 2009.

Glass D, *Freight Forwarding and Multi Modal Transport Contracts*, 2nd edition, Informa, 2013.

Goode R, McKendrick E, *Goode on Commercial Law*, 4th edition, Penguin, 2004.

Ramberg J, *ICC Guide to Incoterms 2010*, ICC, 2011.

Eder B, Foxton D and Berry S, *Scrutton on Charterparties and Bills of Lading*, 22nd edition, Sweet & Maxwell, 2013.

Severn A and North of England P&I Association, *Shipboard Petroleum Surveys: A Guide to Good Practice*, 2nd edition, North of England P&I Association, 2009.

Sparks A and North of England P&I Association, *Steel Preshipment Surveys: A Guide to Good Practice*, 2nd edition, North of England P&I Association, 2009.

Coughlin T, Baker A, Kenny J and Kimball J, *Time Charters*, 6th edition, Informa, 2008.

UCP 600, ICC, 2011.

Cooke J, Taylor A, Martowski D, Kimball J, Young T and Lambert L, *Voyage Charters*, 3rd edition, Informa, 2007.

INDEX

All references are to paragraph numbers in the practical guidance, theory and electronic bills of lading sections. Paragraph numbers in orange are in the practical guidance section, numbers in green are in the theory section and numbers in purple are in the electronic bills of lading section. A yellow G denotes that the term is explained in the Glossary (appendix I) and a yellow A followed by a number means there is a copy in the appendix of that number.

	Paragraph(s)
Accomplished, when	50, 248
Ad valorem bills	10, 196, G
Agents, authority of	128
Amending bills of lading	130
Ante-dating bills of lading	3(c), 188
Apparent order and condition	4, 134, 159, 172
As presented, master to sign bills of lading	18(c), 115 – 122
Authority of agents	128
Authority of charterers	128, 273(a)
Authority of sub-charterers	273(a)
Backdating – see Ante-dating	
Bearer	223, 224(c)
Before issue of bills of lading, cargo damage	170
Blank endorsement	224(a)
Blending or co-mingling of oil cargoes	16, 266 – 269
Both-to-blame collision clause	51.5
Cargo claims	240, 241
Carrier – see Introduction	
Certificate of origin, quality, quantity	205
Change of destination	23, 34, 232, 239, 250, 254, 265, AIV
Charterers, authority of	128, 273(a)
Charterer's bills of lading	271 – 279
Charterparty	4, 271 – 279
Charterparty, incorporation in bill of lading	6, 45, 274
CIF/CFR	13, 72 – 74, 199
Claused bills of lading	1 – 18, 175, 176 – 178
Clausing, typical	4(b)(vi), 177, 204
Clausing, distinct from endorsing – see Introduction	
Clean bill of lading	171 – 174, 176 – 178
'Clean on board'	174
COGSA92	98 – 100
Co-mingling or blending of oil cargoes	16, 266 – 269
Codes and conventions	69 – 93
Common law	67, 69(e)
Completion of loading	190
Conclusive evidence	242 – 244

INDEX

Condition	4, 159 – 168
Consignee	37, 224
Consignment of a bill of lading	224
Congenbill	35
Contents of the bill of lading	3, 133 – 140
Contract of carriage	63
Conventions and codes	69 – 93
Correcting bills of lading	129
Customs document	260
Damage after loading but before issue of bill of lading	8, 194, 170
Date of loading	188
Date of issue	54, 188
Deck cargo	44, 187
Delay	234 – 236
Delivery, at wrong port – see Change of destination	
Delivery, to whom it should be made	22, 223, 261
Delivery of cargo without presentation of a bill of lading	23, 250
Delivery orders	288
Demise clause	G
Demurrage	124
Description words of	155 – 170
Deviation	229 – 231
Discharge, request to issue after	131
Discharge port	41
Dispute as to condition of cargo	1 – 18, 179 – 181
Dispute as to quantity loaded	1 – 18, 179 – 181
Document of title	61
Draught survey	207 – 208
Due diligence	237
Duress	18, 123
Electronic bills of lading	299 – 324
Endorsement	224
Endorsement in blank	224(a)
Endorsing, distinct from clausing – see Introduction	
Evidence	242 – 244
Faxed bills of lading	257
Final destination inland	9, 195
FI0ST/FI0S/FI0	12, 198, 239 G
FOB	75
For customs purposes only	8, 194, 260
Foul bill of lading – see Claused bill of lading	
Free in, free out	12, 198, 239 G
Freight	4, 45, 46, 52, 122, 124
Freight pre-paid	124, 119, 120, G
Freight forwarder	G
General endorsement	224(a)

INDEX

Groupage bill of lading	G
Hague rules	51.2, 82 – 90, 134 – 137, AV
Hague-Visby Rules	51.2, 82 – 90, 134 – 137, AVI
Hamburg Rules	91 – 93, 124, 140, AVII
Handling the bill of lading	216 – 225
Hire	122
Holder of the bill of lading	98, 99, 224
House bill of lading	G
ICC	71
Identity of carrier clause	G
Incoterms 2000	70 – 75
Information contained in the bill of lading	4, 133 – 140, 200 – 214
Inland destination	9, 195
Inspection	206
Instructions which are at variance with the bill of lading	105
Insurance	21, 101 – 104
Invoice number	10, 196
Issue, date of	188
Issue, place of	189
Issue, to whom	193
Issue, when	190 – 192
Issue after discharge	131
Law	69
Letters of authority	AII, 273
Letters of credit	10, 196, 220
Letters of indemnity	17, 26, 28, 182 – 184, 254 – 256
Liens	5, 124
Liner terms	239
Loading, completion of	190
Loading, date of	188
Loading broker	G
Loading port	40
Lost bill of lading, delivery against	25, 253
Lost bill of lading, replacement of	132
Mate's receipt	211 – 214
Mixing of dry cargo	270
More than one copy of bill of lading issued	14
More than one bill of lading presented for delivery	32(b)
Multiple sets of bills of lading	14, 30, 32(b), 50, 53, 258
No bill of lading presented for delivery	23, 250
Non-negotiable or negotiable	224(b)
Notify address	38, G
Notify party	38, G
P&I cover	21, 101 – 104
Packaging and marking	134, 159 – 169, 200, 201
Paperless trading exclusion	310
Parcel, bill of lading for each	15, 191

INDEX

Photocopy bills of lading	29, 257
Place of issue	189
Post-dating – see Ante-dating	
Pre-dating – see Ante-dating	
Preparation of bill of lading, by whom	113
Pressure – see Duress	
Prima facie evidence	242 – 244
Purpose of bill of lading	56 – 64
Quality	4, 169
Quantity	4, 155 – 158
Receipt	58
Received for shipment bill of lading	192, G
Retla clause	185, G
Refusal to sign	18
Rotterdam Rules	94
'said by shipper to contain'	155
'Said to be'	156
'Said to contain'	156
'Said to weigh'	156
Sale contract	10, 69, 196
Sea waybills	167
Seaworthiness	237, 241
Security issues	295
Service bill of lading	G
Set of three	14, 30, 32(b), 50, 53, 258
Ship's bag	11, 197
Ship's name	39
Ship's delivery orders – see Delivery orders.	
Ship's stamp	4(c)
Shipped bill of lading	181, G
Shipper	36, 42
'shipper's figures'	155
Shipper's load and count	155
Shipping documents	217
Shipping marks	134, 200, 201
Shipping note	208
Signing the bill of lading, who may sign	50, 55, 125
Signature, position of	50, 55
Signature, electronic	308
'So near thereto as she may safely get'	233
Special endorsement	224(a)
'Split' bills of lading	293
Statute law	69(e)
Steel cargoes, clausing for	4(b)(viii), 62, 186
Straight bills of lading	24(f), 224(b), 286, 287, 323(d)
Sub-charterer, authority of	273(a)

INDEX

Surveyor	204
'Switch' bills of lading	293
Tally	4(b)
Terms of carriage	51.1 – 51.6, 63, 65 – 68
Three in a set	50, 53, 258
Time charterparty	6, 271 – 273
Timber cargoes, clausing for	4(b)(viii), 62, 186
Transferring bills of lading	224
Transferring title	61, 215 – 225
UCP600	76 – 79
Ullages	209
Vessels, name of	39
Voyage charterparty	6, 45, 51.1, 271 – 273
Without presentation of a bill of lading, delivery	23, 250
Words of description	155 – 169
Waybills – see Sea waybills	
'Weight, measure, quantity, condition, contents and value unknown'	49

INDEX